Words from Our VIP Spiritual Editor

Dear Celeste,

1. As usual ... you feed my soul! Your Scripture knowledge and walk with God fills the pages. I always receive insight accompanied with "soul fatness" when reading your thoughts.

2. Extremely practical! Very thorough. Processed well.

3. Your willingness to be vulnerable connects so well with those who will read and lead.

4. It's obvious that you have immersed yourself in what you teach and know your calling intimately. Your experience allows you to train the leaders thoroughly. If you missed a step in directing them, only God would know! To me ... you missed nothing!!

5. Your continued use of Scripture as foundation and support is fantastic!

6. Your wisdom in how to handle different and difficult situations and people is helpful.

One last observation: Your commitment to your work is apparent in your writing. You will attract that type of person to this ministry. We attract who we are, not who we want. It seems to me that your ministry will appeal to sincere seekers of truth and people with a high commitment to discipleship.

Prayers, Love, and Blessings on you and ALL that you touch. You are making a deep eternal impact on many!

John C. Maxwell

SERVE LIKE JESUS

Triumph Servant Leadership Training

You are our letter, written in our hearts...
2 Corinthians 3:2

CELESTE LI, M.D.

Triumph Series
By Celeste Li, M.D.

Book I:
Triumph Over Suffering
A Spiritual Guide to Conquering Adversity

Book II:
Triumph Of Surrender
A Walk of Intimacy With Jesus

Book III:
Triumph in Warfare
A fight for the territory of our hearts (Vol I & II)

Serve Like Jesus
Triumph Servant Leadership Training

No profits are ever made from the sale of these books. All proceeds are given directly to the church or used to minister to the Body of Christ at large. Thank you for your love, prayers and support. May God bless you and your family with hope and healing.

-The Plum Tree Ministries Team

**The things which you have heard from me
in the presence of many witnesses,
entrust these to faithful men
who will be able to teach others also.**
2 Timothy 2:2

Dedicated to the bond-servants of the Lord

Jupiter, Florida
plumtreeministries@gmail.com
"The surviving remnant of the house of Judah will again take root downward and bear fruit upward." Isaiah 37:31

Serve Like Jesus
Triumph Servant Leadership Training
Copyright © 2020 by Celeste Li
Celeste.Li.Triumph@gmail.com
Visit our website: TriumphOverSuffering.com

Plum Tree Ministries
210 Jupiter Lakes Blvd., #5105, Jupiter, FL 33458 USA

ISBN-978-0-9841515-6-1
Printed in the Unites States of America.

All Scripture quotations, unless otherwise indicated, are taken from the New American Standard Bible. Copyright © 1960, 1962, 1963, 1968, 1971, 1972, 1973, 1975, 1977, 1995 by The Lockman Foundation. Used by permission.

Scripture quotations marked NIV are taken from the Holy Bible: New International Version, NIV, Copyright © 1973, 1978, 1984 by International Bible Society. Used by permission of Zondervan. All rights reserved.

Scripture quotations marked AMP are taken from THE AMPLIFIED BIBLE. Old Testament Copyright ©1965, 1987 by The Zondervan Corporation. The Amplified New Testament Copyright © 1958, 1987 by The Lockman Foundation. Used by permission.

Scripture Quotations marked AMPC are taken from Amplified Bible, Classic Edition AMPC, Copyright © 1954 1958, 1962, 1964, 1965, 1987 by the Lockman Foundation.

Scripture quotations marked NLT are taken from the Holy Bible: New Living Translation, copyright © 1996, 2004. Used by permission of Tyndale All rights reserved.House Publishers, Inc., Carol Stream, Illinois 60188.

Scripture quotations marked NCV are taken from The Holy Bible, New Century Version ®, Copyright © 2005 by Thomas Nelson, Inc.

Cover photography and design by Alec Li
Interior design and layout by Anna Pizzoferrato
i.a.m.pizzoferrato@gmail.com

*If you find anything in this book helpful for yourself or your ministry –
whether your ministry is a formal teaching or reaching out to a friend –*
without taking it out of context, you are welcome to teach it,
reprint it, copy it, quote it, or reproduce it in any format,
including written, visual, audio, or electronic,
without our express permission.
If you are using something that is footnoted,
please acknowledge the original author.
May the Lord bless you and others with this book.

Contents

Foreword	ix
Preface	xi
Introduction: Triumph Ministry	xiii
Chapter 1: We Are Called and Anointed	1
Chapter 2: To Set the Captives Free	21
Chapter 3: Establishing Our Identity In Christ	43
Chapter 4: Running With Endurance	67
Chapter 5: Temptations Leaders Face	97
Chapter 6: In Step with Holy Spirit	135
Chapter 7: Leading the Class	157
Chapter 8: Avoiding Traps in the Classroom	201
Chapter 9: Handling Challenges in the Classroom	223
A Final Word	247
Appendix I: Investment for *Triumph Leadership*	
Triumph Rhythm	254
Count the Cost	256
Qualifications to Begin Triumph Leadership Training	258
Appendix II: Registration Paperwork	
Registration Summary for *Triumph* Classes	262
Triumph Over Suffering (TOS) Registration Form	264
Triumph Of Surrender (T2) Registration Form	265
Triumph In Warfare (TIW) Registration Form	266
Triumph Course Description	267
Triumph Classroom Guidelines	268
Commitment and Confidentiality Agreement	270
Sample Course Schedule TOS	272
Triumph Course Evaluation	273

Appendix III: Resources for Leaders

    Leading Someone to Christ   276

    How to Study Your Bible for Participants   281

    Summary How to Study Your Bible   288

    For Leaders: How to Study Your Bible   290

Appendix IV: *Triumph* Prayer Guide

    Your *Triumph* Prayer Team   294

    TOS Prayer Guide   296

    Percolation Time/Leaders' Restoration Prayer Guide   305

    Bible Study Prayer Guide   307

    T2 Prayer Guide   309

Resources   319

Endnotes   321

Acknowledgements   327

Triumph Ministry Mission Statement

The Spirit of the Sovereign Lord is on me,
because the Lord has anointed me
   to preach good news to the poor.
He has sent me to bind up the brokenhearted,
   to proclaim freedom for the captives
   and release from darkness for the prisoners,
to proclaim the year of the Lord's favor ...
                                            Isaiah 61:1-2

Triumph Servant Leaders guide hurting people
to the Lord Jesus Christ for healing and freedom.

Foreword

We step into leadership sensing God's call and prompting, often believing we will be of some value and service to others. These are right and true, worthy aspirations for the leader. I have found, however, leadership is often as transforming for me as it is for those I lead. Leadership requires a continual laying down of one's life, a constant surrender of will, a sometimes-painful endurance as we witness the pilgrim's dance of two steps forward, one step back. If we enter into leadership thinking we will receive accolades and acknowledgments, slaps on the back, and props for a "job well done," we will be more than disappointed.

We want to Serve Like Jesus. What did we witness in Jesus' journey on earth? We read of disciples falling away, doubting their Messiah, betraying, lying, and missing the point over and over. We hear of those walking away because the call was too high. If Jesus, the perfect Servant King, experienced less-than-perfection from His followers, it seems natural we can expect much of the same. Of course, we will have those few and far between who are ripe for the picking – those who will experience tremendous growth while we walk with them. Praise God! However, the majority of this journey in leadership will be slow. The change will be subtle and it will be our privilege to pay attention. We must continually bring those we love and lead before our Heavenly Father who knows them much more intimately than we do. Eugene Peterson explains,

> My primary pastoral work had to do with Scripture and prayer. I was neither capable nor competent to form Christ in another person, to shape a life of discipleship in man, woman or child. That is supernatural work, and I am not supernatural. Mine was the more modest work of Scripture and prayer – helping people listen to God speak to them from the Scriptures and then joining them in answering God as personally and honestly as we could in lives of prayer.[1]

It stands to reason that great leadership begins with a great leader. This is definitely true but I would submit that every great leader is a submitted leader. Ministry leadership begins with you. You are here because you have found deep satisfaction and freedom through Jesus' work in you. You have committed to wellness in yourself and now, you want to love others as He has loved you.

The call is high for leaders. It is ever imperative that you dig deep, that you continue the work in your own relationship with Christ so you can accurately reflect His heart to those you lead. Celeste knows this well and she lives it well. I have had the honor of knowing and observing Celeste and have seen this play out so beautifully – in her personal life and in those she leads. Celeste knows leadership is a deep call to submission, surrender, humility. She lives it, embodies it, and now, through this book, explains it.

As I read through Celeste's words, my first impression was her deep love for God and His Word. I am believing this hunger will be transferred to you as you learn and lead. My next observation was how many chapters she devoted to you, as the leader. She commits to you first, knowing your own freedom will be the catalyst to your leadership of others. Finally, Celeste has supplied many practical resources for your use. She has lived these principles out in real life at our church and has learned what works well. I am believing God will do exponentially more through you as you implement her hard-learned lessons in your own discipleship setting.

I am praying as you read Celeste's words, you will grow in the confidence that God lends those of us who follow Him wholeheartedly. I am believing your journey will be one of beautiful, hearty fruit that will bear and grow in all seasons. I bring before our loving Father those who will join you on this journey toward more surrender and freedom. It's what He has for all of us. What a joy to see Him work this out in each life He draws toward Himself!

"If you want to be my disciple, follow me and you will go where I am going. And if you truly follow me as my disciple, the Father will shower His favor upon your life."
John 12:26 TPT

Andrea Parsley
Christ Fellowship Church

Preface

This book is intended for use as a specific leadership training program for leaders of *Triumph Over Suffering* and the *Triumph Series*. It does contain general leadership development tools that could be valuable for leaders in other areas, but it is specifically designed for *Triumph* Servant Leaders.

If you are studying this book at the invitation of the *Triumph* Leadership Team, you have already walked through *Triumph Over Suffering* (TOS) and *Triumph of Surrender* (T2) classes multiple times, and processed and embraced these teachings on a deep level. You have invited the Holy Spirit to sanctify your heart, and have received His healing touch in profound and sacred ways. You have observed that these classes invite in those who are hurting, meet them at their point of need, and point them to the Lord for healing, freedom, and growth in intimacy with Him.

This course is your next step in leadership training. This book is intended to be studied over ten weeks under a *Triumph* leader, and to be followed by hands-on training with a *Triumph* leader live in the classroom.

If you have acquired this book on your own, you are welcome to work through it, but do realize that it was written to complement the journey from *Triumph Over Suffering* student to *Triumph* Servant Leader.

As *Triumph* Servant Leaders, we invest in those the Lord brings to us, aiming to make disciples so participants will come to know Him deeply and be equipped to fulfill their Kingdom purposes. In Appendix I, you will find a section titled *Triumph Rhythm*, the discipleship plan to teach our people how to position themselves to receive His healing and equipping. Following this is *Count the Cost,* which details some information on the investment of time and energy necessary for *Triumph Leadership.* Go ahead and read those two sections of Appendix I now, and meet me back here when you are finished.

How will we have the strength to do all this? *Only through the Holy Spirit.* I am praying that the Holy Spirit will anoint us and fill us and strengthen us as we continue to pursue our abiding walk of sanctification.

I deeply believe that the most important preparation for us as leaders is the purification of our hearts. Therefore the first part of this leadership training will focus on seeking the Lord's sanctification. I believe that once our hearts are ready, the remainder of leadership training and logistics will flow easily from there.

I have filled this book with my own personal experiences as a leader, and in the last part of this book have provided tips, recommendations, and suggestions gathered from the fifteen years I have been teaching these classes. But in the end, I'm not going to teach you how to lead. As our hearts are made right with Him, the anointing of the Holy Spirit will teach you all you need to know.

As for you, the anointing which you received from Him abides in you, and you have no need for anyone to teach you; but as His anointing teaches you about all things, and is true and is not a lie, and just as it has taught you, you abide in Him.

1 John 2:27

Introduction:
Triumph Ministry

*M*y heart is so full and I am so deeply grateful that you have answered God's call to serve on the *Triumph Leadership Team*.

When you came into *Triumph* Classes, you experienced firsthand God's rich and powerful message to you. You received His touch personally, and also watched Him touch the hearts of the other participants – healing, freeing, delivering, and restoring.

The anguished hearts that the Lord brings into *Triumph* Classes are so very precious to Him. I believe His plan is to prepare these people to be His letter to the world – His message of grace and hope and healing that He wants proclaimed to the far corners of the earth. And He has chosen to write His message not with paper and pen, but with His Holy Spirit – on the tablets of human hearts.

You are our letter, written in our hearts, known and read by all men; being manifested that you are a letter of Christ, cared for by us, written not with ink but with the Spirit of the living God, not on tablets of stone but on tablets of human hearts.

2 Corinthians 3:2-3

He has called us to *be* these letters – and also to *care for* these letters. *This is Triumph Ministry.*

So hold each of these tender hearts ever so carefully. As teachers and leaders of *Triumph* Classes, we are called to love graciously, unconditionally, nonjudgmentally – and to direct our people right into the heart of God. We teach our people how to seek God, how to open their hearts to His infinite love, how to repent and forgive and surrender as He calls, and how to receive His unconditional grace and acceptance. As we release the outcome of these classes to His control, He is free to reveal Himself to the participants and to answer their deep heart questions as only their Creator can. We fully trust Him to work

His metamorphosis – His extraordinary transformation from caterpillar to butterfly (Rom 12:1-2).[1]

What an incredible blessing and honor it is to be His ambassadors to those who are distressed in their trials, bringing His words of love and peace to them. Come with me as we seek the Lord together for His equipping. He who has called us will not forsake us, but by His grace shall provide everything we need to accomplish His will. One of His primary ways of equipping is sanctifying us, that we may be well-pleasing in His sight, and ready to walk worthy of this calling we have received. (2Cor 5:20, 1:3-4, Heb 13:20-21, Col 1:10, 2Cor 5:9.)

Now the God of peace, who brought up from the dead the great Shepherd of the sheep through the blood of the eternal covenant, even Jesus our Lord, equip you in every good thing to do His will, working in us that which is pleasing in His sight, through Jesus Christ, to whom be the glory forever and ever.
Hebrews 13:20-21

I'd like to pray for you.

> *Lord, I pray for these courageous and humble Triumph Servant Leaders, that Your Spirit will rest upon them. I pray that You will grant them revelation and discernment. I pray You will overflow them with Your Spirit of wisdom and understanding, Your Spirit of counsel and strength, Your Spirit of knowledge and fear of the Lord. I pray that they will delight in fear of the Lord, and that Your lovingkindness will embrace them. I pray that they will make no decisions and speak no words based on what their eyes see or what their ears hear, but only by what their hearts hear from Your Spirit. I pray that as they put their trust in You, they will go out in joy and be led forth by Your peace. Amen.[2]*

Ready? Grab your journal and a pen and let's press in for our equipping.

Chapter 1
We Are Called and Anointed

God has called us to Kingdom work from *before the foundation of the world*. From all eternity, before He created the world, He created our Kingdom purposes – and then masterfully designed us and created us and crafted us just so in order to enable us to *fulfill* these purposes.

He chose us in Him before the foundation of the world ... For we are His workmanship, created in Christ Jesus for good works, which God prepared beforehand so that we would walk in them.

Ephesians 1:4, 2:10

"You did not choose Me but I chose you, and appointed you that you would go and bear fruit, and that your fruit would remain ..."

John 15:16

Chosen, from all eternity. Chosen, to bear eternal fruit. He has indeed called us to a holy calling. He has consecrated us, and set us apart for His purposes. He called us into His Kingdom work not because of anything we have accomplished or earned, not because of our own merit, talents, or abilities, but because *it pleased Him to do so.* He has set us apart for Kingdom work simply for His own unfathomable reasons – and He will accomplish His work through us by His unstoppable grace. (2Tim 1:9, Eph 1:5, 1Cor 15:10, 2Cor 3:5.)

As we seek Him with all our heart, He will unveil the work He has hand-picked for us. If you are reading this book, you are probably feeling nudges or even strong callings towards *Triumph Ministry*. I pray that the Holy Spirit will give you His utmost clarity on the special assignments that He has created *just for you.*

Ponder, Pray, and Journal

Pause and let the richness of this next passage sink into your heart, and then journal what the Lord is telling you.

> **He delivered us**
> **and saved us**
> **and called us with a holy calling**
> **[a calling that leads to a consecrated life—**
> **a life set apart—**
> **a life of purpose],**
> **not because of our works**
> **[or because of any personal merit—**
> **we could do nothing to earn this],**
> **but because of His own purpose and grace**
> **[His amazing, undeserved favor]**
> **which was granted to us in Christ Jesus**
> **before the world began [eternal ages ago].**
> 2 Timothy 1:9 AMP

Because He has called us, and strategically positioned us,

He has placed a special anointing upon us to enable us to fulfill His plan and purpose in this ministry. This anointing that He has given us abides in us, dwells in us, tarries with us. This anointing is the Holy Spirit Himself (1Jn 2:20, 2:27, 3:24).

Now He who establishes us with you in Christ and anointed us is God, who also sealed us and gave us the Spirit in our hearts as a pledge ... The anointing you received from Him abides in you.
2 Corinthians 1:21-22, 1 John 2:27

Only Jesus, by the will of the Father, through the power of the Holy Spirit, saves, heals, frees, redeems. So take a deep breath and relax. Jesus, according to the will of the Father, will do all the work. The Holy Spirit, living and dwelling and breathing in us, will touch and change hearts for all eternity. We must merely surrender, and be led.

When God calls us and anoints us, and we respond in surrender and a willingness to be led, *we become His bond-servants.* There will be a cost involved as we allow Him to take us by the right hand and lead us where *He* wants us to go. Let's evaluate that cost. (Lk 14:25-33, Ps 73:23-24, Jn 21:18.)

Triumph Servant Leaders are F.A.T.

I have heard it said that leaders who are ready to be led by the Spirit are F.A.T.

- Faithful
- Available
- Teachable

As you go through this chapter, don't be concerned if you suddenly feel you don't have everything necessary to lead. We are going to walk through this leadership development *together* and with the Holy Spirit at our side. If you are called to this ministry, God will anoint you and equip you. In this chapter, we are going to simply explore these indispensable characteristics, and, as we work through this book, we will learn together how to become increasingly F.A.T.

Faithful

The most important characteristic of a Servant Leader is an active and vibrant relationship with Jesus. The more intimate we are with Him, the more clearly we will hear Him, and the more profound our leadership will be, because *He* will be the One leading, not us. This type of abiding relationship must be *pursued*, as we continually grow up in Him, surrender to Him, and walk with Him. Our closeness with God and time spent praying for our people impacts our ability to create an encouraging environment that promotes spiritual growth and accountability.

Faithfulness also includes integrity. Integrity means we are imitators of Jesus no matter who we are with, what we are doing, or wherever we are. It means we trust God enough to be vulnerable with our participants. We don't glorify past sins, but we are open and transparent. We allow our people to see the authenticity of our walk with the Lord, our everyday struggles and victories in Him.

Deep faith means trusting in and relying upon God's goodness, power, wisdom, and grace. Deep faith is believing that God cares enough about us to respond when we call out to Him. Deep faith means we trust God to guard what is precious to us, and we demonstrate that trust by surrendering all to Him. (Heb 11:6 MSG, 1Tim 1:12.)

Ponder, Pray, and Journal

Be still before Him. Ask Him if there is anything you are holding back from Him right now. Allow the Holy Spirit to gently nudge and convict. He is preparing you to step into leadership and wants you to be fully ready, with no barriers between Him and you, and able to hear Him in unhindered communication.

Journal your prayer of surrender to Him.

We are next going to explore a few areas where our faithfulness is critical: His Word, our spiritual disciplines, and our church family.

Faithful to His Word

As leaders, we are also faithful to the truth of His Word. We do not set ourselves up as the authority. *God's Word* is the authority, and our foundation of faith is built upon Scripture. We will need a strong grounding in the Scriptures, and specifically a solid understanding of the Biblical principles and Scriptures taught in the *Triumph* books.

Be diligent to present yourself approved to God as a workman who does not need to be ashamed, accurately handling the word of truth.

2 Timothy 2:15

The Amplified says **accurately handling and skillfully teaching. Handling** literally means "to make a straight cut ... to rightly divide."[1] The King James translates it **rightly dividing**. I've heard it explained as cutting it according to God's pattern, upright and true.

As teachers and leaders, we treasure God's Word, and desire to teach it with the utmost integrity. For God has entrusted us with His sheep for a season, to teach, mentor, and guide, and we must not lead them astray. Remember what Jesus said of the Pharisees,

"They are blind guides of the blind. And if a blind man guides a blind man, both will fall into a pit."
Matthew 15:14

We steep ourselves in study of the Word, so we do not lead His sheep into a pit. As teachers and leaders, God holds us to a higher standard. He has called and anointed us, and He holds us to greater accountability.

Let not many of you become teachers, my brethren, knowing that as such we shall incur a stricter judgment.
James 3:1

Don't let this drive you to a place of fear, but let it drive you to be a perpetual student of the Word, desiring to constantly grow in knowledge of the Lord, cultivating and maintaining a fear of the Lord.

Thus says the LORD,
"Let not a wise man boast of his wisdom,
and let not the mighty man boast of his might,
let not a rich man boast of his riches;
but let him who boasts boast of this,
that he understands and knows Me,
that I am the LORD who exercises
lovingkindness, justice and righteousness on earth;
for I delight in these things," declares the LORD.
Jeremiah 9:23-24, emphasis added

While knowing Scripture verses and where to find them in your Bible is an important component of leadership, and a discipline we constantly desire to be developing, of parallel importance is simply *knowing God*. Knowing deeply in your heart His character, His nature, His ways. When we know Him in this way, we will recognize when our people are trapped in lies of the enemy, even if we cannot quote a specific Scripture verse to counteract that lie. We will still need to find that Scripture, because the power is in the Word and our people will need the Scripture to take down that lie and renew their minds with truth, but simply *recognizing* when someone is speaking words that are not in alignment with who God is will be a crucial first step.

Understand that God holds each of us to a different level of accountability, dependent upon our spiritual maturity and the position in which He has placed us. As we keep seeking Him, fully surrendered and growing in Him, we can trust Him to cover us when we have made honest mistakes.

Faithful to the Spiritual Disciplines

In addition to Scripture immersion, God calls us to the spiritual disciplines of prayer, fasting, worship, stillness, solitude, listening, and journaling.

Ponder, Pray, and Journal

Grab your journal and take a spiritual check-up. Ask the Holy Spirit to search your heart, to show you if anything in your heart is not pleasing to Him, and to lead you in the everlasting way. Here are some areas to evaluate.

- Scripture study
- Prayer
- Worship

- Stillness and listening and solitude
- Fasting

"Be still, and know that I am God; I will be exalted among the nations, I will be exalted in the earth."
Psalm 46:10 NIV

I find stillness and listening to be challenging! If this is an area that you are struggling with, try these suggestions:

- Start with worship or the Word. When you are focused on Him, maybe on one of His attributes, or a Scripture of praise, then ...
- Try to sit in silence and stillness for five minutes.
- Whenever your mind wanders off, gently bring it back to focus on Him. (Notice I said "whenever," not "if.")
- As you develop this sweet time with God, you may find that He will hold you in His Presence for longer periods of time.

Faithful to Your Church Family

**Planted in the house of the L<small>ORD</small>,
They will flourish in the courts of our God.**
Psalm 92:13

In order to flourish, a Christian must be *planted*; for us as leaders, this is even more critical. Being planted includes weekly services to receive teaching from your pastor, to worship, and to connect with the Body of Christ. Being planted means being part of church events, such as leadership training. It also includes regular time spent with small groups of friends from your church in order to connect and grow. The *Triumph Leadership Team* meets regularly for fellowship, accountability, and prayer. In the next sections, we're going to discuss accountability and authority in greater detail.

Accountability

The need for leaders to have an accountability partner cannot be overstated. We need someone we can speak to regularly – and we must take the initiative to contact them, and have the courage to confess to them. I have had a few different accountability partners over the years. At this time, I speak to one of my accountability partners once a week and another several times a month. I also have a wise woman who was my counselor for many years. She speaks into my life when she sees something to address, and I can also go to her on an as-needed basis. Finally, I have a group of five women who have been my faithful prayer team for ten years. I meet with them monthly for confession and prayer.

Here are some characteristics I consider indispensable for an accountability partner:

- Same-gender friend with a strong walk with the Lord, who is willing and available.
- Possesses a nonjudgmental heart.
- When I confess, won't minimize my sins or make excuses for me, won't try to fix me or solve my problems, but will simply listen, love, point me to Jesus, and pray.
- Understands confidentiality.
- Wisdom and insight are an added bonus.

But not only do I need a safe place to confess, I am also in need of people who are willing to speak into my life when I am in need of correction. Who see my faults when I do not, and have the courage to bring it to my attention. It can be hard to find people like this. International speaker, author, and leadership expert Dr. John C. Maxwell explains why:

> People often tell leaders what they want to hear, not what they need to hear. So that means as a leader, you have personal blind spots *plus* you don't always receive the honest feedback from the people who know your faults.

He then goes on to explain how he overcomes this problem, by directly asking people, and giving them

> ... permission to speak truth into my life ... The answers I discover are not always comfortable, but if I maintain a good attitude, they can help me to be self-correcting.[2]

I see I need to add another bullet point to my list of indispensible characteristics:

- Have the courage to speak into my life if they notice something is out of integrity – preferably with gentleness.

Ponder, Pray, and Journal

It is important to develop your accountability team. Who is on your team at this time? Pray and ask God to bring you more accountability partners if needed.

Authority

Being planted also means coming up under the authority

of the pastor to whom you are assigned for your *Triumph Classes*. If you do not know the pastor you will be under, it will be important for you to learn the structure of leadership at your church, ask which pastor you will be under, and request permission from that pastor to lead class. Large churches may have senior pastors, campus pastors, discipleship pastors, and pastors that are over classes and groups. You could be assigned under any one of them. Smaller churches may place their groups under a campus pastor or a discipleship pastor, or even directly under the lead pastor.

It is important to develop a relationship with the pastor assigned over your class. Let them know about the course and what it entails (we will talk about summarizing the class in Chapter 7). You will also want to share about the transformational impact the classes have had on you personally, and provide books for your pastor also.

Your pastor is the one you will go to for wisdom to handle difficult situations, guidance in making decisions about the class, logistics, prayer, and confession if needed for yourself. I go to my pastor if there has been a problem in class, such as if a participant withdraws from the class because I have misstepped or misspoken, or if I have difficulties in class that I need prayer and wisdom to handle.

We are next going to explore the "A" of F.A.T. – Available.

Available

In this section, we will examine four areas *Triumph Leadership* will require us to be available: mental, emotional, spiritual, and physical.

Mentally Available

Triumph Leadership is *mentally* taxing. If you are handling significant life-changing events such as a recent divorce, loss of a loved one, family crisis, a new serious medical diagnosis, a major move, or other challenges, your attention will be drawn away from the hurting ones God has brought to class – and rightly so. Your focus needs to be on yourself and your personal life in this season as you process these events and receive your own healing from the Lord. We will discuss this more in upcoming chapters.

I have had a number of leaders move in and out of leadership seasons and healing seasons. I myself have done the same. The Lord will make it clear when you are ready.

Emotionally Available

Triumph Leadership means having a heart for the hurting. Serving in *Triumph Leadership* will draw deeply from our *emotional* wells. Stability of our personal lives and of our significant relationships will be important. We'll do a check-up now, and then we will go deeper later.

Ponder, Pray, and Journal

- Do I take responsibility for my mind and my emotions?
- Do I focus on God or do I focus on my circumstances?
- Am I disciplined in my thought life? Do I take every thought captive to obedience to Christ?
- Am I controlled by my emotions? Or do I control my

emotions by focusing my thoughts on God, who He is, and His power and provision – and thus receive His peace in the storms of life?

If the Holy Spirit is beginning to uncover some heart issues, don't be alarmed. It simply means you are open to His gentle nudging. We will talk about how to fortify our emotional lives in upcoming chapters.

Spiritually Available

Triumph Leadership calls for a certain kind of spiritual *readiness*, and a certain level of spiritual *maturity*. Let's explore.

Spiritual readiness comes from a season of deepening of our relationship with the Lord through the healing He has granted us in the fires of life. This season will have most likely entailed a wrestling through to surrender, a process of forgiveness, and a significant degree of spiritual healing. As leaders, we fight to live in freedom – freedom from addictions, impurity, anger, unforgiveness, pride, idolatry, or other strongholds. We do whatever it takes to receive that freedom and walk forth in it.

For most of my leaders, levels of freedom came through seasons of surrender, healing, and spiritual growth through *Triumph* classes. Other leaders worked through *additional* healing classes, such as Grief Share, Divorce Care, Sexual Abuse Recovery, Abortion Recovery, Celebrate Recovery, Addiction Recovery, Trauma Classes, or Freedom Courses. Other leaders needed a season of mentoring or Christian counseling to be able to walk in greater freedom. I, too, have needed healing classes, mentoring, and counseling.

Equally important is *spiritual maturity*. Paul instructs Timothy to seek out a leader who is...

> **...not a new convert, so that he will not become conceited and fall into the condemnation incurred by the devil.**
>
> 1 Timothy 3:6

I am thinking this warning includes not only someone who is new to the faith and thus not mature yet, but also someone who may have been a believer for a long time but has not yet grown up in the Lord. We are all susceptible to pride, but we can see from this verse that someone who is new in the Lord, or not matured in the Lord, may be more susceptible to falling into pride – and Satan's subsequent condemnation. As we grow in Christ, the Holy Spirit will help us to recognize the pride in us and teach us how to be increasingly victorious over this stronghold and to walk in deeper humility.

As *Triumph* Servant Leaders, we are daily engaged in the battle of tearing down strongholds of not only pride, but also selfishness, independence, fear, guilt, shame, anger, anxiety, depression, unforgiveness, control, and many others. Our goals are our rebellion vanquished and replaced with submission to authority, our offensiveness eradicated and replaced with gentleness and forgiveness, our fear banished and replaced with trust and surrender. We know we haven't "arrived" and we count on Jesus to carry this work through to completion in us.

> **... being confident of this, that he who began a good work in you will carry it on to completion until the day of Christ Jesus.**
>
> Philippians 1:6 NIV

As *Triumph* Servant Leaders, we have wrestled with the sovereignty of God, and His sovereignty now gives us great peace. We are humble enough to know that we need mentors and accountability partners. Day by day, we are increasingly manifesting the fruit of the Spirit and the fear of the Lord. We are not on an emotional roller coaster ride; we **have learned to be content** (Phil 4:11).

Of course our sanctification is a life-long process, culminating in our glorification in eternity. I like how Hebrews explains it:

For by one offering He has perfected forever those who are being sanctified.
Hebrews 10:14 NKJV

Already perfected, yet still being sanctified. Holy, yet being made holy. An unfathomable mystery indeed.

Ponder, Pray, and Journal

Journal where you are in spiritual readiness and spiritual maturity, and your journey that brought you to this place.

Physically Available

Physically available doesn't mean just showing up for class. It also means ready to prayerfully seek out and invite potential participants. It means coming to class prayed up and spiritually ready. And it means ready to pour into the participants, from a few weeks before class starts, throughout the months of the course, and afterwards as we guide them into their next steps.

Physically available also means we take proper care of our physical bodies, including a healthy diet, exercise, and sufficient sleep. This is necessary to sustain the stamina and mental alertness needed to minister to the participants.

Ponder, Pray, and Journal

Ask the Holy Spirit to show you if you are ready mentally, emotionally, spiritually, and physically to move into *Triumph Leadership*. When you're finished your time with the Lord, we'll move into the "T" of F.A.T. – Teachable.

Teachable

Ah, teachable. This is paramount for leadership. No one is ready for *Triumph Leadership* without this deep heart characteristic. Let's talk about what this includes.

- We will open our hearts to the Lord as a student each time we lead a class. We will lead by example.

- We will continue to pursue additional seasons of healing for our own deep wounds.

- We will meet regularly as leaders for deep sharing, fellowship, prayer, and continued development of leadership skills. We will also take advantage of leadership training offered by our church, knowing that there is always more to learn.

- We must be willing to be a perpetual student of the Word, praying constantly for an insatiable hunger to understand even more deeply the mysterious truths of God. Because Satan is always pushing against us, if we are not growing, we are not merely stagnant, *we are going backwards*. We will be steering our ship without a rudder. This would be dangerous enough for ourselves, but since we have people on our ship, we are also leading them into treacherous waters. We will be headed for a shipwreck.

All these traits are very important. Yet perhaps the most difficult aspect of being teachable is being *humbly correctable*. What will that look like?

- *Actively seeking* guidance, accountability, and training by pastors, mentors, and those ahead of us on the journey.

- Open to suggestions for improvement – from our participants, other leaders, our pastors and those we serve under, or whomever God may choose to speak through.

- Willing to receive correction with all humility. Not falling into a trap of blaming, excusing, or defending. Taking full responsibility, and learning from our mistakes.

As you do the next exercise, keep in mind that there are a number of reasons we may not be as teachable as we'd like to be. Pride can certainly thwart teachability, along with self-idolatry and fear of failure. But another factor may be unhealed wounds. If we have endured bitter or repetitive criticism, especially when we were young, or by an important person in our life, we may be particularly sensitive to correction. Deeper healing may be needed to enable us to become more teachable.

Ponder, Pray, and Journal

Let's ask ourselves some tough questions:

- Am I leading to learn – *or to tell others what I know?*
- Am I doing more listening – *or talking?*
- Are my answers to edify the body of Christ – *or to satisfy my own need to be heard or to demonstrate my knowledge?* Spirit-led, or *from the flesh*?

- Am I open to learn from the Holy Spirit when He is correcting me – *even if He is speaking through a Christian whom I believe is less mature than me?*

Of course when we are seeking advice and wise counsel, we will go to the most spiritually mature person we know. But sometimes, seemingly out of nowhere, God may even speak to us through a less mature Christian, a fallen away Christian, an unbeliever – or even a donkey (Num 22:8). Be ready.

One more heart-searching moment. Be still before the Lord and allow the Holy Spirit to bring to mind how you responded to a recent correction, suggestion, or recommendation. Journal what He shows you.

Bond-Servants of the Lord

In my mind, the title "Servant Leader" denotes both humble and teachable. The word in the Greek I am thinking of is *doulos*, translated servant, or even more clearly, bond-servant. *Doulos* means "a slave, one who is in a permanent relation of servitude to another, his will being altogether consumed in the will of the other."[3] Philippians tells us that Jesus **emptied Himself, taking on the form of a bond-servant** (Phil 2:7). Similarly, Peter, Paul, James, Jude, and John all refer to themselves as bond-servants of Christ. As Servant Leaders, we will be, like Jesus, like these apostles, *altogether consumed* with the will of God.

Additionally, Paul writes,

For we do not preach ourselves but Christ Jesus as Lord, and ourselves as your bond-servants for Jesus' sake.

2 Corinthians 4:5

As *Triumph* Servant Leaders, we are first and foremost bond-servants of Jesus Christ, and we are also bond-servants of our participants and our fellow leaders. Our English word doula, the one who provides support and assistance to a pregnant woman throughout her labor and delivery, comes from the word *doulos*. That is a stirring word picture.

Do nothing from selfishness or empty conceit, but with humility of mind regard one another as more important than yourselves; do not merely look out for your own personal interests, but also for the interests of others.

Philippians 2:3-4

Ponder, Pray, and Journal

Take a few moments to journal your thoughts about what it means to be *doulos*, bond-servant.

Dr. John C. Maxwell truly exemplifies a servant's heart. He discloses that his heart's intent is to "add value to people." After just a few moments in his presence, you will discover that those are not idle words.

In his book, *Developing the Leader Within You 2.0*, he shares his strategy when he is asked to speak. He first asks questions such as "What do you want me to say that would help you the most?" And then,

> I'll develop a speech to fit their specific agenda because I know it's not about me. The question I'm asking at the end of my time with them is, "Did I help you?"[4]

When I read this, my heart was deeply stirred. Here is a man so famous that he's a household word, and yet he is developing a speech to fit *their* agenda! That is undeniably a servant's heart.

At the end of this chapter in his book, he shares vulnerably his heartfelt requests, asking God to grow him more as a leader. This very personal prayer culminates with, "I want to be a foot washer!"[5]

I want to be a foot washer. Yes, I want to serve that way too.

Chapter 2
To Set the Captives Free

In order to effectively accomplish our work as *Triumph* Servant Leaders, we must clearly understand the mission God has assigned to us, and then seek Him to prepare us to fulfill it. In this chapter, we will first explore God's overarching Kingdom strategy and our assignment as soldiers in the battle. Then we will discuss how *Triumph Ministry* fits into His strategy. Finally, we will ask the Lord to examine our own hearts to discern what additional heart work may be necessary in order to fully equip us to enter into this calling into *Triumph Ministry*.

God's Kingdom Strategy

After His baptism, when Jesus was about to embark on His public ministry, we read in Luke 4 how He was led by the Spirit into the wilderness for forty days of fasting. After He was victorious in temptation, He returned to Galilee in the power of the Spirit to launch into His Kingdom assignment. In the town of Nazareth, He read in the synagogue from Isaiah:

> "The Spirit of the Lord is upon Me,
> because He anointed Me
> to preach the gospel to the poor.
> He has sent Me to proclaim release to the captives,
> and recovery of sight to the blind,
> to set free those who are oppressed,
> to proclaim the favorable year of the Lord."
>
> Luke 4:18-19

Every time I read these verses, the beauty, excitement, and enormity of this calling takes my breath away. Let's read the original passage in Isaiah:

> The Spirit of the Sovereign LORD is on me,
> because the Lord has anointed me
>   to preach good news to the poor.
> He has sent me to bind up the brokenhearted,
>   to proclaim freedom for the captives
>   and release from darkness for the prisoners,
> to proclaim the year of the LORD's favor ...
>
> Isaiah 61:1-2

Jesus was sent to earth on assignment, and this is *His* mission. Now let's take it up a level. When Jesus met with His disciples after His death and resurrection, He said to them,

> "Peace be with you; as the Father has sent Me, *I also send you.*"
>
> John 20:21, emphasis added

As the Father has sent Me, I also send you. So this is also *our* mission. We have been commissioned to be His instruments as He sets the captives free.

Ponder, Pray, and Journal

Read the above verses from Isaiah and Luke again. Then take a few minutes to write in your journal each part of our calling from these passages, and sit in stillness before Him.

How Triumph Ministry Fits Into His Strategy

In order to effectively lead, a leader must know the destination. But only God knows the purposes He has for each individual, only He knows the intended path to their destiny. So only the Holy Spirit, who knows the mind of God, can lead them. We cannot. Nor should we try. But as *Triumph* Servant Leaders, we do have an assignment, and that assignment is to lead our people into the heart of God. We may not know the actual steps or the final destination, but we do know the Way to that destination.

Thomas said to him, "Lord, we don't know where you are going, so how can we know the way?"
Jesus answered, "I am the way and the truth and the life. No one comes to the Father except through me."

John 14:5-6 NIV

Only Jesus frees, heals, delivers, saves. Only Jesus sets the captives free. And He chooses to do that *by His Holy Spirit working through us*. The *Triumph Series* is a vehicle God employs to bring people to repentance and surrender, to demolish strongholds, to heal and restore and transform and free and deliver. To open blind eyes, to lift burdens, to heal broken hearts, and to proclaim great joy. We, as Servant Leaders of *Triumph*, are the weapons in His hand as He releases those captives and opens those eyes and heals those hearts. It is an honor beyond words.

Let's go to Second Timothy for some insight into *how* He may use us as His weapons as He sets captives free.

To Set Free Those Who Are Oppressed

The Lord's bond-servant must not be quarrelsome, but be kind to all, able to teach, patient when wronged, with gentleness correcting those who are in opposition, if perhaps God may grant them repentance leading to the knowledge of the truth, and they may come to their senses and escape from the snare of the devil, having been held captive by him to do his will.

2 Timothy 2:24-26

I am filled with horror realizing that Satan holds those who are in opposition *captive to do his will.* But in these verses we can also see God's plan for escape.

Ponder, Pray, and Journal

Re-read this passage, and journal God's part, His bond-servant's part, and the entrapped one's part.

My *Greek Word Study* elaborates on the phrase **come to their senses:** "to awake out of a drunken sleep and become sober."[1] That is an important word picture for me. When people are ensnared, they are stuporous, drunken, asleep in the Light. In order to receive freedom, they must awaken to their state of captivity and come to their senses and repent. How will they awaken? How will they come to repentance? Journal what the Lord is speaking to you here.

Second Timothy shows that *God* is the one that grants repentance. Romans 2:4 echoes this teaching: **the kindness of God leads you to repentance**. God *grants* the stirring towards repentance, He *leads*, but those in opposition must *choose* to repent. Repentance of their opposition opens them up to come to know the truth. As they repent, the Holy Spirit opens blinded eyes and brings them out of denial. He arouses them out of their drunken stupor and draws them into the Light where lies are exposed. By renouncing lies and embracing truth, they can escape.

God is the only One who frees, by His Holy Spirit graciously convicting us of sin, by His kindness bringing us to repentance. We point our people onto God's path with kindness, patience, and great gentleness, and we will stand in the gap beseeching God to bring them to that repentance. And as they repent and truth is revealed to them, then *they* must escape. **Escape** is an *action word*.

> **Our soul has escaped as a bird**
> **out of the snare of the trapper;**
> **The snare is broken and we have escaped.**
>   Psalm 124:7

God breaks open the trap, but they will have work to do. They must walk out of that snare. *They must run free.* And as His bond-servants, we will point out the way to them, run alongside them, and support them as they run.

To Proclaim the Lord's Favor

I'd like to read that passage from Isaiah 61 again.

> **The Spirit of the Sovereign Lord is on me,
> because the Lord has anointed me
>   to preach good news to the poor.
> He has sent me to bind up the brokenhearted,
>   to proclaim freedom for the captives
>   and release from darkness for the prisoners,
> to proclaim the year of the Lord's favor ...**
>
> Isaiah 61:1-2

I have heard that the year of the Lord's favor is a reference to the Jubilee Year – when debts were cancelled, slaves were freed, and property was returned to the original owner (Lev 25:1-55). We will want our people to recognize the profound joy of freedom from sin, of release from debt because Jesus has paid that debt. To recognize that the Victor of the war has already been determined – and we will reign with Him at the end of time.

I believe that this time of *Triumph* Class is a season of His favor. This is the "now time" that God has ordained for healing and freedom. There are no coincidences with God. He has called these people to this class at this time because He desires to bless them.

But, as Pastor Julie Mullins of Christ Fellowship explains, we must *position* ourselves to receive His favor. By immersing in class and doing the hard work of repenting and surrendering and forgiving, our people will be positioning themselves to receive His favor and blessing.

We Are Called to a Ministry of Redemption, Restoration – And Beyond

Triumph Ministry is a place people receive the Lord's redemption and restoration – and even beyond. Let's explore together.

We teach our people to invite Jesus to transform their hearts through their willingness, repentance, and surrender. By His miraculous metamorphosis (Rom 12:1-2),[2] He begins to redeem and restore. *Redemption* is setting free for a ransom.[3] *Restoration* is "to mend ... to put a thing in its appropriate condition".[4] Restoration is a rebuilding of a brokenness, a way of settling something *back into its former state*.[5] Restoration may be the way He rescues a broken marriage, heals a fractured relationship, or renews fragile health, bringing something back to its *original condition*.

Sometimes, God is even more gracious, giving *more* than just a restoration to original condition. For example, we read in Scripture that when God's heart work in Job was complete, not only did He restore Job's property and other physical elements, He actually doubled them (Job 42:10-12).

What an honor for *Triumph Ministry* to be used as His instrument to restore. And yet, there's more. It seems that there are other times when Jesus wants to use *Triumph Ministry* to take His people *beyond restoration*. At these times, He takes an entire situation and turns it upside down on its head, vanquishing the enemy, so there can be no question who the Victor really is. This is hard to adequately put into words, so I will let these verses in Isaiah explain:

> **... to bestow on them a crown of beauty**
>   **instead of ashes,**
> **the oil of joy**
>   **instead of mourning,**
> **and a garment of praise**
>   **instead of a spirit of despair ...**
> **Instead of your shame**
>   **you will receive a double portion,**
> **and instead of disgrace**
>   **you will rejoice in your inheritance.**
> **And so you will inherit a double portion**
>   **in your land,**
> **And everlasting joy will be yours.**
>
> Isaiah 61:3,7 NIV

This incredible reversal, this transposition from the tail to the head, is an inconceivable exchange, a mighty miracle where we trade in the ashes of our lives and He gives us beauty. Where we give God our mourning, and He converts our mourning into joyful dancing. Where we place into His hands all that causes us despair – our shame and sins and failures and pain – and in return, He showers us with unimaginable blessings that erupt into praise. Where our shame melts away and is replaced with a double portion infused with everlasting joy. Where He brings purpose out of our pain – not *despite* our pain, but *out of it.* My daughter Jenna describes this as "God turning your wounds into a storehouse of blessings."

Restoration is the couple on the brink of divorce, now transformed and healed and restored. They are raising their children in the Lord and serving in church. But *beyond restoration* occurs when they begin ministering to other hurting couples, using the equipping they have received through their pain.

Restoration is the suicidal man, now freed and healed and delivered, back to work, taking care of his family. He moves *beyond restoration* when he volunteers as a mentor to suicidal teens.

Restoration is the former addict, now delivered, her strongholds demolished. She has now graduated and is looking for work in her field. But she walks *beyond restoration* as she accepts a job as a counselor in the field of addiction.

Beyond restoration, tables are overturned and the enemy is outmaneuvered once again. God deftly takes what Satan meant for evil, and in a miraculous brilliantly blinding move, uses every bit of Satan's diabolical plan for His own good (Gen 50:20). Of course the *ultimate beyond* is the glory God wrought out of the crucifixion: the resurrection of Jesus Christ, the defeat of darkness, the gates of heaven opened, the veil torn in two, our sins forgiven, and captives set free!

Fasten your seatbelts, we're going to the next level. For besides *restoration* and *beyond restoration*, there seems to be other times when God may grant beyond *without* restoration. Let me explain.

Sometimes, when damage is truly irreparable and restoration is not possible, when consequences are already rolling forth and cannot be altered without turning back the clock, God may skip over restoration and go right to *beyond*. He gives beauty for ashes *without changing the circumstances.* Here's what I mean. God did not resurrect Job's ten children. He did not put Job's family back to its original condition on earth. Instead, He went right to *beyond* – giving him ten more on earth – meaning twenty in eternity (Job 42:13). I call that *beyond without restoration.*

Beyond without restoration is also a woman who has had two abortions now being used as God's instrument as He saves lives in a crisis pregnancy center. It is an author being called by God to write more books – after knowingly improperly footnoting the first one. These *beyonds without restoration* would never have happened if I had not surrendered my efforts to try to restore something that is over, that is finished, that can never be restored. These beyonds would never have happened if I had not given Jesus my ashes.

As we deeply repent and surrender, as we place into His hands the ashes of our failures – all of them, holding nothing back – He will indeed transform our defeat into His greatest victory. Because what Satan meant for evil, God meant for good. He laughs at the enemy. He is the Victor, and He always has the last word. That is entering into His beyond. (Gen 50:20, Ps 37:13, Pr 16:9, Dan 2:20-22, 4:34-35.)

And the result of beyond? Oh, so much richness! We will grow up in Him, strong and true, and He will be glorified! Let's read further into Isaiah 61.

> **They will be called oaks of righteousness,**
> **a planting of the LORD**
> **for the display of his splendor.**
>
> Isaiah 61:3 NIV

We will be His instruments as He rebuilds our lives and demolishes the curses that have afflicted our families for generations:

> **They will rebuild the ancient ruins**
>   **and restore the places long devastated;**
> **they will renew the ruined cities**
>   **that have been devastated for generations ...**
> **Their descendants will be known**
>   **among the nations**
>   **and their offspring among the peoples.**
> **All who see them will acknowledge**
>   **that they are a people the Lord has blessed.**
>   Isaiah 61:4,9 NIV

We will minister, and intercede as His priests:

> **And you will be called priests of the Lord,**
>   **you will be named ministers of our God.**
>   Isaiah 61:6 NIV

And we will glow with beauty as a bride or bridegroom would:

> **I delight greatly in the Lord;**
>   **my soul rejoices in my God.**
> **For he has clothed me with garments of salvation**
>   **and arrayed me in a robe of his righteousness,**
> **as a bridegroom adorns his head like a priest,**
>   **and as a bride adorns herself with her jewels.**
>   Isaiah 61:10 NIV

This is the healing and redemption, the restoration and beyond that God has graciously granted us. And this is the healing and redemption, the restoration and beyond that we so desperately desire for our people. And the pathway to position us to receive God's restoration and beyond is walking into the Light, casting down lies, repenting, forgiving, surrendering – and doing the hard work of running out of that trap and into freedom. This is the path we must direct our people down. There is no other way.

On Mission

Our goal as Servant Leaders is to fan into a flame their glowing embers of desire for deeper relationship with God. To teach them truth, to disciple them, and to teach them to hear God's voice. To show them how to position themselves to receive from the Holy Spirit by immersing in the Word, spending time in worship, prayer, and stillness, and connecting into their church family. To walk with them and gently guide them as they journey the difficult paths of forgiveness, repentance, and surrender. And, as we invite the Holy Spirit into our classes, into our lives, and into our participants' lives, we rely on Him to deliver and transform and grow and purify and heal.

But thanks be to God, who always leads us in triumph in Christ, and manifests through us the sweet aroma of the knowledge of Him in every place. For we are a fragrance of Christ to God among those who are being saved and among those who are perishing; to the one an aroma from death to death, to the other an aroma from life to life. And who is adequate for these things?

2 Corinthians 2:14-16

What a privilege to be His instrument as He leads our people in triumph in Christ. What a blessing to be the sweet aroma of the knowledge of Him. And I say with Paul, who is adequate for these things?

Such confidence we have through Christ toward God. Not that we are adequate in ourselves to consider anything as coming from ourselves, but our adequacy is from God, who also made us adequate as servants of a new covenant ...

2 Corinthians 2:3-6

We are not qualified ourselves. Our competency comes from God. We can absolutely trust God to fully equip us, to make us sufficiently qualified, to furnish us with everything that we need so that He can work His plan through this ministry. As we rely on Him steadfastly, He will, through Jesus, make His servants adequate. As Pastor Todd Mullins of Christ Fellowship declares, "We walk in God-fidence."

We must be humble + confident. What an oxymoron! We are to be *humble*, because God opposes the proud but gives grace to the humble. Humble, because it is God who bestowed this leadership position upon us. Humble, because everything comes from God, including our abilities, education, talents, gifts, time, and positions – *and the people He sends into class* (Jas 4:6, Ps 18:33, 1Chr 29:14).

Because this is God's class and we have surrendered it to Him, we can trust that He will bring whom He desires to this class. We will partner with Him by issuing invitations and connecting with participants and leading classes as He directs, but in the end, the people He calls and the heart work He accomplishes are *His responsibility*.

I planted, Apollos watered, but God was causing the growth. So then neither the one who plants nor the one who waters is anything, but God who causes the growth.

1 Corinthians 3:6-7

Ponder, Pray, and Journal

Re-read that last paragraph and the Scripture from First Corinthians, and look up the following Scriptures:

- James 4:6
- Psalm 18:33
- 1 Chronicles 29:14

How do you feel after meditating on these passages?

Because everything comes from God – our abilities, education, talents, gifts, time, positions, and even the people He sends in – we are *confident*. Our competence and skill in leading this class is entirely up to God. He has given, and He can take it away (Job 1:21).

It is and always was His class, but when we *surrender* this class to Him, we stop fighting Him for control. When we surrender the class to Him, we *acknowledge* that it is His class, and recognize that *He* is responsible for the growth of the participants. It has nothing to do with us; we are merely His mouthpieces. We can become completely tongue-tied, and the Holy Spirit will *still* accomplish what He has determined to do. The goal of this class is advancement of His Kingdom, spiritual growth, surrendered hearts, people fulfilling their God-ordained purposes. Only the Holy Spirit can advance His Kingdom. It's *our* job to pray. It's *His* job to change hearts.

Earthenware Jars

We have indeed been called to a stunning ministry. To watch the Holy Spirit transform hearts and lives will continually take our breath away. And I believe God wants us to be acutely aware that it is His work, and not our own. I am thinking of Second Corinthians, God's treasure placed in jars of clay.

> **But we have this treasure in earthen vessels, so that the surpassing greatness of the power will be of God and not from ourselves;**
> > **we are afflicted in every way,**
> > > **but not crushed;**
> >
> > **perplexed,**
> > > **but not despairing;**
> >
> > **persecuted,**
> > > **but not forsaken;**
> >
> > **struck down,**
> > > **but not destroyed;**
>
> **always carrying about in the body the dying of Jesus, so that the life of Jesus also may be manifested in our body.**
>
> 2 Corinthians 4:7-10

I have a few clay flower pots in my garage, most of them in pieces. And I see in Scriptures how earthenware jars can be shattered. The Lord instructed Jeremiah to smash an earthenware jar before the elders and the priests to symbolize the shattering of Israel because they had forsaken the Lord, worshipping other gods and sacrificing their children to them (Jer 19:1-14).

And I also see that God can miraculously hold earthenware jars intact when it suits His purposes to do so. A few chapters later in Jeremiah, when Babylon was besieging Jerusalem and the Israelites were about to be decimated, God instructed Jeremiah to *purchase land in Israel!* Jeremiah, imprisoned for prophesying the fall of Israel, obeyed the Lord and purchased the land (Jer 32:1-13). God gave him specific instructions about the deeds to the land, which Jeremiah carried out in front of witnesses:

> **Thus says the Lord of hosts, the God of Israel, "Take these deeds, this sealed deed of purchase and this open deed, and put them in an earthenware jar, *that they may last a long time.*" For thus says the Lord of hosts, the God of Israel, "Houses and fields and vineyards will again be bought in this land."**
>
> Jeremiah 32:14-15, emphasis added

Moments before their destruction and exile, the Lord promised Israel that He would bring them *back from* captivity and restore their land to them! God instructed Jeremiah to put the deeds in earthenware jars for safekeeping, **that they may last a long time**, vowing that He would miraculously protect Israel's right to this land and bring them back to prosper.

I am also thinking how the Lord miraculously preserved the Dead Sea Scrolls. These scrolls, containing writings from nearly every book of the Old Testament, were hidden in caves and housed for *thousands of years* in earthenware jars. It seems God miraculously protected them from the elements and from human discovery – until His perfect timing unearthed them. A rock carelessly thrown into a cave by a teenage boy shattered a clay jar, and the scrolls were unveiled.[6] I think the Lord wants us to know that He is well able to protect earthenware jars, both physically and spiritually.

Back to 2 Corinthians. We can be shattered as easily as an earthenware jar – but He miraculously guards us. We are attacked on every side, but His extraordinary protection shields us from destruction. When it seems we have no way out, we do not despair, trusting He will supernaturally open doors that no man can shut. When we are persecuted, we know He will never fail or forsake us. Even when we are struck down, the enemy cannot destroy us, because He intervenes, protecting His earthenware jars from shattering. (Ps 121:8, 18:4-6, Rev 3:7-8, Dt 31:6, Rom 8:31, 1Jn 4:4.)

People will expect us to shatter, but we do not. All this to show that we have no power of our own to prevent us from breaking; it is His Holy Spirit within us who is holding our clay jars intact. And as we choose humility and are revealed to be mere earthenware jars, Jesus is made manifest.

Our adequacy is from God. We do not preach ourselves but Christ Jesus as Lord, and ourselves as bond-servants for the sake of Christ. We determine to know nothing but

Jesus Christ and Him crucified. We are constantly dying to ourselves so that the Risen Christ can take His rightful place in our hearts (2Cor 4:5,10 1Cor 2:2, Rom 8:12-13, Gal 2:20).

Therefore we do not lose heart, but though our outer man is decaying, yet our inner man is being renewed day by day. For momentary, light affliction is producing for us an eternal weight of glory far beyond all comparison, while we look not at the things which are seen, but at the things which are not seen; for the things which are seen are temporal, but the things which are not seen are eternal.
                                            2 Corinthians 4:16-18

Ponder, Pray, and Journal

The eternal work of the Holy Spirit is accomplished through our humble earthen vessels. Let's bow our hearts before Him in astonishment and deep gratitude.

Only People Who Are Free Can Help Set Others Free

Imagine a captive still imprisoned in a dungeon. He won't be able to set his fellow prisoners free until he secures his own freedom himself. Spiritual freedom is parallel. Jesus has called us to this ministry of freedom and deliverance, but we will not be ready to be used by Him until we have broken out of captivity ourselves. Pastor Todd Mullins summarizes it this way: "Freed people free people."

Pastor Julie Mullins adds, "Our journeys of freedom will last a lifetime." We studied in *Triumph of Surrender* how, as we grow in the Lord and surrender more deeply, and He demolishes strongholds and grants greater measures of healing, we will walk in more expansive freedom. As we forgive in deeper and deeper measure, we will receive greater freedom. More freedom and healing allows the Holy Spirit to flow without hindrance through us.[7] Then we, His earthen vessels, are more available for Him to flow through us to reach other people. John Bevere, speaking tenderly about Holy Spirit, cautions,

> Someone who sees God's Spirit as an influence or supreme power will constantly say, "I want more of the Spirit." On the contrary, someone who sees Him as a wonderful Person will say, "How can I give more of myself to Him?"[8]

To be used as His weapons in His battle to free others, our equipping demands that we give more of ourselves to Him. It will require some of our strongholds to be destroyed and a certain degree of freedom and healing ourselves. We will need a safe place to work through these battles. Additionally, this journey of freedom and healing is a lifetime journey, and will not be fully consummated until we see Jesus in eternity. So how do we know when we are free enough to step into *Triumph Leadership?*

There is no easy answer to that question, and indeed the answer will be unique to each person. God knows; He will show you. He has placed you here to bear fruit, fruit that remains, and He desires to bring victory through you (Jn 15:16, Rom 8:31, 2Cor 2:14). Trust Him to show you, your pastor, and those who are training you when you are ready.

The Lord has equipped me through many on-going seasons of healing and sanctification. I have watched Him do the same for other *Triumph* leaders. From that vantage point, I have compiled some questions over these next few sections that may help us discern if we still need more healing before we are ready for *Triumph Leadership*. Prayerfully allow the Holy Spirit to reveal the answers to these questions. If He unmasks anything here, don't be alarmed! The Lord simply wants you to be fully equipped and ready, and we will work through these issues and seek His healing in the next chapters.

Ponder, Pray, and Journal

Search me, God, and know my heart;
  test me and know my anxious thoughts.
See if there is any offensive way in me,
  and lead me in the way everlasting.
                                    Psalm 139:23-24 NIV

Ask the Holy Spirit to search your heart, then answer these questions.

Do I have a need to ...

- "Tell my story"?

- Let people know that I have been wronged, hurt, suffered unjustly, or been afflicted with illness, suffering, or pain?

- Demonstrate how "spiritual" I am or show people what my relationship with God is like?

- Prove to people that God is using me?

There will be times when we are with our participants when the Holy Spirit calls us to share pieces of our story, for *His* purpose of ministering. To let our people know that we, at least in some small way, can relate to their pain. To let them see us as His earthen vessels, broken and now gloriously healed, and therefore a beacon of hope.

Sometimes, though, if we still have some unhealed areas, we may cross the line here. We may find ourselves sharing to seek comfort of the members in class, to garner pity, to set ourselves up on a pedestal, or to toot our own horn.

Ask yourself ...

- Are my emotions in balance? Can I talk about hurts in my life without an overflow of emotions?
- Do my trials and tragedies define me? Is my trial part of every introductory conversation? Do I want everyone to know this about me? Do I see myself as a victim?
- Do my hurts and offenses dominate my conversation?
- Am I still offended – or easily offended?

Triggering

Another indicator we can use to discern if more healing is necessary before we are ready to be in a place of ministering is "triggering." Triggering is the experience of having an emotional reaction out of proportion to the circumstances. Most whom God calls to *Triumph Leadership* are compassionate and full of empathy. But triggering goes beyond empathy into a place of emotional distress because painful memories or emotions have been stirred up. I'll use myself as an example to help us better comprehend.

For many decades I was triggered by violence. If someone was talking about violence, or I witnessed violence, or I heard about violence, or I saw violence in a movie or on television, an uncontrollable churning would begin deep inside of me. Overwhelming fear would well up. Although these fears and emotions were so intense I didn't even know how I would survive, most of what was going on was deep inside of me;

no one observing me would even guess something was amiss. Other times I couldn't contain this painful cascade of emotions, I couldn't rein in my reaction, and I would speak or act in terror or anger or helplessness. I was clearly not in a position to minister to people with pain. Over a number of years, the Lord walked me through many seasons of classes and counselors and mentors, granting me much healing from pain of my past, and equipping me for *Triumph Ministry*.

I had many more triggers besides violence. My husband describes my trigger points as "land mines." That imagery helped me to understand how John feels when he inadvertently sets one off.

When the Lord first began to teach me about triggers, He showed me that I had an entire minefield in my heart! As I have partnered with Him over many years, searching out and dealing with the root issues, He has gently defused those bombs and graciously removed them one by one. Yet, as I just saw last week, they are not all completely cleared out. However, they are isolated bombs now, not an entire minefield.

Ponder, Pray, and Journal

Has the Lord revealed anything to you through these past few sections and questions you have pondered? Are you experiencing triggering? Spend some time with the Lord, and ask Him to reveal the root issues here.

Am I Ready?

The decision as to when someone is ready to *begin training* as a *Triumph* Servant Leader, and to be *released* as a *Triumph* Servant Leader, will be made by the Lord through your pastor, church leaders, and/or the *Triumph Leadership Team* who are part of your training. As you are working through this book, you can see that your degree of freedom, deliverance, and healing is just one of many factors that will affect that decision. And of course, only God is the One who will set our feet upon our high places (Ps 18:33, Hab 3:19).

Through this chapter, the Holy Spirit may have exposed some unhealed areas. Do not be alarmed. **God is greater than our heart and knows all things** (1Jn 3:20). This is His perfect timing. I believe you are here because it is His season of favor for you.

One of the most powerful tactics Satan uses to thwart our freedom is distortion, fracturing, or outright destruction of our identity. Let's go together into the next chapter and seek Him to heal and to establish our identity in Christ.

Chapter 3
Establishing Our Identity In Christ

In order to direct people into the heart of God for healing, freedom, and growth in intimacy with Him, we ourselves must deeply know and understand *the heart character of God*. We must be ever so secure in *our own* relationship with Him. We must unshakably know who *He* says we are: our *identity* (Eph 5:1-14, Hos 6:6).

"... but let him who boasts boast of this, that he understands and knows Me, that I am the Lord who exercises lovingkindness, justice and righteousness on earth; for I delight in these things," declares the Lord.

Jeremiah 9:24

See how great a love the Father has bestowed on us, that we would be called children of God; *and such we are.*

1 John 3:1, emphasis added

And such we are. I believe that knowing the depth of God's heart, as well as what we mean to Him, is more important for our equipping as leaders than any training or experience we could garner. Get ready for some heart work, because we are going to settle in and spend some time right here.

We will start by seeing how lies blind us to the love of God and prevent us from receiving His healing and walking in freedom. We will look at repentance and surrender as the doorways to freedom.

Next, we will ask the Holy Spirit to show us if there are any lies our own hearts still believe regarding who God is, and regarding our own identity. Then we will learn how to dismantle those lies and replace them with truth.

Finally, once we are secure in our identity, we will learn how our own transparent walk can inspire our participants to vulnerably open their hearts to God and to the class. We will also discuss how we, as leaders, will handle our own seasons of additional healing. Before we start, let's pray together.

Holy Spirit, please shine Your Light into our hearts. Search us and reveal if there is anything in our hearts that does not align with Your truth. Shake us, stir us, awaken us to truth; expose the depths of our hearts so that these lies cannot fool us anymore. Please grant us the courage necessary to admit any lies or deceptions, and the willingness to come into the Light, inviting You to expose, purify, and heal. Amen.[1]

Veiled Hearts and Blinded Minds

Let's start by focusing in on a few verses in Second Corinthians. These verses are describing those who don't know the Lord, but we are going to see how they may apply to us also.

But their minds were hardened ... a veil lies over their heart; but whenever a person turns to the Lord, the veil is taken away ... And even if our gospel is veiled, it is veiled to those who are perishing, in

whose case the god of this world has blinded the minds of the unbelieving so that they might not see the light of the gospel of the glory of Christ, who is the image of God.

2 Corinthians 3:14-16, 4:3-4

I can so relate. At the time of my salvation, the heavy dark curtain was indeed pulled back and I was able to see Jesus and experience His love and forgiveness for the first time. But when I think about my abiding walk with the Lord, I realize that this passage applies to my heart even now.

As I continue to seek Him, it seems that He continues to reveal additional veils. Some are flimsy gauzy curtains. But others are thick opaque veils, curtains of blindness shrouding parts of my heart in deep darkness.

It seems that these veils, whether opaque or translucent, are composed of lies, wounds, my own sins, generational sins, or any combination. Satan has blinded me even to the existence of these veils. Only God fully knows what veils are left, for only He knows my heart. I remain dependent upon Him to reveal, in His timing. As He mercifully reveals, and as I partner with Him, repenting of sins and casting down the lies that He has exposed, it seems He views that as an invitation to heal, to penetrate the veil and to remove it. And as He removes these veils, He enables me to see Him – and myself and others – more clearly.

If our lives and thoughts are not aligned with God's ways, if our wounds are not yet healed, if we are affected by generational sins, Satan may have blinded our minds with lies so that we cannot fully comprehend who our Heavenly Father is, who our Lord and Savior Jesus Christ is, and who we are as children of God and followers of Christ.

Now this is key: ***Whenever a person turns to the Lord, the veil is taken away.*** When a person turns to the Lord in repentance and surrender, the veil removed. Paul puts it another way in this same chapter:

Now the Lord is the Spirit, and where the Spirit of the Lord is, there is freedom.

2 Corinthians 3:17 NIV

John Bevere expounds on this verse in his book, *The Holy Spirit: An Introduction.*

> "Is there freedom *everywhere?*" ... We have proven that He [the Holy Spirit] is *everywhere*, so again, is there freedom *everywhere?* The answer to this is, absolutely no. There isn't freedom in brothels, bars, prisons, and hospitals. I've been to neighborhoods, schools, homes, and even churches where there is no freedom. So what is Scripture declaring here? I suggest that this would be a more accurate translation:
>
> Wherever the Spirit is *Lord*, that's where there is freedom. (2 Corinthians 3:17, author's paraphrase)
>
> ... The Holy Spirit is not permitted to be in authority in most bars, prisons, hospitals, or homes, and even in many churches. Where He is welcomed as supreme in authority, that is where you will find freedom and justice for all.[2]

Where the Spirit of the Lord is. Let's think of it this way: *where the Spirit is Lord.* Where the Spirit is ruling and reigning. Where we have bowed our hearts to our Almighty God in repentance and obedience. That is the door to freedom. That is our invitation to God to tear down the veil. We must pray for the eyes of our hearts to be open; we must walk in repentance and surrender; we must pursue the love of God and the steadfastness of Christ.

Our Own Humble Walk

We were all once blinded by Satan. Only God's choice of us brought light into our hearts.

For God, who said, "Light shall shine out of darkness," is the One who has shone in our hearts to give the Light of the knowledge of the glory of God in the face of Christ.

2 Corinthians 4:6

"Let there be light" (Gen 1:3). God is the Source of all light; Jesus is the Light; we did not enlighten ourselves. Only by God's grace and mercy did He graciously grant us the stupendous gift of His Light shining in our dark hearts. He opened the eyes of our hearts so that we could, in some small way, comprehend His glory. It was His sovereign choice to enable us to grasp that Jesus is the full reflection of Himself. This was not of ourselves. He shone in our hearts.

Yet even now, we can still fall into Satan's traps, and must rely on the Holy Spirit's revelation of our own blindness. We must continually ask God to search our hearts and reveal any lies we believe or anything that is displeasing to Him. God calls us as Servant Leaders to live a life of repentance and surrender. We are constantly dying to ourselves for Jesus' sake, so that the life of Jesus may be manifested in our bodies (2Cor 4:10-11, Gal 2:20).

Ponder, Pray, and Journal

You will find this to be a lengthy exercise; be sure you set aside enough time. As you do this exercise, mark off what your heart believes, not what your *head* believes. I know that you know the Word of God and your head believes truth. But your heart may be a different story. What God is interested in right now is the depth of your heart. Your heart drives your thoughts, decisions, emotions, mind, and will. In the battle between your head and your heart, your *heart* will win every time. I believe you can feel the Spirit even now stirring and revealing the difference to you.

Read each lie and its contrasting truth. Put a checkmark on the scale where your heart belief is, whether closer to the lie or closer to the truth. If your heart is completely believing the lie, instead of using the scale, simply circle the lie. Likewise, if your heart is completely believing the truth, circle the truth instead of using the scale. (Just focus on the lies and truths now. We will return to the column referencing Scripture verses later.)

This work is between you and God. Answer with the utmost of integrity.

	Lie	Scale	Truth	Scripture
1	I am unworthy of God's love and attention, so He does not pour out His love and attention on me.	☐☐☐☐	Jesus makes me worthy. He loves me unconditionally and always has His eye on me.	Isa 49:16 1Jn 4:10
2	I am unwanted.	☐☐☐☐	I have been chosen and adopted as His child.	Rom 8:15
3	I am worthless.	☐☐☐☐	I am made in His image and precious and honored.	Gen 1:27, Isa 43:1-4
4	God is disappointed with me when I have not read my Bible or prayed enough.	☐☐☐☐	God does not condemn me; He simply wants to spend time with me.	Rom 8:1 Heb 10:14 Ps 103:14 Rom 8:38-39
5	I will never be good enough or pleasing enough to earn His love and acceptance.	☐☐☐☐	Although I will never be good enough, I still don't need to earn His love and acceptance, because I've already got it.	Eph 2:5-6 Rom 8:31 Rom 5:8
6	God does not care about me, does not notice me, or has forgotten about me.	☐☐☐☐	God fully sees me. He suffers when I suffer. His good thoughts towards me are endless.	Rom 8:35, 38-39; Ps 139:17-18
7	If God loved me, He would have answered my prayers by now.	☐☐☐☐	God treasures my every prayer, and answers every prayer, in His way and His timing, with "Yes," "Not yet," or "I have something better!"	Ps 116:2 NLT

	Lie	Scale	Truth	Scripture
8	God is not really all that good.	☐☐☐☐	God's nature is loving kindness, and He is always working for my good.	Ps 36:5-6, Rom 8:38-39
9	I must be obedient and perfect to earn His love and acceptance.	☐☐☐☐	I don't need to earn His love and acceptance, because I've already got it.	Eph 2:5-6 Rom 8:31 Rom 5:8
10	The work God has for me is not as important as the work He has for others.	☐☐☐☐	The Holy Spirit distributes gifts for the common good, as He wills. When I compare myself with others, I do not understand the love of God.	Heb 12:2, 1Cor 12:4-11 2Cor 10:12
11	God has rejected me because of what I have been through, or what I have done.	☐☐☐☐	I have been chosen, adopted, anointed, and appointed for Kingdom purposes.	Eph 1:3-8
12	I cannot take a rest because then I will miss some work God has for me.	☐☐☐☐	Most important to God is my *relationship* with Him. Apart from Him I can do nothing.	Jn 15:5 Jer 9:23-24 Mt 11:28-30 Jer 6:16
13	God loves other people more than He loves me.	☐☐☐☐	God is *infinite*, and He showers me with His infinite love, just as He showers each person with His infinite love.	Rev 21:6 Isa 64:4
14	I will never be enough. I will never be good enough, smart enough, holy enough, strong enough ...	☐☐☐☐	His grace is sufficient for me. I find when I am weak, His power is even stronger in me.	2 Cor 12:9-10 1 Cor 1:26-29
15	I am not attractive enough, beautiful enough, handsome enough ... I'm not worthy of being attractive.	☐☐☐☐	Man looks at physical appearances, but God looks at the heart.	1Sam 16:7 Isa 53:2 1Pt 3:3-4 1Tim 4:8
16	I am not spiritually mature enough; I should be farther in my walk by now.	☐☐☐☐	As I continue to open myself to God, He will grow me in Him – in His timing.	1 Cor 3:6 Ph 3:20-21 Jn 16:13
17	God abandons me when I have sinned.	☐☐☐☐	God will never leave me or foresake me.	Josh 1:9 Ps 139:7-8 Ps 103:2-4

Lie	Scale	Truth	Scripture
18 God's sovereignty cannot be trusted.	☐☐☐☐	God's sovereignty is a great source of peace and security.	Isa 26:3-4 Ps 31:14-15 Rom 8:28-29
19 Some of my sins are too great to be forgiven.	☐☐☐☐	God has forgiven all of my sins, past, present, and future, through Jesus.	Ps 103:3,12 Eph 1:7-8 Col 1:13-14
20 If God really loved me, He would have shielded me from this trial.	☐☐☐☐	The depth of God's love for me is proven by His promises in Scripture and His death on the cross. What happens in this world does not define God's love for me.	Jn 16:33 Jer 31:3 Rom 5:8
21 God doesn't answer my prayers.	☐☐☐☐	My prayers ascend to the very throne room of God, and even when I don't know how to pray, He hears and answers each faltering prayer.	Rev 8:3-4 Rom 8:26-27
22 If I am doing the work He assigned me, He will accept me.	☐☐☐☐	If I fail, I am not a failure; I do not lose His acceptance. I don't need to earn His acceptance – I've already got it.	Jer 9:23-24
23 There are just some things that He doesn't intend to free me from.	☐☐☐☐	In Him, I am a new creation. Where the Spirit of the Lord is, there is freedom.	2 Cor 5:17 2 Cor 3:17
24 God cannot be trusted.	☐☐☐☐	God alone is our Refuge and our Strength, our everlasting Rock, the One who rescues us from the enemy and will never forsake us.	Ps 46:1-3 Isa 26:3-4 Ps 18:1-3, 16-19 Josh 1:5 NLT
25 Praying is a waste of time.	☐☐☐☐	I can enter His throne room with confidence to find help in time of need.	Heb 4:16 Jer 29:12-13 Heb 7:24-25 Rom 8:26-27
26 God is not on my side the way He seems to be fighting for others.	☐☐☐☐	God is fighting for me, and if God is for me, who can be against me?	Rom 8:31 Rom 8:28 Jude 1:24

	Lie	Scale	Truth	Scripture
27	God is not helping me to succeed.	☐☐☐☐	The battle is the Lord's, and He has already conquered the enemy.	1 Sam 17:47 Col 2:13-15
28	God is not concerned about the little details of my life.	☐☐☐☐	God is deeply concerned about and actively involved in every little detail of my life.	Ps 37:23 NLT Ps 138:8 NASB
29	Hearing from God is only for people who are holier than me.	☐☐☐☐	His sheep hear His voice; He is teaching me to hear His voice.	Jn 10:27
30	What I can offer is not valuable or significant. Others can offer more than me.	☐☐☐☐	I am a critical member of His body. If the whole body were an eye, where would the hearing be?	1 Cor 12:14-26
31	I am not really so unique. Anyone could replace me.	☐☐☐☐	I am his uniquely created work of art. No one can replace me.	Eph 2:10 Ps 139:13-16
32	God does not love me.	☐☐☐☐	God so loved the world and He so loves me also.	Jn 3:16 Zeph 3:17
33	I am not valuable to God.	☐☐☐☐	I am irreplaceable.	Acts 1:8 1 Pt 2:9
34	I will never amount to much. My contribution to the Kingdom is insignificant.	☐☐☐☐	I have been chosen and anointed to bear fruit that will remain.	Jn 15:16
35	If I mess up too much, I won't make it to heaven.	☐☐☐☐	I am saved and given eternal life only by His grace, through my faith, His gift to me. I will at times fail and fall short, but as I follow Him, Satan cannot snatch me away from Him..	Eph 2:8-9 Rom 3:23 Jn 8:31 Jn 10:27-28
36	I am not (good enough, smart enough, experienced enough, spiritual enough) to be a leader.	☐☐☐☐	He has called me and He will fully equip me to complete the work He has assigned me.	1 Th 5:24 AMP

	Lie	Scale	Truth	Scripture
37	Holy Spirit will not show up in the classroom to lead and guide me as He does for other leaders.	☐☐☐☐	God is fighting for me, and if God is for me, who can be against me?	Mt 18-20 Jam 1:5

Take some time to be still before Him and ask Him if there are any other lies your heart believes. Write them down, and also the countering truth.

Embracing Truth

Every truth in that chart *that you did not circle* indicates that there is a lie nestled in your heart. Recall from *Triumph Over Suffering* that any half-truth is in reality a lie.[3] The scale can help you see how deep-rooted it is. If you did not circle a particular truth, you are ensnared in a lie. Don't be embarrassed. I used to believe every one of those lies myself – so it was very easy for me to create that chart.

You are at a crossroads right now. You can shrug it off – or, you can partner with Jesus and do the hard work of renouncing these lies and choosing to believe truth. The pain of what has been done to you, the traumas you have witnessed or endured, the lies that have been spoken over you, the agony of living in this fallen world, as well as your own sins and failures have all worked to sear these lies into you. I understand that. God does, too. And right now, you can choose to stay mired in these lies. Or, you can *choose* to believe His truth, no matter how loudly the world, other people, your own thoughts, or the forces of darkness are speaking otherwise to you. Similar to forgiveness, which is not a feeling but a choice,[4] believing truth is not a feeling, but a *choice*.

And the choice is yours. Pause and ask God what He would have you do. If you are not ready, close the book. Seek the Lord in prayer. Meet me back here when you are ready to forsake these lies, because in the next section, we are going to talk about how.

I was praying you would join me here. Now don't rush this part. Be sure you have set aside enough time and privacy to enter the battlefield and break free. I have found that these steps are critical in order to break free:

- Receiving God's Revelation of Roots
- Forgiving
- Repenting
- Renewing Our Minds
- Walking It Out
- Receiving God's Healing and Transformation

You can see that some of these steps will be our responsibility, and some are God's part. I will explain each of these steps below. The order of these steps could be different at different times, and at times may be occurring simultaneously, but they all seem to be very important. **For each lie, do each of these steps, one by one.** If there are some lies that are related and you can group them together, go ahead and do that.

God's Part: Revelation of Roots

Be still before the Lord, and ask Him to reveal to you how this lie was implanted in your heart. Sometimes, the Holy Spirit may immediately reveal. Other times, we may not be ready to hear just yet, but God will answer this prayer by preparing us to hear, and then will reveal in His perfect timing. Asking the Holy Spirit to reveal tells Him that we are open and ready to partner with Him in the destruction of this lie.

Our Part: Forgiving

Often, we begin to believe a lie because we have been wounded. Breaking free involves forgiveness. This forgiveness usually involves several parts to be thorough and complete.

- Start with recalling how much you have been forgiven. Ask the Lord if there are any other sins He wants you to confess and to ask His forgiveness for right now.
- Next, forgive any who have wounded you. Be still before the Lord and ask Him if you are harboring unforgiveness of others, any bitterness, resentment, or hardness of heart. Take the time to forgive and release to God.
- Now ask Him to reveal if you are holding *yourself* in unforgiveness. Don't skip this important step; forgiving yourself is just as important as forgiving others.
- Finally, ask the Holy Spirit to show you if any anger against God is gripping your heart. Take the time as necessary to release God from your anger in order to prepare you for the next steps.

Our Part: Repenting

There was a time when the Holy Spirit revealed that because of wounds of my childhood, I was believing the lie that I needed to earn God's love and approval. I recall squirming under the eyes of my mentor when she suggested that I repent for believing it. I wondered, if this lie took root because I was wounded, why would I need to repent? The Holy Spirit began to teach me that there are two aspects of repentance to comprehend here.

The first component of repentance is turning away. Remember from *Triumph Over Suffering* that repentance is "a 180-degree turn ... a total change of heart, leading to a change of emotions, attitude, thoughts, and actions."[5] Repentance is a choice to *turn away* from a lie and to *choose to believe* the truth of His Word – even if every fiber of your being is telling you otherwise. Turning away is pivotal to breaking free. And when we do our part to turn away as best we can, that invites the Holy Spirit to effect the heart change that will demolish that lie and establish truth.

The second component of repentance as it relates to believing a lie is to ask God's forgiveness *for believing that lie*. Stick with me here. I sense that you have been hurt very deeply. God knows your wounding, too. He sees you. Yet you have grieved God's heart by rejecting His truth, for when you reject His truth, you reject Him (Lk 10:16, Jn 14:6). And right now He is offering a way out of your pain: repent of believing this lie. The pathway to freedom requires forgiveness and repentance.

Our Part: Renewing Our Minds

For each lie, speak these words out loud, with force, definiteness, and boldness:

"I renounce the lie that _____,

and I choose to believe the truth that _____."[6]

By renouncing lies and declaring truth, you have just stepped into a mighty battle. You may be sensing some relief, some lifting, some freedom already. That is beautiful! Realize, though, that you have just embarked on a journey of transformation. We will wear new ruts in our brains by declaring these truths over ourselves daily, and meditating on, immersing in, and memorizing the Scriptures that teach those truths. God calls this wearing of new ruts *renewing your mind*.

Look up the Scriptures from the chart that counteract the lies you are battling. Write down each declaration of truth and its accompanying Scripture on an index card or in your journal or in your phone so you can treasure these truths in your heart and memorize them. Be sure to do this for *each lie or group of lies*. This is the sword in your hand, and the method we will use to renew our minds.

You do not need to renounce the lies again and again; once is enough, and we don't need to keep giving voice to those lies. But we *do* need to keep declaring *truth* over ourselves. Every morning and every night, declare out loud those truths and Scriptures over yourself until your *heart* believes it. Keep these truths and Scriptures handy and use them any time during the day or night that the enemy brings on a fresh round of attacks of lies. This journey into freedom may take many weeks or even longer, so be persistent!

Our Part: Walking It Out

It seems God will graciously give us opportunity to walk out these truths that we are declaring. Be on the alert. Each time you stand at a crossroads, deciding whether to allow your thoughts, words, or behaviors reflect a lie or reflect the truth, the battle is on. And each time you rely on the Lord's strength and choose to make your thoughts, words, or actions reflect God's truth, another battle skirmish is won, and the Lord implants that truth more deeply into your heart.

God's Part: Healing and Transformation

It seems that in order for a lie to be completely eradicated, the heart needs healing. The Lord's healing may come in unexpected ways and at unpredictable times, but as we do the hard work of forgiving, repenting, renewing our minds, and walking it out, we are positioning ourselves to receive His healing of our wounds. And as we wear new ruts of thinking into our brain, God will transform our hearts: **be transformed by the renewing of your mind** (Rom 12:2).

Transformation, the Greek word *metamorphoo*,[7] metamorphosis, is a miraculous heart work of the Holy Spirit. Prior to transformation, we were doing the hard work of choosing truth even when our heart didn't believe it. But when the Lord effects healing and transforms our hearts, He eradicates that lie, and it becomes so much easier, almost effortless, to believe the truth. The enemy may still attack our minds and try to drive us back to believing that lie, but we will be greatly strengthened and enabled to reject that lie and continue in truth.

God will continue to call on us to walk out those beliefs day after day. Once your heart is secure in His truths, hold on to these declarations and Scriptures, so when the enemy attacks in this area again (as we know he is likely to do), you will have your sword of the Spirit ready to immediately take him down.

I am praying that the deep work you have done in this chapter has opened the eyes of your heart to see the nature and character of God in a fresh way. I am praying that together you and Jesus have demolished lies that were fracturing your identity and hindering your effectiveness in Kingdom work. I am praying that you now know in a deeper way the length and breadth and height and depth of His love that passes all understanding. I am praying that your worth is secure in your position as God's child, and that you are able to experience the Holy Spirit's anointing in you empowering you and guiding you. (Eph 1:17-20, 3:18-19, 1Jn 3:1, Eph 3:20, Jn 16:13.)

Now He who establishes us with you in Christ and anointed us is God, who also sealed us and gave us the Spirit in our hearts as a pledge.

2 Corinthians 1:21-22

With our identities secure and the truth of who God is deeply rooted in our hearts, we have been equipped to fulfill a very critical assignment in *Triumph Ministry*: being vulnerable with our participants.

Coming Into the Light

Transparent sharing is vital to *Triumph* classes. Vulnerability is pivotal for freedom of the participants. How can we, as leaders, promote this type of honest transparency? From experience, I have found that *our* transparency invites *their* transparency.

Our participants will walk into the light when they are courageous enough to transparently share their struggles, pains, betrayals, abuses, injustices, failures, fears, sins, weaknesses, and what the Holy Spirit is speaking to them.

This is the message we have heard from Him and announce to you, that God is Light, and in Him there is no darkness at all. If we say that we have fellowship with Him and yet walk in the darkness, we lie and do not practice the truth; but *if we walk in the Light as He Himself is in the Light*, we have fellowship with one another, and the blood of Jesus His Son cleanses us from all sin.

John 1:5-7, emphasis added

Jesus is the Light. Satan and his demons are relegated to places of darkness; they are not free to operate in the light (Jude 1:6, 2Pet 2:4). When people come into the Light, they encounter Jesus. Satan cannot follow them into the Light; he is banished, and captives are set free. This is why it is so critical for our people to share in class. Their vulnerable sharing time invites Jesus to break chains.

Honest and vulnerable sharing with nonjudgmental unconditionally loving people works to drive out shame. Even when a person shares with one other person, Light floods into darkness; a step is taken towards freedom (Jas 5:16). It seems that sharing with an entire class multiplies this work of the Spirit.

Our Participants' Identity in Christ

Go back to the beginning of Chapter 2 and read the passages from Luke 4:18-19 and Isaiah 61:1-2 again.

Did you notice that the passage in Luke doesn't mention binding up the brokenhearted? And Isaiah does not mention opening the eyes of the blind. Puzzling about this, I asked the Lord why not. Surely healing of broken hearts is important. Indeed, it seems to be my constant prayer for my people. As I waited in stillness before Him, His answer came back simply, "When blind eyes are opened, broken hearts are healed." He showed me how the lies of Satan cause such devastation in our hearts, and when we are able to see God as He really is, our hearts are healed and filled in Him (1Jn 3:2).

I believe that one of the greatest hindrances to our participants' spiritual growth and healing is a distorted image of God, and of who they are as a child of God. Ask the Holy Spirit to grant you discernment to see the lies that entangle those you are serving. If you sense that many are not rock solid secure in their identity in Christ, be sure to address that in the first few weeks.

> **"... I am sending you to open their eyes** so that they may turn from darkness to light and from the dominion of Satan to God, that they may receive forgiveness of sins and an inheritance among those who have been sanctified by faith in Me."
>
> Acts 26:17-18, emphasis added

God may bring participants to class – both believers and unbelievers – who have veils over their hearts. If you perceive that a participant's identity crisis is a significant issue, you may want to meet with them individually and guide them through this journey of freedom that you just worked through yourself. If you feel many in the group would benefit from this exercise, pause in your study and set aside a week for establishing identity. Pray for their hearts to be open and willing to walk in repentance and surrender. You may even want to pause in your study and go through the final Bonus Chapter in *Triumph Over Suffering:* Uprooting Lies About Our Identity in Christ. Tell them you are going to take some time to establish identity, and give them a week to work through the chapter.

We want our people to learn that their worth is determined not by their accomplishments or by what other people think of them, but by what God thinks of them – and He sees them *favorably*. We want them to have God-fidence, God-esteem, not self-confidence or self-esteem. We want to teach them that when they are walking with Him, positioned to receive His favor, they can then rest peacefully and quit wrestling with the world; they will now be freed and available for His Spirit to work powerfully through them. As they come to more deeply accept their identity, they will be more surely know that God has set His eyes on them *for good*. He may not be removing the trial, but if they draw near to Him, He will grow them. He is working on their behalf and is on the battlefield fighting for them. They can begin to sense that His hands are open to them, shedding forth love, mercy, and grace, and can begin to start to experience manifestations of their Jubilee Time. (Ps 84:11, Heb 4:14-16, Titus 3:4-7, Eph 3:20-21, Jer 24:6, Jas 1:2-4, 1Sam 17:47, Rom 5:5, Isa 61:2.)

I cannot emphasize this enough: our openness and vulnerability encourages *their* openness and vulnerability. Don't be afraid to share your own wrestling with things such as the lies that you have dealt with in this chapter. When we are courageous enough to allow them to see our own sins and struggles, our failures and weaknesses, our people can begin to feel safe enough to be vulnerable also. They can begin to trust us enough to open their hearts to us. Our transparency is so important that we are going to go into more detail here, and touch on it again in upcoming chapters.

Since We Have This Ministry

Let's go to Second Corinthians and touch on some of our responsibilities as leaders in this realm of transparency.

Therefore, since we have this ministry, as we received mercy, we do not lose heart, but we have renounced the things hidden because of shame, not walking in craftiness or adulterating the word of God, but by the manifestation of truth ... But we all, with unveiled face, beholding as in a mirror the glory of the Lord, are being transformed into the same image from glory to glory, just as from the Lord, the Spirit.
2 Corinthians 4:1-2, 3:18

Ponder, Pray, and Journal

Therefore, since we have this ministry. *Since the Lord has given us this ministry.* Pause and take that in. Grab your journal and let the Lord speak to your heart about this passage.

Since God has given us the gift of this ministry, **we do not lose heart.** We remain steadfast, we fight against discouragement, we rely on His strength, with courage and trust we persevere to the end.

Since God has given us the gift of this ministry, granting us **mercy** ourselves, we are willing to walk in vulnerability and truth. We don't hide in shame; we admit our weaknesses, knowing that His power shines more brilliantly when we are weak, full of mistakes, even downright sinful (2Cor 12:9-10). We choose to come into the light, and to continue to walk in Light as He is in the light, for we know that coming into the light breaks the power of shame. As we share our sins and let our people watch us **renounce** them, as we admit our failures and let our people watch us press forward in the forgiveness and strength of God, we inspire our people to do the same. Our heart's desire is for God's remarkable, undeserved grace to spread to more and more people, so that thanksgiving to God will abound and He will be glorified (2Cor 4:15 AMP).

Not walking in craftiness. We walk in integrity, purity, and truth, not deceiving or deluding. We stand on the truth of His Word**,** not **adulterating**, tampering, corrupting, perverting, distorting, taking it out of context, or twisting it around to suit our needs. We are responsible to know God's Word, and we handle His Word with great reverence and awe, knowing that as teachers and leaders, we are held to a greater accountability (2Tim 2:15, Jas 3:1).

But by the manifestation of the truth ... We are on the alert to lies that we and our people have fallen prey to, and we implore the Lord to expose them and reveal His truth. As He reveals, we renounce the lies and choose to believe His truth – whether we feel like it or not, whether the circumstances of our lives or the words of the world reflect those truths or not. As men and women of truth, we walk in truth, even when it is countercultural, even when the lies we hear from inside ourselves shout louder than His beckoning truth.

As we surrender more deeply, we will see Jesus more clearly. It is an unfolding of our hearts, an unveiling of our eyes. And as we surrender layer by layer, the Holy Spirit will transform us more and more into the image of Christ, bringing us **from glory to glory** as we reflect Him with more radiance. It is a direct correlation: When our faces are **unveiled** and we walk in the fullness of truth, we **behold** Him with greater clarity. When we behold Him with greater clarity, He **transforms** us more into His image. When we are transformed more into His **image**, we reflect His glory with greater brilliance. This is completely a work of **the Lord, the Spirit**.

You know from *Triumph of Surrender* that our surrender, healing, and transformation will come in layers and layers and layers.[8] Sometimes, those are small layers that are not disruptive to ministry work. We can share vulnerably about these freedoms and healings in class. But what do we do as a leader, or a leader-in-training, when the Holy Spirit calls us to address a very deep layer? When He shows us that we are in need of another season of healing? Good question, and one that both my leaders and I myself have had to answer many times over the years.

Continued Freedom and Healing

If the layer the Lord wants to deal with is close to the surface and will not require a lengthy process to work through, it is generally not necessary for a leader to interrupt ministry, but can work through things with the Holy Spirit while continuing to lead.

But other times, the Holy Spirit calls us to a deep season of processing and healing in order to be freed. In these seasons, it is often wisest for the leader to step aside and focus on their own healing without the added weight of ministering to hurting people. In some ways, *Triumph Leadership* is different than other places we may serve in the Body, because it involves a deep giving of heart and soul, and requires us to be mentally, emotionally, and spiritually available, and strong.

For myself personally, fifteen years ago, when the Lord raised me up to write and teach *Triumph Over Suffering*, I was young in the Lord and blind to my need for further healing. The Lord brought only people with physical illness, because, as a physician, that was a realm where I was comfortable, and I was not equipped to minister to any other pain. I served in this ministry for a number of years before the Holy Spirit revealed that my heart was in need of healing, and indicated that He wanted to enter those rooms of my heart that I had unknowingly closed off to Him.

For other leaders, the Holy Spirit may desire entrance into your locked heart rooms *before* He releases you to lead. He will direct each of us individually, and has a perfect timing for each one of us.

The first time the Lord took me through sexual abuse recovery, He made it very clear that I was not to be leading for a season of about six months. He did the same when He called me into abortion recovery. He wanted my intense focus on Him and the work at hand He had for me. After multiple times through both sexual abuse recovery and abortion recovery, on and off over a number of years, He has freed me gloriously from so many layers, but these were indeed deep seasons of Bible study, introspection, prayer, fasting, and wrestling. From this vantage point, I know I could not have been so open to the Lord if I was simultaneously serving. Nor could I have served the participants well while I was in the throes of my own recovery.

Sometimes, a season of deep processing may move us out of *Triumph Ministry* for a time. A significant life-changing event can do the same. Over the years, I have had leaders step aside for a season to handle such things as health issues, a demanding job, a new baby, a daughter's divorce, and a loved one's death. I have had one leader step aside for a year to recover from a car accident. I have had another leader step aside as she relived her own battle with cancer when her daughter was diagnosed with cancer also. I have had several potential leaders realize they needed to go through Step Programs or Celebrate Recovery before considering training for *Triumph Leadership*.

We are warriors in a spiritual battle. If we are wounded, and the Lord is commanding us to rest and heal, but we refuse and we continue in the battle, we are vulnerable to enemy take down. And when Satan takes down the leader, those following will suffer damage also (Zech 13:7, Mt 26:31).

Ponder, Pray, and Journal

- Are there any areas of significant change or instability in your life right now that the Holy Spirit is directing you to focus on before you step into *Triumph Leadership*?
- Are there any areas of your heart or life that the Holy Spirit is calling you to open to Him for deeper healing before continuing into *Triumph Leadership*?

If the Holy Spirit is speaking to you about something here, talk to your pastor or *Triumph* leader. The Lord will guide you to the right place for healing, so you will be equipped to comfort those He brings to your class with the comfort He has given you (2Cor 1:3-4).

This has been a challenging chapter. Do not be discouraged! As God calls you into *Triumph Leadership*, He will fully equip you. Allow Him to lead you on His planned path of equipping, taking you from strength to strength.

**How blessed is the man whose strength is in You,
In whose heart are the highways to Zion!
Passing through the valley of Baca
They make it a spring;
The early rain also covers it with blessings.
They go from strength to strength,
Every one of them appears before God in Zion.**
Psalm 84:5-7

The battles may become more difficult, but His strength will fully match the battles He ordains. And those pathways in your heart that lead to the Lord, already so well-traveled, will become broader and deeper highways as you continue to grow and heal in Him.

Chapter 4
Running With Endurance

Therefore, since we have so great a cloud of witnesses surrounding us, let us also lay aside every encumbrance and the sin which so easily entangles us, and let us run with endurance the race that is set before us, fixing our eyes on Jesus, the author and perfecter of faith, who for the joy set before Him endured the cross, despising the shame, and has sat down at the right hand of the throne of God. For consider Him who has endured such hostility by sinners against Himself, so that you will not grow weary and lose heart.

Hebrews 12:1-3

As we run the race marked out for us, we desire to persevere to the end and finish strong. We are in need of stamina and fortitude, and do not want to collapse in exhaustion or give up in discouragement partway through.

In order to run hard yet avoid collapse, Hebrews instructs us to *fix our eyes on Jesus*, to *lay aside encumbrances*, and to *forsake sins*. In this chapter we will explore focusing on Jesus and throwing off hindrances, and in the next chapter, forsaking sins. In this chapter, we will also look at how stumbling in any of these areas can prevent us from even finishing the race. And we will open our hearts to God's work as we learn how to run our assigned race with endurance, so we can cross the finish line in strength.

For I am already being poured out as a drink offering, and the time of my departure has come. I have fought the good fight, I have finished the course, I have kept the faith.
2 Timothy 4:6-7

Pouring Out Your Drink Offering

We have come to realize that there are ever so many who are in captivity, who are oppressed, brokenhearted, and blinded by Satan. My heart aches for Jesus to free and heal them all. I sense that yours does, too.

Our love runs deep and we are so very willing. We have died; our lives are hidden with Christ in God. His love controls us. We no longer live for ourselves but for Him who died for us, pouring ourselves out like a drink offering (Col 3:3, 2Cor 5:14, 2Tim 4:6). Those in pain will absorb our drink offerings as if they were desert sand, inadvertently drawing out of us until we have nothing left to give.

But what if ... what if ... what if we are pouring ourselves out like a drink offering – *on the wrong altar?*

"If anyone serves Me, he must follow Me; and where I am, there My servant will be also."
John 12:26

Clearly we want to be working *only* where He is working. Yet there is a difference between *desiring* to be working where the Father is working, and *discerning* where the Father is working.

This is very grave. We have only one life to pour out – we don't want to misstep here! I will state the obvious: although God is limitless, *we are not*. Although *God* is at work in infinite places at once, *our* mission is *only* to the people He has assigned us. It will require great discernment to know *where* God is calling us, *to whom*, and *for how long*.

I think that perhaps Jesus wrestled with this same dilemma. Remember how His heart was broken for all of Israel:

"O Jerusalem, Jerusalem, you who kill the prophets and stone those sent to you, how often I have longed to gather your children together, as a hen gathers her chicks under her wings, but you were not willing!"

Luke 13:34

Hear the agony in His voice as His heart ached for the whole nation of Israel. He longed to touch them all ... yet, He was fully human. He had *limited* Himself. Jesus had

... emptied Himself, taking the form of a bond-servant, and being made in the likeness of men.

Philippians 2:7

Jesus had **emptied Himself**. Scripture doesn't exactly explain what or how, but we do know He did not empty Himself of His holiness or perfection. I think He emptied Himself of His powers: His omnipotence, omniscience, and omnipresence. He became fully human. Just what did that look like, for *God Himself* to be fully human?

There arose a great storm on the sea, so that the boat was being covered with the waves; but Jesus Himself was asleep.

Matthew 8:24

God Himself was so exhausted that He slept in the boat during a monstrous storm.

> **So Jesus, being wearied from His journey, was sitting thus by the well ... His disciples had gone away into the city to buy food.**
>
> John 4:6,8

God Himself had become so tired and hungry that He needed to rest, waiting behind while His disciples went off to find food.

> **And He took with Him Peter and the two sons of Zebedee, and began to be grieved and distressed. Then He said to them, "My soul is deeply grieved, to the point of death; remain here and keep watch with Me." ... And being in agony He was praying very fervently; and His sweat became like drops of blood, falling down upon the ground.**
>
> Matthew 26:37-38, Luke 22:44

God Himself was so profoundly sorrowful and troubled about His impending crucifixion and separation from His Father, He was overwhelmed to the point of sweating blood.

Jesus' body became tired, weak, hungry. He could only be in one place at a time. He had relinquished His power and could do only what the Father allowed Him to do.

> **"Truly, truly, I say to you, the Son can do nothing of Himself, unless it is something He sees the Father doing; for whatever the Father does, these things the Son also does in like manner."**
>
> John 5:19

Jesus spoke only what the Father gave Him to say.

> **"I do nothing on My own initiative, but I speak these things as the Father taught Me ... The words that I say to you I do not speak on My own initiative, but the Father abiding in Me does His works."**
>
> John 8:28, 14:10

Jesus did nothing but what the Father was doing. Additionally, He had relinquished His omniscience, and knew only what the Father allowed Him to know. *And yet*, He always knew when to work, and when to rest. He knew exactly what altar to pour Himself out upon.

But how did He know? How *did* He know where the Father was working? How *did* He know what the Father knew? How *did* He know where to go? How *did* He know what altar to pour Himself out on?

Ponder, Pray, and Journal

Read the following passages and journal your answers.

- Luke 4:1-2: What did Jesus do right after His baptism?
- Mark 1:29-39: Jesus in Capernaum. How did Jesus know it was time to leave?
- Luke 5:15-16: What did Jesus do in the middle of amazing Spirit-filled Spirit-empowered ministry work?
- Matthew 14:13-23: What did Jesus do after He taught and fed 5000?
- Read Luke 6:12-16: How did Jesus know which of His many followers to select as His Twelve in order to disciple them, mentor them, teach them, train them, and send them forth? How did Jesus know whose feet to wash?

Pause and sit in stillness before the Lord. Journal what the Holy Spirit is speaking to you through these verses about your prayer life.

Fixing Your Eyes on Jesus

Go back to the beginning of the chapter and re-read Hebrews 12:1-3. Circle this key command to keep us in the race: **fixing our eyes on Jesus.** Fixing our eyes on Him will help prevent us from being pulled off the path by distractions or lured off with enticements. Fixing our eyes on Him is a very intentional absorption with our Savior and His sacrifice for us. Being consumed by Him is an imperative abiding in the Vine (Jn 15:1-11).

God does not want us pulled haphazardly in every direction; He wants us working only where He is working and has called us to join Him. For if we are working where God is not working, we will accomplish ... nothing.

> **Unless the Lord builds the house,**
> **They labor in vain who build it;**
> **Unless the Lord guards the city,**
> **The watchman keeps awake in vain.**
>
> Psalm 127:1

We must remain in deep, abiding relationship with Him. We studied *abide* in *Triumph Over Suffering* and in *Surrender*, learning what it means to be united with Him in heart, mind, and will.[1] Jesus puts it very succinctly:

> **"... apart from Me you can do nothing."**
>
> John 15:5

As we step into leadership, it may be easy to become so busy working and ministering that we find ourselves spending less time with God. Often it seems that when we are overextended, our time with the Lord suffers first. It may be very subtle in the beginning, a little less time reading our Bibles, more infrequent times in stillness before Him. But I believe this distraction of busyness – even being busy with good things, seemingly with Kingdom work – is one of Satan's greatest ploys. For Satan knows that if we are not in close communion with the Holy Spirit, we will soon find ourselves working in our own flesh (translation: accomplishing nothing).

Ponder, Pray, and Journal

As you step into *Triumph Leadership*, and the demands of leading a class threaten your relationship with the Lord, what will you do to ensure that your time with Jesus remains deep and vibrant, "quality time in great quantity"[2]?

Waiting For His Invitation

As we abide in deeper measure, we will more clearly see His work and His movement. We will not merely *desire* to be working where He is working, we will also begin to *discern* where He is working. But there is more. There is yet another difference between discerning where He is working, and *being invited in*.

Where the Father is working and where He has invited us to join Him are *not* the same thing. We may see lots of places where He is working. But we are not *called* to every place where He is working. Where He has invited us to join Him is only a small subset of where He is working. We would be overwhelmed if He sent us everywhere He was at work! Yes, we are to recognize that He is moving, but then wait to be called and assigned. Pause to take that in.

Our churches may be full of the Holy Spirit's activity, making us want to jump in everywhere! But truly, we are not *assigned* everywhere. Our calling and assignments are very specific. We were created and equipped to fulfill the works He planned in advance for us to do. He called us and appointed us, for specific works, before the foundation of the world – so our fruit *will remain* (Eph 2:10, 1:4, Jn 15:16).

If we enter an area of God's Kingdom movement when we are not *assigned* there, we may be able to be part of His move in some small way. But when we wait for His invitation and *enter where we are assigned,* He *anoints* us for that assignment. We can then walk and work in the power of the Holy Spirit, who enables us to bear much fruit for His glory.

Waiting for His invitation also helps to prevent us from exhausting ourselves by working in unassigned areas. We can learn to pace ourselves and maintain stamina to finish the course. I have heard it said that saying "no" to something that God is *not* calling us to allows us to say "yes" to what He *is* calling us to!

For me, it requires a close walk with the Lord to know where in particular He is assigning *me.* I need to wrestle through guilt and fear and idolatry of what people think of me. And if I go where He is not sending me, I will not be available for the mission that He *has* hand-picked for me. I will not have endurance to finish the specific race that He has marked out *for me.* I must develop a greater discernment of His voice and learn to be led by His Spirit if I want to be on mission.

Ponder, Pray, and Journal

Take inventory with the Lord. Make a list of your commitments. For each area, ask Him to reveal the answers to these two questions:

1) Are You working here?
2) Have You invited me to join You here?

If the Lord has uncovered any issues here, ask Him what He would have you do now.

Discerning God's Invitation

How can we know where God is working? How will we discern God's invitation? When the Holy Spirit enables us to see that a heart is open to Him, this is an indication that *He is working here*. And when He brings that open heart to class, He is *inviting us to join Him in His work*.

How do we discern an open heart? I think that one of the methods Jesus utilized to discern an open heart is found in His mission statement. I think we can use this method, too.

Go back to the beginning of Chapter 2 and observe how Luke 4:18-19 and Isaiah 61:1-2 both start. Finish this sentence: **The Lord has anointed me ...**

_____

I believe that the positioning of this sentence at the beginning of these passages is very significant. Note also Jesus' words at the Sermon on the Mount, again in *first position*:

Blessed are the poor in spirit, for theirs is the kingdom of heaven.
Matthew 5:3

This word **poor** in Luke and Matthew is derived from the Greek word meaning "to crouch ... a beggar (as cringing),"[3] indicating that these people are so poor they have nothing to offer. **Poor in spirit** is spiritually helpless; it is a place of utter humility. The spiritually poor realize that they have absolutely nothing to offer, they recognize their helplessness and their desperate need of Jesus. They are repentant, teachable, and hungry to hear His message. They are poised to surrender. They are open and ready because the Holy Spirit has already prepared their hearts.

We know that *Triumph* Classes do not give superficial feel-good messages. We do not point our people to earthly things for restoration. We are not asking God to deliver them from hard times. We *are* praying for repentant hearts that crave to know God more, that are seeking spiritual healing and deliverance from sins and strongholds, that are open to the work of the Lord and ready for His healing. When God shows us that someone is poor in spirit, He is revealing that He is at work here, and inviting us to join Him.

Although we will minister to many people on many levels, meeting them right where they are and pointing them to Jesus, it is the poor in spirit whom I believe we as *Triumph* Servant Leaders are called to minister to most deeply. If we discern that some of our participants or potential participants are not poor in spirit, we may soon discover that they are probably not open for freedom at this time. Captives must *recognize* their prison, *desire* freedom, and be *willing* to forsake whatever is holding them in captivity – things which, from their perspective, may be good or secure or comfortable or at least familiar. Some people may choose to stay in their own dungeons by refusing to forsake lies or turn away from sins when the Holy Spirit convicts. They can fortify their own prisons by withholding forgiveness or by refusing to surrender their idols to God.

Yes, we will often cast a wide net, as Jesus did. With tender love and compassion we will reach out and touch each person that God brings to us in divine encounters. We will intercede and pray for eyes to be opened and the Holy Spirit to move, and we will pray for those who don't know how to pray for themselves. Yet, if we find that we want their repentance, freedom, healing *more than they do*, we may find ourselves working on our own strength. If someone only wants to have their ears tickled (2Tim 4:3-4), investing energy here will drain us and burn us out. Pouring out our drink offering here will probably deplete us of the resources we need to finish the race. If someone is not yet ready to seek His transformation, we will love them and pray for them, but it may be wiser to wait until they are ready before we devote ourselves here.

In order to keep in stride with the Holy Spirit and to run with endurance to the end, our greatest outpouring will be upon those who are poor in spirit, who are humbly open to His transforming work. God calls us to be *on mission*.

Ponder, Pray, and Journal

Although we may want to jump right to the freeing of the captives, it seems that the step preceding freedom involves a deep humility that leads to repentance. So more specifically, I believe we are called to be His vessels as He sets *humble and repentant* captives free. Pause and take that in. Journal anything the Lord is speaking to you.

Read Mark 12:28-34. What made Jesus say that this scribe was not far from the Kingdom of God? How can you apply this to those whom you are burdened for?

Laying Aside Encumbrances

Go back to the beginning of the chapter and re-read Hebrews 12:1-3. This time circle this key command to keep us in the race: **lay aside every encumbrance.**

The NIV translates it **everything that hinders** and the NLT **every weight that slows us down**. It seems in this passage that encumbrances are not the same as sins. I think that encumbrances are neutral things or even good things at the wrong time or in the wrong proportions. When we are weighed down with encumbrances, we are trying to run with a loaded backpack, and are hindered from running well. Unloading the backpack will allow us to move freely under the Holy Spirit's leading.

In the next few sections, we will seek pruning to unload our backpacks, and will explore how to maintain healthy margins to prevent from overloading them in the first place.

Seek Pruning to Unload

I had been working on writing *Triumph in Warfare* for many years. I felt God was calling me to complete it, but I could not seem to find the needed blocks of time to focus on it. As I sought His guidance, He showed me that I was in need of pruning. As I pursued this in prayer, He began to show me that I was involved in many things, good things, like Bible studies and teaching *Triumph* classes and spiritual mentoring and prayer meetings and other Kingdom work, but in this season, they were an impediment to running the race He was marking out. He showed me that these Godly pursuits in the wrong timing were pulling me away from the center of His will. As I partnered with Him and withdrew from these areas as He led, He miraculously pruned away other things and provided the needed time to focus on praying, listening, and writing.

As *Triumph* leaders, it can be easy to become overwhelmed. Between God-ordained responsibilities of leadership, the increased call to more work that we feel is from God, and the heightened recognition of those who are trapped in captivity, we can become truly engulfed. Yes, there will be times when we cry out to God and utterly rely on Him to give us supernatural strength to accomplish His purposes. But there will be other times, probably more frequently, when we must stop and rest, when we must pace ourselves, admitting the constraints of the human body. When we humbly acknowledge that *He doesn't need us.* We will want to diligently seek His pruning – *so that* we can bear *even more* fruit.

" ... every branch that bears fruit, He prunes it so that it may bear more fruit."

John 15:2

Ponder, Pray, and Journal

Earlier in the chapter, we took inventory with the Lord, asking God if He had truly invited us into the areas where we are involved. Let's take it deeper now. Go back to your list and ask Him if there is anything He desires to *prune* so that you can bear more fruit.

Establishing Margins to Prevent Overloading

I call margin "extra space just in case." I think of it as breathing room. Like the margins on a paper that give me a bit more room to write if needed, I think God wants us to work margin into life just in case He brings along something unexpected.

I didn't always live with margin. I used to plan such packed schedules that if one appointment ran over, it caused the entire day to topple like dominoes. There was never any room for something unanticipated to fit into the day.

This is an area that remains a challenge for me, but I am learning. If two people want to meet with me for prayer tomorrow afternoon, and each one estimates an hour meeting, I don't schedule them at 1:00 and 2:00. I schedule them at 1:00 and 3:30 or 4:00 to allow for the first person to be late or to need more time, and also to give me time in between to thank the Lord for His provision, to pray for the next meeting, and to rest in Him for filling and strengthening for the next meeting.

I find lack of margin to be a definite encumbrance to running the race. If I am running with my schedule at 100% capacity, I will be unavailable for an unexpected assignment from the Lord – an assignment that actually *is* the race. Additionally, when I lack margin, it seems my relationships with both God and people take a hit. Earlier in the chapter we discussed how, when we are overextended, often our time with the Lord suffers first. Without margin, "there is not time for silence or solitude, reflection or contemplation, the foundation of intimacy with God."4 Deep connected relationships with God and with those I love require time to develop, and even more time to nurture in order to maintain them in strength and health. Relationships – both with God and people – cannot be cultivated by just fitting them in around the edges of a busy life.

Ponder, Pray, and Journal

Ask the Lord to search your heart and journal your answers to these questions:

- Do I run myself ragged?
- Do I find it hard to admit the constraints of the human body?
- Do I have trouble saying "No"?
- Would people who know me well say that I am "overscheduled"?
- Do I lack margin? If a friend or a participant calls me for prayer, would I be available?
- Additionally, take some time to assess the important

relationships in your life. Are you nurturing and cultivating them, or trying to fit them in around the edges?

If you are out of balance, ask the Lord to show you the depth of your heart that causes this lack of balance.

Count the Cost

"For which of you, intending to build a tower, does not sit down first and count the cost, whether he has enough to finish it — lest, after he has laid the foundation, and is not able to finish, all who see it begin to mock him, saying, 'This man began to build and was not able to finish'?"
Luke 14:28-30 NKJV

I asked some of my *Triumph* Servant Leaders to estimate how much time they dedicate to *Triumph Ministry,* beyond the actual classroom time. Of course the number of participants, and the number of leaders, will be big factors. Some of my leaders have spouses and children; some are single parents. Some are working full time; some are retired. Some care for elderly parents or grandchildren; others are challenged by their own physical illnesses. As you can guess, there is a large range of estimates here. These are just some guidelines to give some understanding of the time commitment involved.

One of my leaders estimates she spends five to seven hours a week, which includes reading the chapter, talking to some of the participants by phone, and time for prayer. "And it can require more time when we have a larger class."

Another leader explains that she reads through the chapter several pages each day as part of her regular devotion time. As she reads through the sections, she prays for the participants as the section seems to relate to them. On the day of the class, she spends about an hour in prayer over the class. She estimates about three to four hours a week in prayer and preparation, and additional time for phone calls.

Another leader would set aside one full day a week to prepare the chapter and pray, seeking the Lord for what He wants covered in the classroom. And one of my long-time leaders relates that the more classes she leads, the less time she spends reviewing the chapter and the more time she spends in prayer. She estimates two to three hours a week in prayer preparation, and additional time ministering with phone calls. She clarified that time required for phone calls is very variable week to week, depending on the needs of the participants and the topic of the chapter.

Ponder, Pray, and Journal

I had you read the Appendix entitled *Count the Cost* when you read the *Preface*. Go ahead and skim through that *Count the Cost* Appendix again for a refresher. Then prayerfully evaluate your commitments. As you take on the responsibilities of *Triumph* leader, how will you continue to live with margin?

Maintaining Healthy Margins

In this section, we'll discuss three concrete strategies we can implement to help maintain healthy margins in order to avoid collapsing before we reach the finish line.

Achieving Holy Spirit Balance

For those of us who are highly motivated and goal-oriented, who like to fix, or have struggled with striving or perfectionism, achieving Holy Spirit balance may be more challenging. Yet learning to stabilize our lives, putting Christ as the fulcrum even in the midst of turmoil, is an indispensible part of our walk. We must seek the Lord's leading in the balance of work and play, people and solitude, exercise and rest. Satan is full of distractions and can so easily orchestrate busyness. It is our responsibility to surrender our moments and our days to the Lord, to *daily* seek Him for His plan and His schedule, and to listen and obey.

When we realize that the race marked out for us is a marathon, not a sprint, we can begin to pace ourselves. We must run with perseverance, keeping in step with the Spirit and allowing *Him* to set the pace.

Connecting in the Body of Christ

You may be wondering how spending *more* time with friends will help with an overly busy schedule. True deep friendships can keep us grounded, and friends who know us well can help us see when we have gotten overextended. Pastoral oversight can also be very valuable here.

Cultivating true, safe, meaningful relationships with family and same-gender friends can give us a place to be vulnerable and to receive prayer and encouragement. Friendships with your co-leaders and other *Triumph* leaders can be special ones to develop, because other *Triumph* leaders will have unique insight from a ministry perspective and understand how to pray for you.

Delegating

I think this one is best understood through the Word. Read Exodus 18:13-27. How will delegating help you maintain margin? Is delegating hard for you? If so, ask the Holy Spirit to show you why.

John C. Maxwell teaches, "If you delegate assignments, you create followers. If you delegate authority, you create leaders."5 What do you think this means? How will you apply this to your leadership?

As we've studied so far in this chapter, some issues that can prevent us from even being able to finish our race include taking our eyes off Jesus, pouring ourselves out on the wrong altar, working where He has not invited us, running with encumbrances, and lacking margin. These missteps can lead to stress, depression, exhaustion, anxiety, and fear. But what if the weights we are carrying are so heavy they are already causing us to collapse in the middle of the race? Experts call this *burnout*.

Definition of Burnout

Burnout is a term used often in the medical profession, so we will tap into research done with doctors and nurses to better understand how we as *Triumph* Servant Leaders are also at risk for burnout.[6] But first, let's look at the similarities and differences between stress and burnout.

Stress can occur when we are overextended and are pressured with overwhelming demands. Stress can cause a sense of urgency, which in manageable doses can help hone our focus and push us to complete a task. In larger doses, however, it can hinder clear thinking and lead to a frenzy of unproductive activity. And in worse situations, it can lead to fear, anxiety, or panic.

Chronic unmanaged stress can eventually lead to burnout, which can occur suddenly, or in a gradual fashion. But burnout is actually much more than just overwhelming stress. Burnout results in exhaustion or even collapse. It seems that burnout involves a physical, emotional, and spiritual *draining*.

Medical research indicates that burnout is marked by these three characteristics:

- Overwhelming exhaustion.
- Inability to be emotionally available.
- Feeling unappreciated, or feeling that our work is having no real impact.[7]

Ponder, Pray, and Journal

These three characteristics seem to be a downward spiral, starting with exhaustion and culminating in the feeling that our calling and our work has no eternal impact. Let's take a look at these three and ask the Holy Spirit to reveal our hearts. In order to do that, I've expounded a bit below, listing some signs that I have noticed in myself or others that seem to indicate current burnout or to portend impending burnout.

Prayerfully mark those that you have experienced in the past, and circle those you are experiencing right now.

Overwhelming Exhaustion

- Are you struggling with depression, fatigue, exhaustion, or trouble bouncing back?
- Are you often sick?
- Do problems seem impossible to solve? Does the workload seem endless?
- Do you feel helpless to keep everything in balance? Do you feel like you are losing control?
- Do you wonder how much longer you can keep up this pace?
- Are you having trouble admitting mistakes or taking responsibility? Are you shifting blame or making excuses?
- Are you procrastinating?
- Are you focusing too much on details at the expense of the big picture?
- Are you having difficulty making decisions?
- Are you more frequently falling into temptation?

Inability to be Emotionally Available

The medical profession calls this characteristic "compassion fatigue".

- Do you find yourself listening out of obligation instead of listening to understand, or maybe even find yourself not listening at all?
- Are you starting to lack compassion and empathy?
- Are you withdrawing from family and friends? Are you detaching? Isolating?
- Are you becoming resentful, easily offended, easily angered, irritable, or short with people? (Hint: look at your family life. We may be gracious to our participants, but short and irritated with our spouse, children, co-workers, friends.)
- Are you seeing interruptions and changes to the planned schedule as *frustrations* instead of as *divine appointments?*
- Are you griping, complaining, or criticizing?
- Have you become sarcastic or cynical? Do you find yourself constantly venting?

Feeling Unappreciated,
or Feeling That Your Work Has No Eternal Impact

- Are you becoming disillusioned with *Triumph Ministry* or with your calling?
- Are you having trouble seeing the Lord at work in your ministry? Does your work seem ineffective?
- Has it been a while since you have seen any real breakthroughs in your participants' hearts and lives?
- Are you feeling alone or unappreciated, or feeling that no one understands?
- Have you lost motivation? Are you feeling hopeless?
- Are you no longer content?
- Are you questioning your calling into this ministry?

- Is your time alone with the Lord becoming routine and mundane?
- Has it been a while since the Lord has spoken to you?

Jesus' Definition of Burnout

Let's quit using the euphemism "burnout" and call it as Jesus does:

"If anyone does not abide in Me, he is thrown away as a branch and dries up; and they gather them, and cast them into the fire and they are burned."
John 15:6

Burnout is a branch no longer abiding in the Vine — dried up and good for nothing. I think this makes it pretty obvious how to treat burnout – *and* how to prevent it.

Prevention and Treatment of Burnout

"Come to Me, all who are weary and heavy-laden, and I will give you rest."
Matthew 11:28

Now that sounds like a good way to prevent burnout. Simply by going to Jesus for rest. But then Jesus goes on to say,

"Take My yoke upon you and learn from Me, for I am gentle and humble in heart, and you will find rest for your souls. For My yoke is easy and My burden is light."
Matthew 11:29-30

Now this seems confusing. Taking up Jesus' yoke makes me think of oxen plowing, and plowing and rest seem mutually exclusive to me.

It wasn't until I traveled to Israel that I understood more clearly what Jesus meant. In Israel I learned that in rabbi-speak, the rabbi's "yoke" is his teaching. "Taking up his yoke" means fully committing to his teachings, living the way he lives. I have heard it said that a rabbi's students wanted to follow so closely behind their rabbi that they became covered with the rabbi's dust.

Ponder, Pray, and Journal

- How can committing yourself to follow Jesus with all your heart be restful?
- Is the Lord calling you to take steps to treat or prevent burnout?

We were created us to be in harmony with our Creator, and when we are aligning our lives with what pleases God, obeying His commands and seeking to follow His will, then our souls, spirits, bodies, minds, and hearts will be at peace. That is true deep rest, soul rest even when we are physically working. But before I can use this concept of rest to excuse lapses into overworking, I must acknowledge that aligning myself with my Creator happens through study of the Word coupled with stillness so deep and thorough that He is able to illuminate what I have studied and reveal where I am misaligned. For me, this means *less* work, and more time alone *in the secret place of His Presence.*

When we enter this secret place, we can position ourselves in a place of utter humility, with nothing to offer – in fact, not even *trying* to offer anything. Soaking in gentle worship music, allowing His love to infiltrate our dry cracked hearts. In order to heal, we need sweet times in the tent of meeting, allowing Him to do what He so deeply desires to do: to pour His unearned love into us and thus restore our souls. To reveal to us how valuable we are to Him, and to unveil the miracles He is accomplishing in us and through us.

I believe that the only true *prevention* of burnout, and the only *treatment* for burnout or near-burnout, is such deep rest in the Lord that we return to abiding in Him. And if we have hit burnout, or near-burnout, I don't think this will be resolved in just one or two visits.

As we rest in Him, He may certainly prune. But we won't be receptive to His pruning without sacred time alone with Him. Because He loves us and wants what is best for us, His pruning will eventually come, but if we aren't abiding, we may find ourselves fighting the Gardener's hand instead of partnering with Him in the pruning.

An Unusual Tactic

Let's take a little tour through the gospel of John and watch Jesus in action. Read the following passages. Observe what Jesus said and did and how the people responded, and watch for a pattern.

- At the multiplication of the loaves and fishes:
  - Step One: John 6:2-14
  - Step Two: John 6:51-58
  - Outcome: John 6:60-69

- At the feast:
  - Step One: John 8:12, 30
  - Step Two: John 8:31, 44, 47
  - Outcome: John 8:59

- In Bethany and Jerusalem:
  ○ Step One: John 11:43-45; John 12:9,11; John 12:12-13; John 12:19
  ○ Step Two: John 12:24-26; John 12:32-33
  ○ Outcome: John 12:37

Ponder, Pray, and Journal

Journal what you saw in these passages. Why do you think Jesus used this method?

Jesus' Litmus Test

Jesus attracted large crowds, then escalated the depth of His teachings – and the crowds dispersed. At first glance, this hardly seems a likely way to grow a ministry.

Jesus, the Fisher of Men, seemed to cast a large net, then searched for those who were willing to fully devote themselves to Him. He sought the poor in spirit who would put their hand to the plow and not look back (Mt 5:3, Lk 9:62). He had three years to pour into them. He needed to know whom to pour Himself into. Did this method work?

After teaching "eat My flesh and drink My blood" (Jn 6:53), many disciples withdrew and were not walking with Him (Jn 6:66). But watch how the Twelve responded:

So Jesus said to the twelve, "You do not want to go away also, do you?" Simon Peter answered Him, "Lord, to whom shall we go? You have words

of eternal life. We have believed and have come to know that You are the Holy One of God."

John 6:67-69

If we are to serve like Jesus, we can expect our Kingdom work to look similar. *Triumph Ministry* is not about attracting large crowds; it's about *making disciples*.

"Go therefore and make disciples of all the nations, baptizing them in the name of the Father and the Son and the Holy Spirit, teaching them to observe all that I commanded you; and lo, I am with you always, even to the end of the age."

Matthew 29:19-20

Ponder, Pray, and Journal

What does it mean to be a *disciple* of Christ? Read the following passages and journal your answer.

- John 8:31
- John 15:18-19
- Matthew 16:24-25

Those Who Leave

I am thinking of the many in Jesus' time whose first encounter with Him involved healing. *Triumph Ministry* indeed seeks to point hurting people to Jesus for His healing, and that is often their first touch point with the Lord. But ultimately, we desire to make our people *disciples*. We will encounter those who start out very excited, but then walk away because they are not willing to allow the Holy Spirit to work His sanctification and healing process. They are not ready to allow Jesus access into the deep recesses of their hearts. They are not yet open to His ways of touching and healing. They are not yet ready to walk in obedience.

I am thinking with heavy heart of the rich young ruler.

Jesus looked at him and loved him. "One thing you lack," he said. "Go, sell everything you have and give to the poor, and you will have treasure in heaven. Then come, follow me." At this the man's face fell. He went away sad, because he had great wealth.
Mark 10:21-22 NIV

Ponder, Pray, and Journal

How will we handle those that leave? Follow Jesus' example. Read again Mark 10:21-22 to see how Jesus treated the rich young man. Be still before the Lord. Will this be hard for you? What will you do to ensure that you do not take rejection personally?

Some May Reject

If people are rejecting us, *it means they are rejecting God.*

"The one who listens to you listens to Me, and the one who rejects you rejects Me; and he who rejects Me rejects the One who sent Me."
Luke 10:16

Sometimes, no matter how much we and our prayer team pray and fast, no matter how much we love and reach out and connect and lead and guide, we still witness no move of the Lord. Some of our participants seem to remain closed off to the work of the Holy Spirit. Do not view this as a failure. Remember, it's our job to pray and walk forth in obedience; it's God's job to move. Sometimes, God may have directed someone into class *whom He knew would remain resistant to Him* – for the express purpose of your prayer. Sometimes, *there may be no one else praying for these people.* God may have brought them onto your radar screen because He knew you would pray.

Each of us is on our own journey, growing in God's perfect timing, according to His perfect plan. His plan has already taken into account our participants' – and our own – free will. We can plant and water, but only God makes someone grow (1Cor 3:6-7). We must look at those who leave and love them. It is God's class. We must trust God to shape these classes exactly as *He* desires, and pray for Him to do just that.

And Some Who Reject May Return

I want you to see something else very important here. Recall how Jesus was completely abandoned. At His arrest, **they all left Him and fled.** (Mk 14:50). Yet, we see John at the foot of the cross (Jn 19:26), and we know the Eleven all returned to bring the gospel to the world. And although the crowds were shouting, "Crucify Him!", a few weeks later, three thousand received Christ and were baptized on Pentecost.

So then, those who had received his word were baptized; and that day there were added about three thousand souls. They were continually devoting themselves to the apostles' teaching and to fellowship, to the breaking of bread and to prayer.

Acts 2:41-42

Notice that these three thousand are *disciples*. They *received* the Word, were *baptized*, and then were continually *devoting* themselves to the apostles' teachings, fellowship, breaking of bread, and prayer. Sometimes, those who walk away, return in surrender to become devoted disciples.

The Crown of Righteousness

We have studied in this chapter ways to run with endurance and to avoid missteps that prevent us from finishing the race God has marked out for us. But not only do we want to *finish* the race, we want to *finish well*. We want to receive the reward of the crown of righteousness from our Lord and Judge.

For I am already being poured out as a drink offering, and the time of my departure has come. I have fought the good fight, I have finished the course, I have kept the faith; in the future there is laid up for me the crown of righteousness, which the Lord, the righteous Judge, will award to me on that day; and not only to me, but also to all who have loved His appearing.
2 Timothy 4:6-8

Let's ensure we are pouring ourselves out like a drink offering – on the altar God assigns.

Let's ensure we are fighting the good fight – against the real enemy.

Let's ensure we finish the course – without collapsing partway through.

Let's ensure we are keeping the faith – fearing the Lord, abiding in Him, and walking in step with the Him as we rely on Him and trust fully in Him.

In the next chapter, we will pursue deeper sanctification as we learn about temptations we will face as leaders, knowing that as we give more of ourselves to Him, He can work through us in greater measure. As we humble ourselves before Him, He is glorified, and will grant us a **crown of righteousness** – *so that* we can cast it at His feet.

... the twenty-four elders will fall down before Him who sits on the throne, and will worship Him who lives forever and ever, and will cast their crowns before the throne, saying,

> **"Worthy are You, our Lord and our God,**
> **to receive glory and honor and power;**
> **for You created all things,**
> **and because of Your will they existed,**
> **and were created."**
> Revelation 4:10-11

Chapter 5
Temptations Leaders Face

> *... let us also lay aside every encumbrance **and the sin which so easily entangles us**, and let us run with endurance the race that is set before us ...*
> Hebrews 12:1, emphasis added

In the last chapter we studied fixing our eyes on Jesus and laying aside encumbrances in order to cross the finish line in strength. In this chapter, we will focus on the third command: forsaking sins. While encumbrances can hinder us or weigh us down, sin actually **entangles us**. It trips us up and causes us to stumble or even fall. We will be entering the classroom in the next chapters, so it is paramount that our hearts are ready. Realize that, as Hebrews 13 explains, our sanctification *is* our equipping.

> Now the God of peace, who brought up from the dead the great Shepherd of the sheep through the blood of the eternal covenant, even Jesus our Lord, equip you in every good thing to do His will, *working in us that which is pleasing in His sight*, through Jesus Christ, to whom be the glory forever and ever. Amen.
> Hebrews 13:20-21, emphasis added

And as He sanctifies us, we become useful vessels to the Master.

Therefore, if anyone cleanses himself from these things, he will be a vessel for honor, sanctified, useful to the Master, prepared for every good work.
2 Timothy 2:21

I have read a number of leadership books that caution about temptations of leaders. But instead of quoting from them in this chapter, I thought I would just share personally my own battles with temptations and invite the Holy Spirit to speak to you.

Teaching *Triumph* Classes for fifteen years and training leaders for ten, I think I have managed to fall into every possible trap Satan has laid out for me. Last year I even prayed, "Lord, can I *please* get through just one semester without making a mess?" Apparently not. I may *think* that these classes are for the participants, but even more so, they seem to be for me. He is exposing, purifying, pruning, training, teaching, honing, and equipping me. I have found it invaluable in this journey to have places for confession, wisdom, and guidance: several accountability partners, a few mentors, a dedicated, loving, non-judgmental prayer team, and my pastor.

I don't know about you, but deep heart work can drive me to places of shame, false guilt, self-deprecation, fear of rejection, and low self worth. I have found that especially in seasons of purification, there are some specific spiritual disciplines that are key in order to maintain my identity in Him, to keep me humble and recognizing of Who is in control, and to remind me of the unshakeable depth of His love for me. I call them the three S's:

- Soaking
- Stillness
- Solitude

This is a deep and lengthy chapter; we will cover fourteen areas here. Be sure the three S's are top priority for you as we work through this chapter together.

As I share some pitfalls I have faced, ask the Holy Spirit to search your own heart and bring any dark areas into the Light. Please understand that the intent of this chapter is not to remove you from leadership! You have been prayerfully invited onto the *Triumph* Leadership Team because we believe God is calling you. This season is merely a time to seek our Heavenly Father to fulfill His call by making you holy:

**Faithful is He Who is calling you [to Himself] and utterly trustworthy,
and He will also do it
[fulfill His call by hallowing and keeping you].**
    1 Thessalonians 5:24 AMPC, emphasis added

Temptation: Pride

I recall a time when *Triumph of Surrender* was about to be published. I was very concerned about whether my church would place it on the shelves in their bookstore, next to *Triumph Over Suffering*, and began to ask the bookstore questions about that. The Holy Spirit stopped me in my tracks, asking me *why I* was asking these questions. He showed me that my focus was on my position as a *Triumph* leader and my status as an author. Nothing like a little three-letter word like "Why?" to expose pride and to humble me.

Pause and take a look at the cover of this book. *Triumph* leaders are *Servant* Leaders.

"If I then, the Lord and the Teacher, washed your feet, you also ought to wash one another's feet."

John 13:14

We are servants first, and leaders second. We serve our King, we serve His people, and we serve our fellow *Triumph* Servant Leaders.

"But the greatest among you shall be your servant. Whoever exalts himself shall be humbled; and whoever humbles himself shall be exalted."
Matthew 23:11-12

Ponder, Pray, and Journal

Ponder these verses:

- Philippians 2:3
- James 1:21
- Galatians 2:20
- Colossians 1:10-12

Which one of these commands will be the hardest for you to obey? Why?

When I am walking in pride, I start to become concerned about how I look to others. My desire for participants, friends, or pastors to compliment me becomes greater than my desire for the healing and freedom of the participants. I begin to focus on the *outcome* of the class instead of on my *relationship* with God. I have begun to think of myself more highly than I ought.

Do not think of yourself more highly than you ought, but rather think of yourself with sober judgment, in accordance with the measure of faith

God has given you. Just as each of us has one body with many members, and these members do not all have the same function, so in Christ we who are many form one body, and each member belongs to all the others. We have different gifts, according to the grace given us.

Romans 12:3-6 NIV

Ponder, Pray, and Journal

Why do you think God uses the analogy of the Body of Christ for His people? How does that relate to pride and humility?

Jesus' life was all about glorifying His Father, not about glorifying Himself.

Jesus answered, "If I glorify Myself, My glory is nothing; it is My Father who glorifies Me."

John 8:54

But the crowds had a different agenda, **intending to come and take Him by force to make Him king** (Jn 6:15). It is the same temptation Satan enticed Jesus with in Luke 4:5-12.

Seeking glory for myself may be one of the greatest temptations for me as a leader. I may not exactly be thinking about being crowned king, but there are other subtle draws that may cause me to try to steal away from God's glory, such as ...

- Focusing on the numbers, instead of on the deep surrender and spiritual growth of the people.

- Allowing, or even encouraging, people to become dependent on me, for comfort, for advice, for wisdom and counsel, for finances – instead of teaching them to depend on God.

- Drawing attention to myself instead of pointing people to God. If I am bigger-than-life, people will not see past me to find God.

Here are two of my life verses:

"He must increase, but I must decrease."

John 3:30

For you have died and your life is hidden with Christ in God.

Colossians 3:3

Ponder, Pray, and Journal

- Another aspect of pride may involve the desire to be in charge over others, or the temptation to lord it over others. Read Mark 10:42-45 and ask the Lord to search your heart.

- Look up John 6:15 and see how Jesus handled the temptation to glorify Himself. Think about the places God has stationed you. What will you do when temptations to glorify yourself arise?

As we continue to work through these traps, you will see that pride seems to be at the root of many of them. It would be easy to gloss over these other angles and just consider them covered under the blanket of pride. However, pride can be very insidious, so let's go into some additional details, pondering each facet and inviting the Holy Spirit to search our hearts.

Temptation: Comparisons, Competition, and Jealousy

When I am seeking to know where He has invited me to join Him, I can get tripped up when ...

- I start comparing and competing.
- I take my eyes off Jesus and look at my friends or other leaders or other Christians.
- I get jealous of how He is using others, and prideful about my reputation.

Then, the idol of them and the idol of me get in the way, and I can't hear clearly from Him. I may start pouring out my drink offering on the altar of myself, or on the altar of the idol of my friend, or on the altar of people-pleasing. The Word reminds me of the dangers of comparing:

We do not have the audacity to put ourselves in the same class or compare ourselves with some who [supply testimonials to] commend themselves. When they measure themselves by themselves and compare themselves with themselves, they lack wisdom and behave like fools.

2 Corinthians 10:12 AMP

The **audacity** to compare myself to others. That's *beyond* pride. When I compare, I lack wisdom and am behaving like a fool. When it is unchecked in my heart, comparing morphs into jealousy. I need to keep my eyes fixed on Jesus, and stop measuring and comparing, so I can work where He is working *and* has invited me to join Him. To know nothing **except Jesus Christ, and Him crucified** (1Cor 2:2).

Ponder, Pray, and Journal

Set aside some time to sit in stillness. Ask the Holy Spirit to search your heart and expose any comparing, envy, or jealousy.

Temptation: Judgment

"Do not judge, or you too will be judged. For in the same way you judge others, you will be judged, and with the measure you use, it will be measured to you. Why do you look at the speck of sawdust in your brother's eye and pay no attention to the plank in your own eye? How can you say to your brother, 'Let me take the speck out of your eye,' when all the time there is a plank in your own eye? You hypocrite, first take the plank out of your own eye, and then you will see clearly to remove the speck from your brother's eye."

Matthew 7:1-5 NIV

Condemning judgment involves a heart that looks down upon someone. When I am judging, I think I am better than the other person, perhaps thinking I am holier or smarter or more righteous. It starts with comparing, but instead of taking me down the path towards jealousy, it leads me to a place of superiority. When I judge, I set myself up as God, who is the one and only Judge. You can see how pride, self-idolatry, and rebellion are underlying roots of judgment. Contempt and disdain can then grow out of judgment.

Some of us can get tripped up here if we do not understand the difference between condemning judgment, and *discernment*. Discernment is the ability to determine if something is right by God, or displeasing to Him. Discernment is the ability to distinguish between good and evil, between Light and darkness, between God and Satan. As followers of Christ we are expected to develop discernment, as we can see when we read further into Matthew 7. Jesus teaches us not to invest our lives in those who are not receptive to the things of God, and how to recognize false prophets by their fruit (Matt 7:6, 15-20).

As we will see in upcoming chapters, a nonjudgmental heart is crucial for *Triumph* leaders to help our people feel safe enough to open up in class. A nonjudgmental heart does not come naturally to me, so this is a place of constant prayer for me.

Ponder, Pray, and Journal

Look up the following Scripture verses, and allow the Holy Spirit to examine your heart.

- Romans 2:1-3
- James 4:11-12
- John 8:7

Temptation: Hypocrisy

We're going to take it up a notch and touch on a sin that is an extreme opposite of humility: *hypocrisy*. This sin unites pride and deception. We like to think that Jesus reserved this scathing word for the Pharisees. But as we just read in the passage from Matthew 7, Jesus also cautioned *His own disciples* against hypocrisy.

The word hypocrite comes from the Greek; it was originally a word used for actors in a play, meaning "playing a part on the stage, pretending to be something one is not."[1] That derivation really pierces my heart.

Hypocrisy may involve trying to persuade people that I am better than I really am (maybe by exaggerating or omitting or even lying) because I want them to think more highly of me. Hypocrisy may be manifested as seeking to prove that which isn't true, to persuade people to think that I am something other than what I really am. To deceive people into believing that I am holier or smarter or more capable than I really am. To convince them that I know and understand Scripture better I we really do, or that my walk with the Lord is more intimate than it really is.

For me, shame was a strong impetus to create a façade, as I only allowed people to see the carefully crafted person that I wanted them to see. Fear of failure, deception, self-idolatry, people-pleasing, and pride all played into it. Although the Lord has really done much demolition work of this stronghold of shame in me, it still can at times rear its ugly head.

I can recall times when I have not wanted to admit that I didn't have the answer, because I wanted people to think that I am smarter than I really am. Indeed pride is at work here, but also deception, because I was trying to delude people into thinking I am something that I am not. Pride plus deception resulting in hypocrisy.

Only God has all the answers. As we humbly acknowledge our lack and pray and ask for wisdom and knowledge, the Holy Spirit will often give us answers, for as His *Triumph* Servant Leaders, we are walking in His anointing. But there will be times – lots of times – when we don't have the answer.

Ponder, Pray, and Journal

This is a strong word picture, of an actor on a stage. Be still before the Lord and allow Him to show you if there are times you have masqueraded in deception.

Temptation: Self-Protection and Self-Defense

A few weeks ago I found myself expounding with a wordy defense of myself and my actions. Unjustly accused, I felt a need to uphold my reputation and justify my decisions. Later, I wondered why I was so driven. I asked the Holy Spirit, and He showed me that my need to defend myself came out of pride. That I needed to prove myself, instead of trusting Him to defend my reputation and protect my work, if He so desired. As I sought Him in prayer, He strengthened my identity in Him and brought me to a new level of trust – and then let me be tested again. I was surprised to find such a peace in the midst of accusations, and not even a desire to defend or explain. I knew God would do all the defending necessary.

Ponder, Pray, and Journal

Read Psalm 18:1-3. Journal what it means to you for God to be your Stronghold, Fortress, Rock, Refuge, and Shield.

Think about a time when you have been your own shield. How would things have turned out differently if you allowed God to shield you as He desired?

Temptation: Fear of Failure and Perfectionism

A number of months ago, my prayer group posed an introspective question: What do you fear the most? I prayed and the Holy Spirit quickly revealed. I wrote down my answer: I feared missing the Kingdom work God has assigned me. It was an honest answer, and at the time, I thought it was quite a good answer. I thought that it showed that I was focused on the Lord's work. But something seemed not quite right here. Over the next day or two, the Holy Spirit would not let me brush Him off. Apparently He didn't think it was such a good answer.

Eventually, when I stopped to get alone with Him and listen to what He was saying, He showed me that what I was focused on was me, me, me. That my fear of failure demonstrated my selfishness and pride, my obsession with what *I* would be doing for the Kingdom – instead of focusing on the Lord, on His glory, and on the Kingdom itself. Horrified at my own heart, I prayed and repented and worshipped God instead of myself, and God then banished that fear.

Fear of failure has manifested itself in me as perfectionism and as the need to be right. It will be a walk of humility to grapple with and admit that I am human, and being human means that I will fail. Trying to be perfect sets me up in competition with the only perfect One. Fear of failure and perfectionism are both self-idolatry and idolatry of my reputation. And the root again is pride.

God is Light, and in Him there is no darkness at all ... If we say that we have no sin, we are deceiving ourselves and the truth is not in us ... in Him there is no sin.

1 John 1:5, 1:8, 3:5

The Greek word translated **sin** in these verses is derived from an archery term which means to miss the mark.[2] And of course Jesus is the only One who never misses the mark.

Seeing things from God's perspective can help overcome this fear. I go forth on His authority, not my own. He has sent me. His work is bigger than me; it doesn't depend on me, but He invites me to join in. He will accomplish His Kingdom plan, with or without me.

**He does as he pleases
with the powers of heaven
and the peoples of the earth.
No one can hold back his hand
or say to him: "What have you done?"**

Daniel 4:35 NIV

Ponder, Pray, and Journal

Let's ask the Holy Spirit to expose pride and its many manifestations, including some of the areas we addressed so far in this chapter: self-idolatry, people-pleasing, perfectionism, fear of failure, hypocrisy, self-preservation, self-defense, comparing, judging, jealousy. Some additional indications that pride may be at work may include

- Avoiding vulnerability and transparency.

- Comparing, judging, and jealousy can deteriorate into persecuting and criticizing in order to build ourselves up.

- Becoming unteachable and unable to accept constructive criticism. Ken Blanchard in *The Servant Leader* expounds, "One of the quickest ways you can tell the difference between a servant leader and a self-serving leader is how they handle feedback, because one of the biggest fears that self-serving leaders have is to lose their position."[3]

Meditate on the following Scriptures, ask the tough questions and invite Holy Spirit to reveal. Journal what He shows you.

- Read Matthew 9:6-8 and Matthew 5:16. Am I here to glorify myself, or to glorify Jesus? So people will look at me, or at Him? For my agenda, or His agenda? So people know my name, or His Name? So people remember me, or remember Him?

- How do I handle feedback? Do I embrace it because I want to improve my service, or do I defend myself because I am afraid of losing my position as leader? Read Psalm 18:33 as a reminder of Who strategically positioned us here.

- Do I tell my tips and secrets, or do I hide things and withhold information? Look up John 15:15 to see how Jesus led.

- Am I interested in training other leaders? Am I dedicated to multiplying? Or do I want subsequent courses to fail if I am not the leader? How would I feel if those I trained surpassed me? Look up John 14:12 to see how Jesus led.

Temptation: Self-Sufficiency

When I first began leading *Triumph Over Suffering*, I was in a place of healthy fear, which led to deep reliance upon the Lord. I spent a lot of time praying, fasting, and preparing physically, mentally, and spiritually for class. As I have become a more experienced leader, self-sufficiency beckons, a more enticing trap. I can be tempted to rely on my experience, knowledge, efforts, abilities, talents, or gifts.

Alert to this trap, I take definitive steps to remain connected to the Lord. When I am in a semester of leading, instead of spending less time with the Lord because I am busy preparing, ministering, leading, I deliberately spend more time with Him. I mark off in my calendar specific times and days to be alone with Him in prayer, worship, solitude, listening, fasting. I work hard to keep these times sacred, protecting these appointments with God, not allowing other things to infringe upon these times. Setting aside specific times to go into the tent of meeting is a discipline I adhere to all year round, but in a season of leading, I am even more intentional.

Ponder, Pray, and Journal

Take some time to ask the Lord how He wants you to continue your deep abiding in Him even during the busy season of a class. Journal your prayer of commitment to do as He asks.

Let's look at another manifestation of self-sufficiency: an unwillingness to allow our needs to be met. We may have learned to rely on the Holy Spirit to lead a class, but *admitting our needs* may be a completely different issue.

When I first came to the Lord, I was so independent that I was reluctant to even admit that I had *any* needs. I would not ask for help, and would even refuse offers of much-needed help. For example, if someone offered to bring in snacks for class, I would turn down their offer because I felt guilty and ashamed that I couldn't "do it all." This again is pride and perfectionism, coupled with striving and earning as I relied on my own work to "keep the participants in the class." Additionally, the low self worth of not being able to acknowledge that it was acceptable for me to have any needs also played a part here. As I am now seeing this from another angle, I recognize that this behavior deprived others of the opportunity to be used by the Lord to serve.

Another way this self-sufficiency manifested in me was in the area of prayer. When I first came to the Lord and began praying for people, I was completely unable to *receive* their prayers for me in return. I would actually shut down anyone who offered to pray for me. I welcomed their prayers for the participants of class, but not for me personally.

The Holy Spirit did indeed get hold of my heart, and revealed the pride and independence behind these behaviors. It required a walk of humility to accept help and prayer. As He has transformed me, I am now seeking and asking for help, and ever so grateful for any offer, no matter how small. I am also crying out to God to send me people to pray for me. If someone genuinely asks if I have any prayer requests, if I sense that they have been sent by God, I am willing to be transparent and open in order to receive their Spirit-led prayers.

Ponder, Pray, and Journal

Read the following Scriptures, and ponder, pray, and journal.

- Psalm 20:7 NIV
- Proverbs 16:9
- 2 Chronicles 32:7-8
- Isaiah 31:1-3

Temptation: Isolation

Early in my walk with the Lord, self-sufficiency morphed into isolation. I felt very alone as a leader. It seemed that no one was carrying the same burdens that I did. I found it hard to relate and to connect.

Ponder, Pray, and Journal

Why is this a very dangerous place to be? Pause and journal your thoughts.

Isolation was a place of pride for me. Thinking how important I was, that no one could relate, no one could understand. Pridefully thinking that I was an important part of the Body, like a hand or an eye, I forgot that we are all equally important members of the same Body. Detached from the Body, I was not accountable to anyone. Self-reliant, I smoothly justified my mistakes and errors.

The Lord revealed my need for accountability. He showed me that I needed people to whom I could ...

- Confess my sins.
- Admit my struggles and fears.

- Seek wise counsel and perspective.
- Unload my burdens.
- Receive prayer.

As He revealed these things, I could see my need, but then I discovered that *I had to seek it out*. And when I asked, He graciously provided me with mentors, accountability partners, and counselors. He also gifted me with a devoted prayer team who not only prays with me and for me, but also keeps me accountable.

The next revelation He granted me was that it wasn't enough just to have these people in my life; *I needed to be honest with them*. To confess my mistakes and sins and failures and short-comings. To be transparent with them and to ask them to hold me accountable. To give them permission – in fact, to beg them – to call me out when they noticed something out of integrity in my walk.

And next I learned that *I needed to be receptive to them* when they spoke into my life. Sometimes, my sins and shortcomings are concealed from my own perception. It is as if I am blind to them – so they are called *blind spots*. And, in that sweet way God has of keeping me humble, sometimes He ordains that I be dependent upon others in the Body to point out my weaknesses to me.

As leaders, we do indeed have need for accountability, but we have an equally important need for a safe place. This safe place is not a place to gossip or complain, but to unload burdens, confess sins, and receive prayer. This is especially critical for leaders who are ministering to hurting people. We will need filling, because we want to be able to deeply connect with our hurting people *without needing them to give back*. Of course the Lord will be our first and most important Safe Place, and the only One who fills us. But I believe He also offers us *His people* as safe places, people who will pray for us for filling, who will shore us up and encourage us, in order that we are equipped to be sent out.

Some of these safe places will be where we leaders are for the most part not doing any ministering, but are only *receiving*. Other safe places will be places perhaps with other leaders, where we both regularly *give* and *receive* encouragement, edification, and prayer.

These safe places are necessary to provide strengthening and refreshing so that we are ready to go forth to serve broken people. Leaders need others in the Body to pour into them so they can pour into others, because we want to minister to the hurting from a place of strength. I think that pride, fear, or an earning, striving mentality can thwart us from seeking out these safe havens. Humility will facilitate our coming up under the prayers of these people who have been sent by God.

I am thinking of Joshua on the battlefield and Moses, Aaron, and Hur up on the mountaintop praying (Ex 17:8-13). Joshua was a strong man of prayer himself, who spent much time in the tent of meeting (Ex 33:7-11). But when the Lord sent him into battle, he needed the prayer power behind him for victory. And when the Lord sends *us* into battle, leading a class, we will also need the prayer power behind us for victory.

Our Paul, Silas, and Timothy

I recall Pastor Tom Mullins of Christ Fellowship teaching us that we all need a Paul, a Silas, and a Timothy.

We need Paul, a spiritual mentor, someone ahead of us on our journey, someone to go to for advice and perspective. Our Paul must be willing to speak into our lives, challenge us, and call us up to more demanding work. And we must be willing to humbly receive Paul's wise counsel.

We need Silas, someone about in the same place as we are spiritually, so we can run together this race marked out for us. Someone to encourage us and hold us accountable.

And we must be willing to be open with Silas and to be held accountable by our Silas.

And we need Timothy, someone whose walk is not yet as deep with the Lord as ours is, yet is teachable and eager to learn. Our Timothy is the one we are mentoring, pouring into as our Paul is pouring into us. And we must be willing to be available to Timothy as our mentors have been available for us.

Our Silas will have multiple responsibilities, so it is important that we develop a true deep connection with Silas. Leaders may find their most helpful Silas to be a leader in a similar position who shares parallel challenges and struggles. Silas should also be a person we can come to bounce ideas off, and also for prayer. Actually, I think we may need a few Silases.

Our "Inner Three"

Realize that Jesus did not admit His exhaustion and limitations to the crowds. He shared some of His personal needs with His twelve disciples, letting them know He was hungry or exhausted. And deeper experiences He didn't even reveal to all twelve, but reserved for Peter, James, and John. Jesus allowed these three disciples inside the house to see Him raise the young girl from the dead. These same three were witness to His mountaintop transfiguration. And these "inner three" were also invited to be with Him during His agony at Gethsemane. They witnessed His fear, His human struggle, and His ultimate surrender. He also asked these three for prayer.

Like Jesus, we will need deep close friends, people who will run this race with us. And like Jesus, we will also need a smaller and closer group to share with them about our private encounters with the Lord, and to bring to them heavy prayer requests. We need an "inner three." Two or three same-gender friends who are safe when we are vulnerable and transparent. A few strong Christians who will not be afraid to speak out when we are off track. A few friends who will pray for us and encourage us when we are down, and keep us accountable when necessary. We will rely on our "inner three" to point us to God for the answers.

Yet – we must also be careful of becoming dependent on a person. We must remain dependent *upon God*. Jesus is the only One who completes us. The Holy Spirit is the only One who matures us, and the only One who will fill us. He is the One who will give us the answers. Human wisdom is but foolishness to Him. Our God is also the only One who will never fail us. Remember how all Jesus' disciples left Him and fled when He was arrested. Humans will fail us, and we will fail them. It is part of being human. (Jer 17:5-9, Col 2:6-10, Acts 4:31, 1Cor 3:18-19, Mk 14:50, Ps 20:7, 33:16-21.)

Additionally, the Holy Spirit can and will move people in and out of our lives at will.

"The wind blows where it wishes and you hear the sound of it, but do not know where it comes from and where it is going; so is everyone who is born of the Spirit." John 3:8

We must be reliant upon God, not upon other people. We want our inner three to be people who understand that concept also.

Ponder, Pray, and Journal

Ask the Holy Spirit if you have any tendencies to isolation. Journal your Paul, your Silas, and your Timothy. (Of course you will have lots of Timothy's in your class!)

Who are your inner two or three that you can fully confide in, and who will hold you accountable? These are probably your Pauls or Silases. What are you doing to cultivate and maintain these connections?

If you don't have these crucial relationships in your life right now, ask the Lord to graciously bring you into connection with them. And remember from Chapter 4 how vibrant relationships cannot be cultivated in a life lived without margin.

Temptation: Co-Dependency

When I first began leading *Triumph Over Suffering* Classes, it seemed I was a magnet for every hurting crying soul on the planet. I was excessively burdened, I was available day and night, and it wasn't long before I was run ragged. I felt used and unappreciated. My mentor told me there was something not right in my heart that was attracting all these people. I didn't believe her. I thought I was called to this ministry, and God was sending me people to minister to.

Turns out, my mentor was right. As I continued to seek the Lord and grow up in Him, the Holy Spirit showed me that I had a *need to be needed.* In order to feel useful, validated, and important, something inside of me was drawing in people who were very needy, *but who were not open to the transforming work of the Spirit.* It was a trap of co-dependency: they needed someone to listen to their endless woes; I needed people to "help."

Although the other pitfalls we have covered are really applicable to any type of leader, this one of co-dependency is probably a more dangerous and more insidious trap for leaders who are called to minister to those who are hurting.

As I sought the Lord to reveal the root issues here, the Holy Spirit uncovered a few deep roots. He showed me that lack of depth of relationship with Him opened me up to this trap. He wanted me to come to Him to meet all my needs – my need for love and acceptance and approval, my need for validation and encouragement and companionship, my need to feel valued and useful and appreciated.

He also exposed self-idolatry: I thought I could help them. Instead of pointing them to Jesus for healing and comfort and answers, I was drawing them to myself. I was playing god. Although I could give some temporary human comfort and maybe some "good" answers, I was thwarting them from going to God for eternal comfort, healing, wisdom, freedom. This was why I was drawing to myself people who did not want to do the hard work of sanctification, who were resistant to opening themselves up to His transforming power.

Additionally, He revealed to me that co-dependency was thwarting my ability to set Godly boundaries. I had trouble saying no, and I had difficulty discerning where He was working and where He was not. The idols of the people I was "helping" and the idol of myself interfered with my hearing clearly from Him.

Finally, He showed me that this tendency towards co-dependency also extended to my friends. The pendulum in my heart had swung from isolation and self-sufficiency to co-dependency. I had begun to rely on people for encouragement and prayer instead of seeking Him to fulfill all of my needs. He wanted me to call on Him instead of calling up one of my friends.

"Call to me and I will answer you and tell you great and unsearchable things you do not know."
Jeremiah 33:3 NIV

The only way out of this mess was repentance, and spending more time with Him – quality time in great quantity.

I needed to grow to know Him more, to learn to receive from Him more, and to seek Him first and always for all my needs.

I have learned in greater measure to be led by His Spirit, to work only where He is working and has called me in on assignment. I am learning to point people to Jesus for the miraculous instead of drawing them to myself for the limited. I am increasingly seeking Him instead of people for encouragement, validation, comfort, guidance, wisdom, companionship. Of course I won't always get it right, but as I seek Him desperately I can trust Him to correct me if I have gotten off track.

Ponder, Pray, and Journal

Now it's your turn. Give yourself over to the Holy Spirit to examine, and journal what He reveals. Ask Him to unveil the motives of your heart.

If God is revealing issues of co-dependency, study these Scriptures:

- Jeremiah 17:5-9
- Colossians 2:10
- 1 Corinthians 1:25, 3:18-19
- Psalm 33:16-21

We do indeed have a heart for the hurting – or we wouldn't be called as *Triumph* Servant Leaders. And I love your compassionate loving hearts! But sometimes ... we can cross that line from a Godly work of meeting people's needs – to bearing burdens God never intended us to bear. Because it seems that this trap of co-dependency is a common one for those ministering to the hurting, before we leave this topic, we will look at another facet: bearing another's assigned load.

Temptation: Bearing Another's Load

To keep me alert to my tendency to fall in this trap, I have created a list of signals that could indicate I am slipping here. As you go over my list, think about the last class you were in – or about leading one upcoming. Go ahead and circle anything in the list below that pertains to you.

- Feeling overwhelmed with the needs of the class.
- Feeling you cannot possibly minister to each one.
- Constantly worrying about the participants.
- Constantly thinking about what to say to them to bring them to surrender or to forgive.
- Repeated concerns about whether a participant will complete the class.
- Fear that you will fail in your job as leader because the participants won't learn the material.
- Fear that no one will show up to class.
- Feeling their pain and not being able to let it go after class.

If we persist on this path, we may collapse, burn out, break down, and even abandon the ministry. Or, we may harden our hearts so that we no longer feel their pain. Neither is God's plan. In order to avoid this trap, Galatians teaches us to bear **burdens** but not **loads**:

Bear one another's burdens, and thereby fulfill the law of Christ ... For each one will bear his own load.

Galatians 6:2,5

How can we bear another's *burdens* but not their *loads*? As I researched the Greek here, I see the word **burdens** focuses on "pressure,"[4] seeming to indicate the weight and crushing heaviness of overwhelming sufferings. But the word **load** is defined as "the burden of one's own responsibilities and failures."[5] **Load** seems to indicate our *own* personal duties and our *own* responsibilities for our sins and failings.

I have heard **burdens** described as huge boulders that one person cannot shoulder alone, and **load** described as one's own personal knapsack that he is responsible to carry. A team is needed to help carry a burden. We are here to support, love, encourage, comfort, empathize and pray with those who are suffering as they endure the anguish of their trials. Yet we are not to take on the consequences of their choices or the responsibilities that are assigned to them. We must be cautious that we don't fall into enabling patterns. Each is to run with perseverance the race marked out for them. It will require a close walk with the Lord to discern if we have crossed the line from helping to bear a burden to carrying someone's assigned load. It is crucial that we do not short-circuit their spiritual growth by carrying their loads for them.

As we discussed in the previous section, realize that if we begin to take on loads that have been assigned to another, we may at first feel very important and quite useful, because we think we are in a position to "help" someone in need. But that feeling of being "useful" will probably be very short-lived, as we suddenly find ourselves drowning in their problems, and as God opens our eyes to our pride, self-idolatry, and co-dependency.

Yes, we are called to help bear one another's burdens, to weep with those who weep, to comfort the afflicted with the comfort we have received from God (Rom 12:15, 2Cor 1:3-4). Yet we are not called to identify with them so closely that we put on their garments of pain. That's Jesus' job.

In order to help bear their burden but not carry their load, I use the friendship of David and Jonathan as my model. When David was running for his life from Saul, hiding in caves, it would have been easy for Jonathan to avoid David, to let David suffer alone. But Jonathan was not afraid to meet with him, to spend time with him, to listen to him and comfort him. Yet, Jonathan did not provide weapons or warriors; he did not rescue David or lead him to a new hiding place. Jonathan simply **helped him find strength in God** (1Sam 23:16). God was using this time of trial to equip David to be the warrior king He had purposed him to be. If Jonathan had rescued him, David would have missed this crucial time of preparation.

Don't think this is easy – rescuing someone may be much easier than helping them find their strength in God! But as we do what God calls us to do, and move out of the way so God can do what only He can do, we will enter into a sweet partnership with the Creator of the Universe. We are seated in the front row to watch His magnificent work and astounding miracles.

If we have fallen into carrying another's assigned load, there is only one way out: repentance and surrender. We must step off the pedestal of being god to our participants and make room for God to be God. We must surrender our people, and the outcome of this class, to God. We must learn to lovingly step into their pain with them, and then hand them off to Jesus.

Stormie Omartian teaches that releasing someone into God's hands ...

> ... doesn't mean you have given up on him or her. You're not saying, "You take him, God. I can't deal with him anymore." Or, "That's it, Lord. I've had it. She's all Yours now." It means you have surrendered the burden you have been carrying ... to the Lord so He can take it off of our shoulders. Then the burden you carry is in prayer.[6]

Surrendering them *without giving up on them* is not easy. Recall how Paul labored in prayer, and how Jesus agonized in prayer (2Cor 1:11, Lk 22:41). Realize a burden of prayer is vastly different than a physical, mental, or emotional burden. When the Lord burdens us to pray, we are led to partner with the Lord, open to the Holy Spirit's leading on when to pray and how to pray and even what to pray. When the burden lifts, the Holy Spirit says our prayer is finished for now. We surrender to Him the answer to our prayers, and walk away until He calls us to intercession or other action again. The enemy may try to drive us to worry and fret and fear – but we must differentiate the enemy's voice from our Lord's voice and refuse to succumb to Satan's tactics.

Ponder, Pray, and Journal

Ask the Lord to show you if carrying another's load is a danger for you. How will you set Godly boundaries?

Temptation: Prayerlessness

Prayer is another area I can skimp on when I am "too busy" leading a class. Other times, I find myself excusing myself from prayer for the participants because "the prayer team is praying." And indeed they are, but I believe God requires and expects my prayers also. As leaders, we will know our participants the most and are best positioned to know their deep spiritual needs and how to pray.

I have committed to prayer in many different ways over the years of leading, but one thing I have discovered, that for me, waiting "until the Spirit moves me" is not reliable enough. Yes, He will indeed bring a burden of prayer at times, but if I don't position myself with lots of alone time with Him, I may not be sensitive enough to His Spirit when He is searching for someone to pray.

Often, I feel like I don't know how to pray for my people. All I know is that I desire His will to be done, but I am not at all certain what His will is. We will discuss more about prayer in the next chapter, and I have written a prayer guide for you in the Appendix. But for now, realize that as we pray, He will show us *how* to pray[7] – but we must come to Him, unhurried and open in order for Him to pray through us.

Temptation: Control

A number of years ago, one of my participants in class was doing a lot of talking, so much so that she prevented others from sharing. I worked hard to control the situation, trying a new strategy each week to limit her sharing and to allow other ladies to have a chance to share. Nothing worked. It was extremely frustrating for me and for the rest of the class.

After a number of weeks, as the situation grew worse, the Holy Spirit spoke to me very clearly, showing me that what was going on here was completely out of my ability to control. And He revealed to me that the reason this disruptive behavior was continuing was because I was so busy controlling *I did not see her heart*. I was so concerned with having a nice little class where everyone behaved properly and took their turn in proper order that I was oblivious to her heart needs.

In Chapter 9, we'll discuss ways to handle these kinds of issues, but in the meantime, let's pause for a heart check.

Ponder, Pray, and Journal

What sorts of things do you try to control? Other people's behaviors? The schedule of the day? What people think of you? Your spouse? Your children? If the Holy Spirit is convicting you of control, meditate on these verses:

- Psalm 115:3
- Daniel 4:35
- Proverbs 19:21

Journal your prayer of surrendering everything to His control. Then meditate on these verses:

- Psalm 37:5
- Psalm 20:7
- Psalm 9:10

Temptation: Forsaking Our Spiritual Covering

It seems that God offers us an extra layer of protection from the enemy: the guardianship of those He has placed in authority over us. Just as He holds us as leaders responsible for the spiritual welfare of those He brings to us, He holds the pastors and leaders over us responsible for our spiritual welfare.

Obey your leaders and submit to them, for they keep watch over your souls as those who will give an account. Let them do this with joy and not with grief, for this would be unprofitable for you.

Hebrews 13:17

The NIV translates it, **Have confidence in your leaders.** Let's read it in the Amplified also:

> **Obey your [spiritual] leaders and submit to them [recognizing their authority over you], for they are keeping watch over your souls and continually guarding your spiritual welfare as those who will give an account [of their stewardship of you]. Let them do this with joy and not with grief and groans, for this would be of no benefit to you.**
>
> Hebrews 13:17 AMP

We come up under this protection when we recognize the authority of our pastors and leaders over us, and observe God's commands to **obey** them and **submit** to them. Wives even have an additional layer of protection through submitting to their husbands in the Lord. This "spiritual covering" is a precious gift of protection that God offers us; if we do not tuck up under that covering, we are *rebelling* against God, and *forsaking* the shield of protection that He is offering us.

Pastor Watchman Nee in his book *Spiritual Authority* refers to the authority that God gives leaders as God's "delegated authority." He writes that he himself is so desirous of the spiritual protection afforded by coming up under God's delegated authority that wherever he goes, wherever he serves, he asks God to show him whom he is to submit to as his spiritual authority. "If you ever once in your life meet authority you will then be able to see God's authority everywhere. Wherever you go, your first question will be: Whom should I obey, To whom should I hearken?"[8]

He also explains that a most important part of our walk with the Lord is obeying His will. He writes that when we are fully submissive to God's authority, and choose to be "restrained" by the authority He has designated for us, *then* "we can begin to be used by Him."[9]

Refusal to obey and submit to our leaders is *rebellion* against God. Pastors and church leaders are anointed by God for their position, and God commands us to support them.

> "... for who can stretch out his hand against the Lord's anointed and be without guilt?"
>
> 1 Samuel 26:9

If there are any church policies or teachings of your church that you are wondering about, do not gripe or complain among your peers or participants. First go to God. He may tell you all you need to know. Then, if needed, go directly to your immediate leader or pastor and respectfully ask questions.

It is important that we as leaders are supportive of our church and church leadership from deep in our hearts. We can't fake it here. Most likely, when we understand why decisions have been made, it will be easy for us to support the decisions. If there is ever a time you do not fully understand, or have not yet had an opportunity to ask questions, God commands us to support our pastors and leaders in trust of Him and His choice of them as our leaders. We may not always be privy to the reasons behind a decision, or may not fully understand all the factors and implications that went into this decision, but we can trust God and in obedience support our leadership.

Sometimes, there may be more going on than policies. If the issue is sin, we will follow the Lord's commands:

> "If your brother sins, go and show him his fault in private; if he listens to you, you have won your brother. But if he does not listen to you, take one or two more with you, so that BY THE MOUTH OF TWO OR THREE WITNESSES EVERY FACT MAY BE CONFIRMED. If he refuses to listen to them, tell it to the church; and if he refuses to listen even to the church, let him be to you as a Gentile and a tax collector."
>
> Matthew 18:15-17

Certainly cover this in love and prayer, and if needed, seek wise counsel.

One last thought. Before you shrug this temptation off, certain that you are not in rebellion against authority, realize that rebellion can involve more than just outright defiance. Leading class in a way that is not in step with the direction of the church can be rebellion. Refusing correction can be rebellion. Criticizing, scorning, even questioning with the wrong heart can also be rebellion. Additionally, keep in mind that the church is the Body of Christ. When we criticize the church, *we are criticizing Jesus Himself.*

Ponder, Pray, and Journal

Read Luke 1:5-20 and Luke 1:26-38. Why did the angel respond to Zacharias and Mary so differently? Journal your thoughts.

Ask the Holy Spirit to reveal any rebellious thoughts or ways in your own heart. If He reveals, you know what to do.

God requires that His servants are connected into the Body of Christ and submitted to leadership, and this is a requirement for *Triumph Leadership* also. God demands from all of us respectful speech about our leaders and pastors. We are also mandated to appreciate our pastors and leaders and esteem them:

But we request of you, brethren, that you appreciate those who diligently labor among you, and have charge over you in the Lord and give you instruction, and that you esteem them very highly in love because of their work. Live in peace with one another.

1 Thessalonians 5:12-13

Live in peace with one another. I see that submitting to our church authority also involves pursuing unity with others in the church. That leads us into our final temptation of this chapter.

Temptation: Division and Strife

We truly desire to be united with our co-leaders in all our decisions. And somehow, we think unity should just "happen" when Christ-lovers are serving the Lord together. But we are made differently, we process differently, we are wired differently and we have different creativities. We won't think the same. Consequently, unity is not humanly natural – so don't be surprised when it doesn't "naturally" happen.

Unity is not *uniformity*. Uniformity is when all are the same. Identical, with no variation. But *unity* seems to *require* there to be differences and uniqueness and diversity in order for there to *be* a melding into oneness. To me, unity seems to be the *opposite* of uniformity, because if we had uniformity, we would have no need for unity. We would already *be* the same. When I think about the infinite diversity and creativity of God's creation, I conclude that He loves variety – and the glorious harmony produced when we are united in Him.

Compromise, or meeting in the middle, is a human method that two dissimilar people can use to work together. But seeking *unity* is an entirely different way, something that can be only achieved in Jesus by the work of the Holy Spirit. Seeking unity involves valuing and *capitalizing on* our differences, diversity, and unique giftings as we rely on God to grant us to be *of the same mind* with one another. Seeking unity means we ask God to weave us into a beautiful tapestry with a singular focus: to glorify Him with one voice and one accord (Rom 15:5-6).

When we do not agree, as we deeply seek His will and surrender to His way, we can count on the Lord to work in our hearts. We may discover that one or the other of us is not aligned with His will. Or, He may show us that neither of us are aligned with His will – and meeting in the middle is not His will either. As we seek Him in prayer, He may unveil a new creative plan that had not even crossed our minds. As we humble ourselves and acknowledge that the plan came from Him, we open ourselves to receive His true deep spiritual unity.

Be sober in spirit and on the alert. Satan is the mastermind behind arguments, division, strife, disunity (1Pt 5:8, Jas 3:14-16). He will sow disunity between leaders, between participants, and between leaders and participants. He will use disagreements to attempt to rip apart these classes and interfere with the flow of the Holy Spirit. He desires to distract us, drain our energy, and cause us to focus on anything but the Lord and His heart work in us.

To overcome the wiles of the enemy, we will need to stop wrestling with each other, recognize who the enemy is, and unite in battle against *our real enemy* (Eph 6:12). Seeking unity will require forgiveness, grace, and mercy. It will entail compassion, understanding, and discernment. And it won't happen without persevering in prayer and humbling ourselves by relinquishing our plan and opening our hearts as we ask the Lord what *His plan* is here.

Ponder, Pray, and Journal

- Read Ephesians 4:1-3. What will you do to preserve unity and protect from falling into division with your co-leaders and your participants?

- Read 1 Corinthians 12:12-27. This is an important passage for *all* the temptations we have wrestled with in this chapter. Why do you think God uses the analogy of the Body of Christ for the family of God?

- Go back and review all the temptations we have covered in this chapter. How will a deep comprehension of the family of God as the Body of Christ help you overcome these temptations?

Behold, how good and how pleasant it is
For brothers to dwell together in unity!
It is like the precious oil upon the head,
Coming down upon the beard,
Even Aaron's beard,
Coming down upon the edge of his robes.
It is like the dew of Hermon
Coming down upon the mountains of Zion;
For there *the Lord commanded the blessing—*
    life forever.
Psalm 133:1-3, emphasis added

Not only is unity pleasing to our Heavenly Father – when we are dwelling in unity, He **commands** His blessing upon us! And no wonder He blesses us in unity, because it is in unity that we can glorify Him with one accord and one voice:

Now may the God who gives perseverance and encouragement grant you to be of the same mind with one another according to Christ Jesus, so that with one accord you may with one voice glorify the God and Father of our Lord Jesus Christ.
Romans 15:5-6

What if We Fall Into These Traps?

As we've worked through these temptations, the Holy Spirit may have shown you some sins and dark areas of your heart. And we are human; we may certainly fall into these traps in the future. What will we do?

First, confess to God for forgiveness and cleansing:

If we confess our sins, He is faithful and righteous to forgive us our sins and to cleanse us from all unrighteousness.
1 John 1:9

Next, as the Lord leads, confess to your accountability team, the *Triumph* leader you are under, and/or the pastor you are under to receive prayer and healing:

Therefore, confess your sins to one another, and pray for one another *so that you may be healed*. The effective prayer of a righteous man can accomplish much.
James 5:16, emphasis added

Finally, take the necessary steps to continue to walk in the Light.

... for you were formerly darkness, but now you are Light in the Lord; walk as children of Light.
Ephesians 5:8

How will we know when we can simply confess a mistake or failure to an accountability partner, and when it necessitates confession to our *Triumph* leader or pastor? As we seek the Lord, the Holy Spirit will inform these decisions.

In Chapter 2, I shared about how I had knowingly improperly footnoted the original version of *Triumph Over Suffering*. When the Holy Spirit brought His conviction heavily upon me, I confessed to my prayer team, my husband

and kids, and my mentor, but in my heart I knew immediately that this was insufficient. As the Holy Spirit led, I confessed to multiple pastors at my church and contacted all the authors. Each one I confessed to gave me forgiveness and incredible unspeakable grace. The Lord told me that He had not let me be hurled headlong:

> **The steps of a man are established by the Lord,**
> **And He delights in his way.**
> **When he falls, he will not be hurled headlong,**
> **Because the Lord is the One who holds his hand.**
> Psalm 37:23-24

Humbled, forgiven, and sanctified, I have been graciously given more books to write and classes to teach. That was ten years ago, and I am still honored and stunned. Yet I know that the outcome may not always look this way. These are the Lord's sovereign decisions. But remember that His desire for you is to finish the race, and to finish strong. He holds your crown of righteousness in His hands.

Chapter 6
In Step with the Holy Spirit

One of the most challenging parts of *Triumph Leadership* is leading in the classroom. You might guess that leading in a way that promotes healing, provides encouragement, and constantly puts the focus on Jesus will come with experience and practice. And experience and practice is indeed a component of strong leadership. But vastly more important is to be *led by the Spirit*.

After the difficult heart work of the previous chapters, I think you will find this chapter to be a breath of fresh air. We will first focus on the importance of allowing the Holy Spirit to lead, and what it will be like for us as leaders when we rely on Him and walk in step with Him. Then I will share some ways that I invite Him in and make Him feel welcome. This positions me to hear from Him, and helps me to submit to His leading.

We will also learn how to help our participants feel comfortable and safe in order to facilitate *their* hearing from the Holy Spirit in the classroom. And in the final part of the chapter, we will discuss how to help our participants learn to hear from the Holy Spirit both inside of the classroom with us, and outside of the classroom on their own as well.

Led By the Spirit

Being led by the Holy Spirit is a most crucial characteristic of a *Triumph* Servant Leader. If we desire the Holy Spirit's leading, we must fully and continually surrender to Him. As leaders, we are responsible to prepare the chapter, to be familiar with the material and seek Him in prayer for His guidance for this specific class. But we must hold our agenda very loosely in our hands. We must have no drive to accomplish anything on our agenda, and simply wait and listen for His direction.

Being led by the Spirit requires us to be comfortable with the unknown. Although I may want the Holy Spirit to lay out the class or the whole day or the whole year right now, I find He generally leads me one step at a time, waiting for me to take the first step in obedience before He shows me His next stepping stone.

As we studied in previous chapters, God desires us to have *laser focus* on the mission He has assigned us, and to be on task without discouragement or distraction. He does not want us pulled away, even by other wonderful ministries or other good things. He wants us to hear from Him and to walk in obedience. The Holy Spirit wants to flow through us unimpeded. We can accomplish this only when we are operating under the Holy Spirit's power and are being led by Him. Listen to how Paul describes the Holy Spirit working through him:

And when I came to you, brethren, I did not come with superiority of speech or of wisdom, proclaiming to you the testimony of God. For I determined to know nothing among you except Jesus Christ, and Him crucified. I was with you in weakness and in fear and in much trembling, and my message and my preaching were not in persuasive words of wisdom,

but in demonstration of the Spirit and of power, so that your faith would not rest on the wisdom of men, but on the power of God.

1 Corinthians 2:1-5

We are **determined to know nothing among you except Jesus Christ, and Him crucified.** We will put aside all positions, statuses, titles, and degrees, considering them but rubbish. My medical degree is useless in the spiritual setting of the classroom where Holy Spirit is Healer. Likewise, our own counseling is pointless when Holy Spirit is the Counselor. Our own teaching is meaningless when Holy Spirit is the Teacher. Our own persuasion is unproductive and our own words of wisdom are but foolishness when Holy Spirit has arrived on the scene (Ps 147:3, Isa 9:6, Jn 14:26).

Jesus Christ sends us to teach His Word,

... not in cleverness of speech, so that the cross of Christ would not be made void.

1 Corinthians 1:17

So that the cross will not be made void. The AMPC says so that it will not be **deprived of force and emptied of its power and rendered vain (fruitless, void of value, and of no effect).** The cross is the power of God and the wisdom of God (1Cor 1:24).

Ponder, Pray, and Journal

We do not speak with superiority of wisdom, so that the faith of our people will not rest on human wisdom, but on the power of God. We do not speak with cleverness of speech, so that the cross will not be emptied of its power. In fact, our human "wisdom" can even hinder His work. Our assignment is to point our people to Jesus, to direct them to the cross of Christ.

This is heavy. Write a prayer of surrender to the Holy Spirit based on the Scriptures we have read so far in this chapter.

Wisdom of the Spirit

Paul goes on to say,

Yet we do speak wisdom among those who are mature; a wisdom, however, not of this age nor of the rulers of this age ... but we speak God's wisdom in a mystery, the hidden wisdom ... For to us God revealed [this wisdom] **through the Spirit; for the Spirit searches all things, even the depths of God. For ... the thoughts of God no one knows except the Spirit of God. Now we have received, not the spirit of the world, but the Spirit who is from God, so that we may know the things freely given to us by God, which things we also speak, not in words taught by human wisdom, but in those taught by the Spirit, combining spiritual thoughts with spiritual words.**

1 Corinthians 2:6-13

So we come to class, not with superiority of speech or wisdom; we come knowing only Jesus Christ and Him crucified – and yet we come ready to speak the wisdom that God has taught us to those who are mature. How will we know who is mature enough to receive the spiritual wisdom God has granted us? And how will we know if we are speaking with our own human "wisdom" or speaking the wisdom of the Spirit? This is going to require a very close walk with Him indeed.

As each one has received a special gift, employ it in serving one another as good stewards of the manifold grace of God. Whoever speaks, is to do so as one who is speaking the utterances of God; whoever serves is to do so as one who is serving by the strength which

God supplies; so that in all things God may be glorified through Jesus Christ, to whom belongs the glory and dominion forever and ever. Amen.

2 Peter 4:10-11

The Holy Spirit has granted us special gifts; we honor Him when we, as jars of clay, are open for His Spirit to flow through us and utilize those gifts. We glorify Him when we allow Him to take over our hearts and minds and even our mouths, and we speak as one speaking the very utterances of God. Only a profound abiding, only a deep walking in fear of the Lord, will result in this flow of the Spirit through us. Only when we have continually and fully surrendered to Him will He take His rightful place: in charge of our lives, in charge of the class.

Relying on the Holy Spirit

I cannot emphasize enough the importance of depending on the Holy Spirit to teach the class. We cannot transform a heart – *only He can*. We cannot persuade someone to repent – *only He can*. We cannot open blind eyes to the lies that ensnare them – *only He can*. We cannot free or heal or deliver – *only Jesus, through His Spirit, can*.

"Not by might nor by power, but by My Spirit," says the Lord of hosts.

Zechariah 4:6

Our words are human and full of nothing – unless they are infused with the Holy Spirit's power and conviction.

... for our gospel did not come to you in word only, but also in power and in the Holy Spirit and with full conviction...

1 Thessalonians 1:5

As we have prayed and surrendered and prayed some more, we can trust that God has strategically placed us in this specific class, for this specific role, for this specific group – and that He did not set us up to fail. The Holy Spirit has promised to show up when we are gathered in His name and invite Him in. We are here on His assignment; when we ask, He comes (Rom 8:31-32, Heb 13:21-21, 12:1-2, Mt 18:20).

When we abide in Him, walking in intimate obedience, He promises to grant us any prayer that we ask according to His will. When we admit our weaknesses, and rely on the Holy Spirit to teach and lead the class, we can trust that He will give us, His anointed ones, the words to say. He promises wisdom if we ask without any doubting. He will certainly teach the class if we, with humility and fear of the Lord, allow ourselves to be led. And He promises to bring forth fruit thirty, sixty, a hundredfold when we abide in Him (Jn 14:26, 15:6-8,16 1Jn 5:14-15, 2Cor 12:9-10, Lk 12:11-12, Jas 1:5-6, Mk 4:8).

Inviting the Holy Spirit To Lead

Of course we know He is always with us, and will never leave us or forsake us (Heb 13:5, Dt 31:6, Josh 1:9). We know that when even two or three of us are gathered in His name, for His purposes, desiring to seek Him, He is in our midst (Mt 18:20). But *recognizing* His Presence, and *submitting* to His leadership, are two different things. I'd like to share some things I do before each class to prepare my heart, to invite Him to lead, and to create a welcoming atmosphere for Him, an environment where He can move.

Please understand that we cannot approach our invitation to the Holy Spirit in a genie-in-a-bottle sort of way. Our prayers before class and in the classroom are merely a continuation of our abiding relationship with Him. If we are spending sweet daily time alone with Him in Scripture and prayer and worship and stillness, if we are walking closely with Him, asking, listening, obeying, if we are daily clinging to Him and being led by Him, then our preparation before class will be an outpouring of our love for Him.

Inviting Him With Prayer

There are certainly lots of ways we can pray in preparation for class. If I can pray in the classroom itself, that is my first choice, but logistically that is not always feasible.

Often, my prayers develop from the recent passages in Scripture I have been pondering or memorizing. In that sweet way that He has, in the days leading up to class, He seems to bring me to the exact Scriptures He wants me to pray.

Additionally, there are some very specific prayers I focus on to open my heart and prepare me for His work. I'll invite you into my prayer closet to listen in.

Worship

I like to spend time in worship first. I like to start with praise music, which helps me to focus my mind and my heart on His tenderness, beauty, love, compassion, and astounding miracles. I bring my Bluetooth speaker and I worship with all my heart. Thanksgiving from a heart full of gratitude overflows.

Worship reminds my heart that He is God, and I am human. That I can do nothing apart from Him, and that He can do anything and everything *without me.* Worship reminds me that nothing is impossible for Him, that He is the Mover of Mountains, the Redeemer of Mankind, the Prince of Peace and the Answer to every prayer ever prayed. That He is Healer of Broken Hearts and Comforter of Grieving Souls, the One who brings dead things to life and the Only One who can bring beauty from our ashes. He is the One who, when He gives us Himself, is all we ever need. (Job 38:4-7, Mt 19:26, Isa 54:5, 9:6,61:1,3, 2Cor 1:3-4,20, Jn 11:25, Col 2:10).

"With people this is impossible, but with God all things are possible." Matthew 19:26

It seems that worship can transform the classroom into a welcoming place for His Spirit. I so want Him to feel comfortable here. I want the classroom to become a secret place of His Presence (Ps 31:20).[1] I think of the classroom as His tent of meeting. I think of myself as an usher, escorting the participants into His Presence.

Worship leads to my surrender and prepares me for His purification. It opens my heart to hear His voice and positions me to be led by Him.

Prayer of Surrender

Generally, I go into my prayer time thinking I have surrendered everything, but sometimes, He shows me there is more. Specifically, I ask the Lord if there is anything I am holding back from Him, or anything I am trying to control in the class or with the participants. Before each class, I pray afresh and anew a prayer of utter surrender to Him from the depth of my heart.

Prayer for Sanctification

**"The heart is more deceitful than all else
And is desperately sick;
Who can understand it?
I, the LORD, search the heart,
I test the mind ..."**
Jeremiah 17:9-10

Who can know the heart? Only God knows my heart, and only He can reveal it to me. I sit in stillness before Him, asking Him, before class starts, if there is anything He wants to address with me. Sometimes, He may reveal sins related to the class, such as judgments, unrealistic expectations, control, idolatry, or fears.

Prayer of Dependence

I remind myself that this is His class, and that He will accomplish what He desires with or without me. I acknowledge that I have nothing to offer, and I thank Him for the opportunity to be His vessel during this time. I know He is hovering, willing to lead, *waiting to be invited* to lead – but I must humbly step off the leadership platform and align my heart under His.

> **Trust in the LORD with all your heart**
> **And do not lean on your own understanding.**
> **In all your ways acknowledge Him,**
> **And He will make your paths straight.**
> Proverbs 3:5-6

When we trust Him with all our heart, and surrender to Him all our plans, we exercise deep faith that what He has promised, He will fulfill.

Prayer of Invitation to the Holy Spirit

I deeply believe that these participants do not need me, *they need Him*. I don't want them to walk away having received only "human" wisdom – I want them to receive wisdom from the Fountain of Wisdom (Pr 2:6). I am interceding for them, beseeching the Holy Spirit to come and meet them right here. I ask Him to send down His tender Spirit, His answers and wisdom, His conviction, His healing touch. I truly desire His Presence, His sweet deep touch upon each participant each week. And I also specifically ask Him to teach and to lead.

Prayer for the Leaders

I pray for myself and my co-leaders, asking the Holy Spirit to fill us and anoint us. I pray for wisdom, discernment, and revelation.

I ask the Lord to make us sensitive to His Spirit and obedient to His leading. I pray that He will lead, and that we will follow, willingly and without resistance, like a ballroom dancer being expertly led by their Dance Partner.

I also pray for Him to fill our mouths.

> **Open your mouth wide and I will fill it.**
> **Psalm 81:10**

If my co-leader or a leader-in-training is leading this week, I pray continually throughout the class for the Holy Spirit to anoint them and be with their mouth as He was with Moses' and Aaron's mouths. I pray that the words spoken by the leaders will touch the participants with the Holy Spirit and with power (Ex 4:12, 1Cor 2:4).

Prayer for Protection

I ask God to protect the leaders and participants from enemy attack, to scatter the enemy and confuse them, and to shield us with His power (Ps 144:6, 18:2). I pray specifically for physical protection and health. I pray against enemy interference as they travel to class. I pray the Lord will defend from strife and dissension in relationships. I pray against counter-attacks of the enemy.

> **He sent from on high, He took me;**
> **He drew me out of many waters.**
> **He delivered me from my strong enemy,**

> **And from those who hated me,**
> **For they were too mighty for me.**
> **They confronted me in the day of my calamity,**
> **But the Lord was my stay.**
> **He brought me forth also into a broad place;**
> **He rescued me, because He delighted in me.**
>
> Psalm 18:16-19

Prayer of Intercession

I ask the Holy Spirit how to pray for each participant, and I intercede as best I can hear from Him. He knows their heart and the work He desires to accomplish in this season, and I rely on Him to reveal and to lead my prayers.

> **The Lord confides in those who fear him ...**
> **The secret of the Lord is for those who fear Him ...**
>
> Psalm 25:14 NIV, NASB

I ask the Lord to create Holy Spirit-connections between the leaders and the participants and between the participants themselves, and that He will develop these relationships and protect those relationships from division.

I pray for my people for their time in the classroom, but even more importantly, for their time in their prayer closet, when they are immersed in this study alone with Him. I ask the Lord to teach them, speak to them, convict them, heal them, free them, deliver them, and grow them up in Him.

I also pray specific prayers for the chapter we are in, such as forgiveness, surrender, casting down of idols, and learning to recognize His voice. In the Appendix I have compiled some direction for prayer related to each chapter for you and your prayer team to pray for your participants each week.

But truthfully, I don't know how to pray as I ought, so I count on the Holy Spirit to intercede with groanings too deep for words.

In the same way the Spirit also helps our weakness; for we do not know how to pray as we should, but the Spirit Himself intercedes for us with groanings too deep for words; and He who searches the hearts knows what the mind of the Spirit is, because He intercedes for the saints according to the will of God.

Romans 8:26-27

Prayer with Fasting

"When you fast ..." (Mt 6:16, emphasis added). As Servant Leaders, we fast for our people. We fast to humble ourselves before the Lord, to remind ourselves of our utter dependence upon Him. To acknowledge that He is everything and we are nothing. To seek *His* will instead of stubbornly pursuing our own. To attune our hearts to His voice. To stand in the gap for our people, asking Him to heal the brokenhearted and release the captives.

**"Is this not the fast which I choose,
To loosen the bonds of wickedness,
To undo the bands of the yoke,
And to let the oppressed go free
And break every yoke?"**

Isaiah 58:6

Ponder, Pray, and Journal

Spend some time alone with the Lord. Ask Him *His plan* for your leadership, and journal your commitment to prayer, fasting, abiding, and utterly relying on Him.

Then read Daniel 9:1-19. Leaping off Daniel's prayer, write a prayer interceding for your participants, confessing your sins and theirs, and asking the Lord to free and heal them.

Helping Our Participants Prepare To Meet the Holy Spirit

Now that we have covered how to make the classroom a welcome place for the Holy Spirit, let's discuss how we can make the classroom a welcome place for our participants. In order for our participants to feel comfortable enough to open their hearts to the Holy Spirit and to share deep heart pains and struggles, they will need to feel secure. In the next sections, we will touch on three ways we can help them feel comfortable: meeting their needs, getting to know them deeply, and creating a safe environment.

Meeting Their Needs

Let's take some time to distinguish between two types of unfulfilled needs that our people may bring to class: their *felt need*, and their *true need*.

- Felt needs are the reasons they came to class. These are the needs they are expecting this class to meet.

- True needs are the reasons God brought them to class. This is what God knows they need.

They may understand their true needs, or be blind to them. Some of their felt needs may match up with their true needs. Some may not. Yet felt needs are still real needs, as best they can comprehend, and none of these felt needs are unimportant, so we won't discount them. Sometimes, when God grants them fulfillment *of what He knows they need*, their felt need may be met also – or may no longer even be an unfulfilled need.

Ponder, Pray, and Journal

Grab your journal and write out some felt needs our people bring to class, the reasons they come to class. No peeking at the next section! Meet me back here when you are finished.

Here's a list I have compiled of some felt needs that I have seen over the years. I'm sure you have listed even more.

- To get answers; to find out why they are suffering.
- To be heard and understood.
- To be accepted right where they are.
- To be encouraged on their journey.
- To have a safe place to share.
- To know that their trials are not unique and that they are not alone.
- To find out how to end the pain.
- To have deep meaningful fellowship with other believers.
- To regain control of their lives.
- To feel peace and joy.
- To change the person who is hurting them.
- To change their situation to alleviate the suffering.
- To figure out how to fix their problem, or how to fix someone else.
- To help others deal with their suffering.

Remembering that our God-assigned mission is *to guide hurting people to Jesus for healing and freedom*, write down some reasons *God* may have brought these people to class. You have been through enough classes to have received His revelation on this. Write down *His* plan for your people through this class. *What He knows they need.* No peeking at the next section!

Here's my list:

- To know who God is, the truth of His character and nature.
- To learn the truth of their identity in Jesus.
- To recognize and renounce lies – about God, themselves, and others – and receive God's truth.
- To be loved unconditionally and nonjudgmentally.
- To realize that they are forgiven in Jesus.
- To forgive those who have wronged them.
- To forgive themselves for their mistakes, failures, and sins.
- To come to know God deeply.
- To learn how to position themselves, through Scripture study, prayer, worship, and connection in church family, in order to invite God to mature them in Christ.
- To learn to love His Word and receive from Him through His Word.
- To learn how to hear from the Holy Spirit.
- To repent.
- To learn to cooperate with God as He sanctifies and matures them.
- To surrender control of every aspect of their lives.
- To learn to want what God wants.
- To discover His purpose for their lives.
- To connect deeply into His family for encouragement and accountability.
- To be healed and set free.
- To understand that they are in a spiritual battle, and to learn to fight with spiritual weapons.
- To receive not merely *answers* from the Lord, but to receive *the Lord Himself.*

As you compare these two diverse lists, hold in your heart all we learned in the last chapter regarding co-dependency, enabling and carrying another's assigned load.

For some of those felt needs, it may not be God's plan to meet them at all.

For other felt needs, God may desire to use us to meet them *in order to help create a place of safety for them.*

And for still other felt needs, we *could* meet them on a human level, but standing back and letting God meet them allows for *eternal* impact.

But I believe the real importance of these felt needs is that they are the open door to *the reasons God brought them to class.* I think that God's plan is to use *Triumph* Classes to bridge the gap between their felt needs, and the needs that He has brought them here to fulfill.

Getting To Know Them Deeply

When our people feel known and loved, they will begin to feel comfortable and secure in class. Our people are most likely to open up to us and to the Holy Spirit when they sense that we deeply know them, that we understand their heart and their pain, and that we fully accept them just as they are. This will require us to hear their story and their heart and to love them unconditionally and nonjudgmentally – *without trying to fix them.* To simply love them and leave all the transforming work up to God.

Ministering to them well will also require that we learn what makes them tick, what upsets them, what drives them, what makes them dig in their heels, what makes them furious, what comforts them, what causes them to build walls, what helps them to break down walls. We explored developing this deep level of intimacy when we talked about what it takes to be available in Chapter 1. Let's go a bit further.

The compassion Jesus had for the sick, blinded, and spiritually lost was so deep the Greek word describes a visceral ache (Mt 14:14, 20:34, Mk 6:34). Recall how Jesus met people where they were comfortable – in the homes of Zaccheus, Levi, the Pharisee. With Nicodemus in the middle of the night. He ate with them, listened to them, discussed deep spiritual issues with them – even tolerated their barbed questions as they tried to trap Him. His love for all people was deep and unshakeable, no matter their sin.

Think about how Jesus was ever so sensitive to the felt needs of the people. He fed the five thousand. He restored the skin of ten lepers. He healed Peter's mother-in-law the moment He walked in the door.

Now think about the paralyzed man lowered through the roof. Think about the man whose child was seizing. Notice how He ministered to both the felt need *and* the spiritual need.

It is true deep *agape* that will make our participants feel welcome and safe.

This is how we know what real love is: Jesus gave his life for us. So we should give our lives for our brothers and sisters. Suppose someone has enough to live and sees a brother or sister in need, but does not help. Then God's love is not living in that person. My children, we should love people not only with words and talk, *but by our actions and true caring*.

1 John 3:16-18 NCV, emphasis added

Ponder, Pray, and Journal

Read John 4:3-26. What was the woman's spoken *felt need?* What was the reason God brought Jesus to this woman? Journal how Jesus started with her spoken felt need, and then transitioned from her felt need to what she truly needed.

Next read John 8:3-11. What was this woman's *unspoken felt need?* What was the reason God brought Jesus to this woman? Journal how Jesus took care of her unspoken need, and then met her deep spiritual need.

We will only know the spiritual needs of our people when the Holy Spirit has revealed them to us. Pray for wisdom, discernment, and revelation, for these are indispensable gifts for *Triumph* Servant Leaders.

Creating a Safe Environment

Besides meeting their felt needs as the Lord directs, and knowing them deeply and accepting them fully, the third area that promotes security is creating a safe environment. I have found three keys that help to develop a safe environment. We will touch on them briefly here, and go into more detail in upcoming chapters.

First, require and protect confidentiality. Our participants will be seeking certainty that the sharing of their heart will not become fodder for gossip. This security can be pivotal in helping your participants open up.

Second, share vulnerably yourself about both your own journey of healing and your right-now convictions and encounters with the Lord. As we learned in Chapter 3, transparency of the leaders invites transparency of the participants. This is a crucial element to create safety, and I cannot emphasize it enough.

And finally, lead with authority. *You have the anointing. You are not here on your own authority; you are here on God's authority.* You are in charge of the classroom. You are responsible for each individual participant, *and the class as a whole.* We will discuss in more detail what this means in the next chapter.

Teaching Our Participants To Hear from the Holy Spirit

When our people perceive the classroom as a safe place, it can become an ideal setting to teach them how to recognize the voice of the Lord. Participants may bring forth problems and request answers and solutions. A participant may have specific questions, such as if they should undergo a particular surgery, or move to another city, or quit their job. They may ask what to do about an adulterous spouse or a rebellious child. They may be asking for spiritual direction, such as if they really need to forgive or if God is expecting them to apologize or attempt to restore a relationship. They may want to know if the promises of the Lord are really for them.

Remember, it is not our job to answer these questions. *It is God's job.* The best way to handle these direct requests for answers is to ask them, "What do you think the Lord is saying to you about that?" In the silence that follows, pray quietly in your heart for the Holy Spirit to speak. Remember, *He is here.* We have invited Him and welcomed Him and beseeched Him to come and make His Presence known. *He* has brought them to this class, and we count on *Him* to speak to them.

For some leaders, this can be difficult, especially if we like to "fix", or if we have trouble standing back and allowing people to struggle in order to grow. But if we always answer our participants' questions, whether with "human" wisdom or truly with God's answer as we are hearing from Him ourselves, we circumvent the voice of the Holy Spirit, and they lose an opportunity to learn to hear from the Lord.

If they say they do not know what God is saying, this is a good time for prayer, asking the Lord to grant them wisdom and direction. If they are willing, encourage them to pray themselves right now. It may be helpful to give them some guidance in their prayer, suggesting they surrender the situation to the Lord and ask for His path. If they agree to pray, take off your sandals, for you are stepping onto holy ground (Ex 3:5). The Holy Spirit is near. Pray deeply in your heart while they are praying, imploring the Lord to open their hearts to hear from Him this very moment.

If they are not ready to pray aloud this way, the leader can pray. Walk with them confidently into the throne room of grace to receive mercy and find grace in this time of need (Heb 4:17). Stand in the gap for them and together place the situation in God's hands, and ask God to speak to them. After praying, ask again, "What do you think the Lord is speaking to you now?" Sometimes, they will know by the Holy Spirit right then and there what He wants them to do.

If they have no answer after prayer, encourage them to continue to ask *and to listen for His answer.* Remind them that stillness and listening is important to hear His voice. Pray for them during the week, and when they come back next week, ask if the Lord has spoken to them on the issue.

Transitioning Hearing From Inside to Out

We want our participants to transition from hearing from the Lord *inside* of the classroom, to hearing from Him *outside* as well. Our prayers can pave the way for them to enter His Presence when they are at home working through the class materials, and when they are seeking Him in prayer, worship, stillness, and Scripture. Recognizing His voice in the classroom may enable them to recognize His voice at home as well.

Teach them to ask the Holy Spirit to speak to them *before* they even open their class materials or their Bible. Asking puts us in a place of openness and submission, and lets Him know He is welcome and we are willing to be led. Additionally, asking helps remind us not to take His Presence for granted.

During the season that we have our people in *Triumph* Classes, we are a bridge to the Lord. But our ultimate goal is to help them learn to seek Jesus *themselves* in order to continue their spiritual growth, sanctification, and healing – *without us*. Some may learn this through one semester. But for many, this will require several semesters and even several years before they are no longer relying on us to guide them into the heart of God.

As we move into the final chapters, we will delve into some practical tips and strategies for the classroom. But before we do, I'd like to share with you some imagery that helps me to understand why God brings His people to these classes, and what He intends to accomplish.

God's Spiritual Hospital

I often think in medical terms, and I think of the *Triumph* Classes as God's spiritual hospital. I realize that to some of you hospitals are scary places, so let me clarify.

From my viewpoint as a physician, hospitals are safe loving places where people can receive healing. They are places of rest and recovery where doctors and nurses provide tender care. Some patients have obvious wounds, and others have mysterious hidden ailments that require patience and study for revelation. Some patients come in with gunshot wounds and are near to death and require time in the ICU. Others just need a quick suturing in the Emergency Room. Others may have a deep-seated infection and need the depth of the infection completely cleared out surgically in order to heal. Still others may require open heart surgery. And others are about to give birth to a miracle and need supporting staff to help them bring forth new life. People come into a hospital battered and broken, and walk out strong and healed. Hospitals are places where the miraculous can happen.

Adopt my perspective and see if you can see *Triumph* Classes as God's spiritual hospital. Our people enter at all different degrees of injury and at all different levels of spiritual maturity. When the Lord has healed, strengthened, and equipped an individual, He will send this warrior forth into battle again. And then, after a season of battling, serving, and working for the Kingdom, some may require a return to *Triumph*, or to a different "spiritual hospital," for another season of rest, healing, strengthening, and equipping.

As we enter the classroom in the next chapter, don't be overwhelmed. Trust the Holy Spirit to graciously teach you all you need to know. And at the moment you are live in class, trust Him to bring to mind exactly what you need at the right moment.

"But the Helper, the Holy Spirit, whom the Father will send in My name, He will teach you all things, and bring to your remembrance all that I said to you."

John 14:26

Chapter 7
Leading the Class

In this chapter, we will walk through the practical details of what it looks like to serve as a *Triumph* leader, starting from the weeks before class begins, through the time in the classroom, and concluding with next steps. Then, in the following two chapters, we will learn how to avoid traps in the classroom and how to handle common classroom challenges.

Your hearts are prepared; you have counted the cost, laid aside encumbrances, and invited the Lord's pruning. By His sanctification process He has equipped you to do His will (Heb 13:20-21). Now we are ready to move into the practical arena.

In the Weeks Before Class Begins

Laying the groundwork before class begins is analogous to laying the foundation before building a house. As Jesus taught, if the foundation is faulty, the house will lack stability and be vulnerable to collapse in a storm (Mt 7:24-27).

> **According to the grace of God which was given to me, like a wise master builder I laid a foundation, and another is building on it. But each man must be careful how he builds on it. For no man can lay a foundation other than the one which is laid, which is Jesus Christ. Now if any man builds on the foundation with gold, silver, precious stones, wood, hay, straw, each man's work will become evident; for the day will show it because it is to be revealed with fire, and the fire itself will test the quality of each man's work. If any man's work which he has built on it remains, he will receive a reward. If any man's work is burned up, he will suffer loss; but he himself will be saved, yet so as through fire.**
>
> 1 Corinthians 3:10-15

Spiritually, we have already laid the groundwork by our deep heart work. Now, starting a few weeks before class starts and continuing throughout the course, I persist in this process by setting aside specific times for prayer with fasting. I want to be in a place of humble submission to the Lord's leading. I want to build with precious stones onto the foundation of Jesus Christ.

In the next sections, we will learn how to position ourselves to meet potential participants and share with them what is involved in the class. We will also discuss how to deeply connect with them even before class starts, how to assess for readiness, and how to guide them to prepare themselves while they are waiting to enter the classroom.

Preparing Your "Elevator Speeches"

An "elevator speech" is a strong pointed summary of the class, brief enough that you can deliver it in the length of time it takes to ride up one floor in an elevator. Your elevator speech for *Triumph Over Suffering* will be your most critical one. You will use it for potential participants, for church pastors and leaders who may be unfamiliar with the class, and also for people who may not be interested in taking the class themselves, but who are wonderful connectors and will direct hurting people your way.

Using the key points below, write your own elevator speech for *Triumph Over Suffering*.

Key Points to Describe Triumph Over Suffering (TOS)

This is a class of freedom and healing:

- To understand why we suffer.
- To grow closer to God in our trials.
- To discover the purpose God has for us *through* our pain. (Not *despite* our pain, but *through* our pain).

Additional details to add if the listener has interest:

- This is a deep Bible study of what God says in His Word about suffering and trials.
- In order to position ourselves to receive His freedom and healing, we will focus on surrender and forgiveness, and will wrestle with the sovereignty of God.

Once you have written your elevator speech, work with it, make it your own, and memorize it so you are ready.

Triumph Of Surrender (T2) and Triumph in Warfare (TIW)

Your elevator speech for these classes will be needed in a different setting. TOS is a prerequisite for T2, and T2 is a prerequisite for TIW. Near the end of your TOS course, you will be giving your class your T2 elevator speech to invite them into T2. And near the end of your T2 course, you will be giving your class your TIW elevator speech to invite them into TIW.

You may also find yourself giving these elevator speeches to pastors and leaders at your church in order to familiarize them with the classes, but you will probably not be describing these classes to people who have not gone through TOS.

Often during the last few classes of TOS, a participant asks about a "sequel," or if the class can stay together, or where they will go from here. I believe this is the Holy Spirit paving the way for us to announce the sequel. Be sure you have your elevator speech ready!

Key Points to Describe Triumph Of Surrender (T2)

This is a class of intimacy, abiding, and hearing God's voice.

- It is a time to get our eyes off our suffering and onto Jesus.
- We will immerse in Scripture.
- We will establish our identity in Christ.
- We will take sovereignty, surrender, forgiveness, and repentance to a deeper level.

Key Points to Describe Triumph in Warfare (TIW)

This is a class to learn how strongholds are built, and how to co-battle with Jesus to tear them down.

- The goal is to spur people to wake up and engage in the battle.
- We will learn how to recognize that our battles are not against flesh and blood, and start to understand Satan's manipulative tactics.

- In order to position ourselves for healing and freedom, we will learn how to close the doors to the enemy by repentance, forgiveness, obedience, and surrender.

- Scripture immersion to know Jesus more deeply as the Victor who came to set the captives free.

Positioning Ourselves to Meet Hurting People

This is God's class, and only He can bring the participants to class. We are totally reliant on Him. He calls us to co-labor with Him, stationing ourselves to meet those who are hurting and invite them in.

Our greatest referral source will be our graduates! They have personally experienced the depth of the course and the Holy Spirit's transformational power, so they are uniquely positioned to direct people our way.

It's our job to seek out people who are interested and willing to come into class. If this is your church's (or your campus') first TOS class, it will probably take some time for the course to develop traction. We will want to be visible and active in our church in order to facilitate connections. Position yourself to meet hurting people at events, and in membership, introductory, and freedom and healing classes.

Get to know your pastors and leaders at your church. People coming out of Freedom Class, Divorce Care, Grief Share, Celebrate Recovery, Abortion Recovery, Sexual Abuse Recovery, and other similar classes may want to continue their healing journey. Leaders of these classes can refer people to you. Be sure you have given them ways to easily contact you (I provide my cell phone and email).

Get to know connecting people at your church. Let these connectors know about the class, and ask them to connect you with people whom they have spoken to who are interested. If they can facilitate a brief in-person meeting perhaps after church service, that can work well as a way to introduce you in a non-threatening way. If the potential participant is interested, arrange for a time for a more in-depth conversation with them.

I am cautious about reaching out to contact a potential participant that a connector is referring to me. The potential participant may wonder what confidential information the connector has told me that would lead me to call them about a class called *Triumph Over Suffering*. Instead, I ask the connector to give the potential participant my cell number so if they are interested, they can contact me.

Most importantly, pray for the Holy Spirit to stir up hearts and bring people in as only He can. In the weeks and months before class, be on the alert for divine appointments. Pray that your words will be full of grace and seasoned with salt, and pray for the wisdom to know how to respond in these God-ordained opportunities (Ex 35:21, Hag 1:14, Col 4:4-6).

Connecting With Potential Participants

Triumph Over Suffering is a doorway into discipleship and spiritual growth for those in pain. TOS meets people right where they are, at the point of pain, doubt, anger, fear. Expect those with physical illness, divorce, wayward children, loss of loved ones, financial woes, loneliness, abandonment, betrayal, abuse, rape, natural disasters, and many different traumatic events to be drawn into the class. Expect also caretakers of those with physical illnesses or other hardships.

We must develop a level of intimacy with our participants that would make most leaders of other groups uncomfortable. I have found that the more deeply I know the people that I am serving, the easier it is for me to receive revelation, direction, and guidance from the Holy Spirit, both in the classroom, and during encounters outside of the classroom. It seems the Lord grants me greater understanding and compassion for the people, and uses me in greater measure as His vessel during the length of the course. This requires an investment of time, a Holy Spirit-created connection, and lots of prayer.

In the weeks before class, make contact with those who have expressed interest. I mean deep phone conversations or face-to-face meetings, not just texts, emails, or other avenues of social media. Go into these conversations with lots of prayer, and set aside forty-five minutes to an hour – you are laying foundation here.

This is a crucial time to get to know the potential participants and to begin to build trust. I find that the more work I do up-front, before class even starts, the more likely the participants are to come to class open and ready. Often, if I have prepared well by forging relationships in these initial conversations, the Holy Spirit begins deep heart work right away. Additionally, as the participants begin to trust us as leaders, that seems to pave the way for them to begin to trust each other, even from the very first day of class.

There are six important parts to this initial connecting conversation. I'll list them below, and then we will go into detail regarding each one.

- Leader shares brief description of the class.
- Leader shares their story, and potential participant shares their story if they are willing.
- Leader assesses spiritual readiness.
- Leader assesses mental and emotional readiness.
- Leader explains depth of the course.
- Leader prays and closes.

Leader Shares Brief Description of the Class

After a bit of an icebreaker, I generally start with a brief description of the class. I take from the first part of my elevator speech:

This is a class of freedom and healing:

- To understand why we suffer.
- To grow closer to God in our trials.
- To discover the purpose God has for us through our pain.

The bulk of the conversation and by far the most important part is what comes next: their sharing of their story. Here's how I invite them to do that.

Leader and Potential Participant Share Their Stories

After I have briefly described the class, I share some about my story, because we know that our transparency invites their transparency. I share about myself so that they know I can in some way relate to their pain, and I share the healing Jesus has given me to provide hope. I invite them to share a bit with me by asking them, "Is this a class that sounds interesting to you?" If they answer yes but do not share anything else, I ask them "What about the class makes you interested in it?" Often, as the Holy Spirit has been working and softening hearts and nudging people into class, these two questions are sufficient to encourage people to open up. I may ask, "Do you feel comfortable sharing your story with me?"

As they share their story, it is critical to *really listen*. For some people, this may be the first time anyone listened to them with a loving nonjudgmental heart. Pray silently in your heart as they share, asking the Holy Spirit to give you the words to respond to their honest outpouring. You will want to thank them for being so open with you and sharing their heart. (We'll talk more about *responding* to participants when we move into the sections to follow regarding our time in the classroom.)

If the Holy Spirit leads, especially if someone is tearful or distraught, I offer to pray with someone right after they have shared.

Some people may not share at all, or may not fully share. Continue to pray that they will feel safe to share with you, and with the class, as they become more comfortable throughout the course.

Leader Assesses Spiritual Readiness

Spiritual readiness only requires an open heart to the things of God. People do not need to be spiritually mature or even saved to come into class, but in order to receive from this class, they do need a spiritual hunger to know the Lord and grow in their relationship with Him. Because we want people to be directed to the right course for where they are in their walk with Christ, it is important to assess their willingness to really seek the Lord for healing and freedom. *Triumph Over Suffering* is a deep spiritual growth course, not a support group. If this course is not right for them, we will want to prayerfully guide them to an appropriate place for growth.

Therefore my next questions relate to their walk with the Lord. "Tell me about your walk with the Lord right now." It is not unusual to hear that they do not feel close to the Lord in this season, or to hear that they are not regularly in church or reading the Word. Reassure them that the Lord often uses this class to help people grow closer to the Lord and to grow in their relationship with Him.

Sometimes, when I ask them about their "walk with the Lord right now" they tell me their salvation story of years ago. This is crucial to know, but I also press in to hear about their relationship with the Lord *in this season* of their lives.

It is not unusual for someone to desire to come to TOS to "help people who are hurting." I acknowledge that tender heart that wants to minister to others for healing, and then I gently explain that the first step is to seek the Lord *for their own healing.* If someone does not recognize that they have had trials and pains that they may need to process with the Lord, they may not be open to receive from Him at this time and may not be ready for the course (Matt 9:12). I do not accept them into class, but send them off to pray about it and reschedule another call.

Leader Assesses Mental and Emotional Readiness

Some people may not be mentally or emotionally ready to process the depth of TOS. Others could be triggered by the challenging material in the course or by the stories of other participants. As we speak to potential participants, we rely on the Holy Spirit to reveal to us if someone may need some other first steps before coming into TOS. We will want these people to be in a safe place for continued healing.

If the Holy Spirit reveals current alcohol or substance abuse, or recent hospitalization for mental illness, or deep trauma, or psychological problems that are not well controlled, He may be showing you that this potential participant may benefit from some other steps before entering TOS. They may need gentler or more basic steps, such as an intorductory class or membership class, a Bible Study, or Freedom class. Or, they may need deeper processing that the TOS Classroom cannot provide, such as individual counseling, or Celebrate Recovery.

If you need help directing them, you can ask if they would be willing to meet with a pastor, church leader, or other *Triumph* leader to help determine if TOS is a good next step for them, or if they may benefit from some preparation work first.

Part of our responsibility as leaders is to match individuals with the right growth opportunities. If you feel TOS is not the right fit for them, let them know, and direct them into another group or study that is appropriate for them. We would much prefer someone to decline the course prior to starting than come in briefly and withdraw because they were not expecting the depth or were not ready for the time commitment. Withdrawal from the course can be painful for both the one dropping out as well as the participants left behind. Participants will be sharing personal pain and forging tentative bonds. This process can be easily be disrupted by people entering or leaving the class at will.

Do realize that even if people decline, or if they drop out, you may indeed see them in a year or two when they *are* ready!

Leader Explains the Depth of the Course

I generally wait until I have assessed for readiness and we have developed a rapport through sharing before explaining the depth of the course. Often, after they have shared, they have become to feel safe and have developed an interest in the course, and are more willing make a commitment.

I have written a brief *Triumph* Course Description in Appendix II. Take a moment to read through it now.

I explain to the potential participant that this is not a support group, but a challenging Bible study to immerse in what God has to say in His Word about suffering and trials. I ask them if they are interested in committing to come weekly for twelve weeks, and to complete 30 minutes to an hour of homework daily. We desire our participants to persevere to the end, so it is important to be truthful about what the course will entail.

I have had people so excited to grow up in the Lord that they plan to take TOS along with another Bible study. While I am delighted to see their fire for the Lord, I generally discourage them from taking two classes simultaneously. I explain that their focus will be splintered, and they will probably not be able to receive all the Lord has for them from either class. I recommend they pray about which one the Lord would have them take, and get back to me with their decision.

Even though we know that TOS is only the first step, and that many participants will take the course multiple times and enter into the sequels and Bible studies, I don't divulge all that to the potential participants up front. That would be too overwhelming for most. Instead, I follow Jesus' example.

When Andrew and another disciple began to follow Jesus, asking where He was staying, He didn't immediately launch into eating My flesh and drinking My blood, or tell them right away that He would require them to deny themselves and pick up their cross to follow Him. He didn't reveal at that moment that if they loved parents or children more than Him they were not worthy of Him (Mt 16:24, 10:37). He said simply, "Come, and you will see" (Jn 1:39).

At this point in our relationship with a potential participant, we are only asking them to commit to a twelve or fourteen week course – and that is a big enough initial commitment for most people. An appropriate time to invite them to come into the next class to continue their healing process is when the TOS class is nearing its end. At that time they can prayerfully make a decision whether to continue or not.

Leader Prays and Closes

If the potential participant is ready to commit, I inform them that I will email them the initial registration forms, and ask them to return them to me "in order to complete your registration." (Appendix II - or email me for electronic copies.) I also tell them that on the first day of class, they will have three or four minutes to share their story *and what they want Jesus to do for them through the class.* Instruct them to pray about what the Lord would have them say.

Finally, I close in prayer. I find potential participants are generally extremely grateful for our prayer. I ask, "How can I pray *for you* right now?" I am specific about asking them for a prayer request *for themselves.* I emphasize that God is calling them into class *for them,* for their own spiritual growth and healing, and tell them that the focus will be *on their own heart.*

While They Are Waiting

Sometimes, potential participants find themselves waiting for class to start. This could be because the next class isn't starting for a number of months, or it could be because they are not yet ready for the depth of the course, or perhaps it is just the wrong season. Give them some steps to take to prepare. Church membership classes or other introductory classes, foundation classes, Freedom Classes, other healing classes, life groups, or Bible studies all provide a good basis for TOS. They can even start reading TOS (it won't spoil the class!).

This time of waiting can be a very delicate time. It is important to be sensitive to the needs of upcoming participants. They may have just shared transparently for the first time during your phone call, and feel ashamed, fearful, or unstable. They may need reassurance, connection, encouragement, acceptance, and prayer. Try to stay connected with them with periodic prayer phone calls in the time of waiting. If you have other co-leaders, or participants who are returning to class a second time, you can perhaps enlist their help here.

In the Classroom

We are now moving into the classroom! In the next sections, we will discuss how to prepare for each class, how to create a welcoming classroom environment, how to structure our time in the classroom, and how to respond to participants as they share.

Preparing for Each Class

As we've discussed throughout this book, your leading in the classroom will be an outgrowth of your intimate relationship with the Lord. In the last chapter, we delved into preparing with prayer. There are two additional areas of preparation that I will highlight here.

In my first few years of leading, each time I led, I would "take the class" again myself. I would get a new book and *Workbook*, immerse in the chapter, and answer the questions in the book or *Workbook*. I highly recommend this method for your first few years of leading.

Now that I have led many classes, I spend more time in prayer than in working through the chapter. I still get a fresh book, and as I prayerfully read through the chapter each week, I ask the Holy Spirit to highlight what He would like covered in the class. I have to admit that it's not unusual for Him to work in my own heart as I prepare.

Additional preparation is my transparent sharing for this week. We will go into more detail below, but here I want to mention how important it is to ask the Holy Spirit what He would like us to share. For me, He will generally bring me a heart conviction or an encounter with Him this week that parallels the teaching in the chapter for the week. In the first few weeks, I often share first to model vulnerability.

Creating a Welcoming Environment

There are three areas we will focus on to help our participants feel welcome: determining the class size, encouraging connection, and promoting safety.

Determining Class Size

Having led classes as large as fifty and as small as two – and everywhere in between – I have found that eight to ten participants seems to be an ideal class size. There are several factors that play into that recommendation.

Most importantly, the goal in *each class* is for *each participant to share*. Participants repeatedly declare that one of the most impacting parts of these courses is sharing time. It is during sharing time that they learn that they are not alone. Sharing time becomes a safe place to share their pains, traumas, and victories in the Lord – for many, this will be the first time they have had this type of safe place. As they give voice to their stories and receive validation, healing can begin. Eight to ten seems to be a good number to allow each to have an opportunity to share within the two hour timeframe.

Secondly, I have found that the more we converse with

our people outside of class, the greater our connection will be. Even ten participants can be a challenge for you and your co-leaders to maintain strong connection with each of them.

And finally, too few participants (five or less) seems to increase the potential to deteriorate into more of a support group instead of sacred place for the Holy Spirit to convict and transform and heal. Although this can happen in any class, it seems that smaller classes are more likely to fall into complaining and criticizing. This is not conducive to the Holy Spirit's intended heart work. If you have a smaller class, I recommend you decrease the classroom time accordingly. Once the Spirit-led discussion has ended, simply close in prayer and end early.

Encouraging Connection Between Leaders and Participants

Give of yourself before and after class. Come early and stay late. A good goal is to have completed your prayer, set up, and other preparations at least fifteen to twenty minutes before class, so when the participants arrive, you can greet them, listen to them, encourage them, and answer questions. Stay about fifteen to twenty minutes after class to do the same.

One of the most powerful means to connect is to learn their names! Knowing someone's name says so clearly, "I care about you." Work to memorize the names of those in your class before the first day, even if you have no faces to put with the names. Address them by name when speaking to them.

Give your participants a way to contact you. It is important that you are *accessible*, but that does not mean you need to be constantly *available*.

I try to connect with one or two participants each week by phone as the Holy Spirit leads. I don't mean leaving a voicemail, or bumping into them after church in a crowd without privacy.

I mean engaging in deep Spirit-led conversations. I find these phone calls average about forty-five minutes. Sometimes, a twenty minute call will do. Sometimes, it will be well over an hour. I make sure to leave enough time to listen to their heart and pray with them.

Encouraging Connection Between Participants

Make it easy for them to learn each other's names and to connect also. Every class, provide nametags and thick markers for both leaders and participants. On the first day of class, provide a roster with names and phone numbers.

I find that most participants do want to connect with other class members, and deep bonds of friendship can be forged through class. It is not possible for the leaders to minister to all their needs, so encourage them to minister to each other.

Be creative, or try "The Connection Game": Each participant writes their name on an index card; scramble the cards and distribute them, instructing them to make phone or in-person contact with the person on the card that week (not just text or voicemail). Let them know participation is voluntary. (I generally don't play; I just call participants as the Lord leads.)

Promoting Safety

In the last chapter, we saw how paramount it is for participants to feel safe in order both to share transparently, and to open their hearts to the Holy Spirit's work. This is so very critical that we will spend a bit of time here. In this section we will expound on the three areas we touched on in the last chapter that create a safe environment: confidentiality and commitment, leaders sharing with transparency, and leading with authority.

Confidentiality and Commitment

The goal of developing a safe environment is to begin to build trust, and confidentiality and commitment are foundational for trust in the class.

As leaders, it is our responsibility to uphold and protect confidentiality. Requiring all participants to sign the *Triumph* Commitment and Confidentiality Agreement prior to class will send a strong message that breaking confidentiality will not be tolerated. I have included the Commitment and Confidentiality Agreement in Appendix II – go ahead and turn to the Appendix and read through it now.

Safety is also promoted when the participants can begin to trust that the other participants have committed to the course also. There is a certain reassurance about seeing the same faces every week; an unsettled feeling pervades when people drop in and out of class at will.

Leaders Sharing With Transparency

Paul's relationship with the Thessalonians is our model here.

Having so fond an affection for you, we were well-pleased to impart to you not only the gospel of God but also our own lives, because you had become very dear to us.

1 Thessalonians 2:8

I cannot stress this enough: *our* transparency invites *their* transparency. Pastor Henri Nouwen, in his book *In the Name of Jesus*, confides,

I am deeply convinced that the Christian leader of the future is called to be completely irrelevant and to stand in this world with nothing to offer but his or her own vulnerable self. That is the way Jesus came to reveal God's love.[1]

As we share openly and honestly, we will invite our participants to connect with us on a deep level. Our sharing should be brief and vulnerable, intended to open the door for our people to follow and share transparently too. Our vulnerable sharing will include two aspects:

- Sharing our journey.
- Sharing our right-now heart struggles.

On our initial phone call, we will briefly and transparently share highlights of our *journey*, focusing on our victory in Christ and how the Lord has healed us. As the weeks progress, there may be other parts of our journey that we will also be led to share. This is not a time to glorify past sins, but a way to let our people know that we can relate to their pain, and are on the journey with them. Our victorious sharing can also give them hope.

In classes, we will share a *right-now heart struggle*. Not something from years ago, but how we wrestled through something with the Lord *this week*, and came to surrender. A *current* battle, a "this week" conviction of sin, or how God is working in our heart or what He has spoken to us *through this week's chapter*. I find that as I share such things as my wrestling with fear and my struggling to trust, or my challenges surrendering my own desires and embracing God's plan, or my difficulties choosing faith in the midst of doubt and pain, my testimony can help my people to recognize my humanness, and they are then less likely to begin to idolize me. This *does not mean* we bring to the classroom our *unhealed* traumas or our *current* grave sins or failures. We have accountability partners for that. It *does mean* that we share with our people our hearts and our lives.

Our people need to know that we are in the battle with them, that we are not perfect, and that we are just one step ahead of them. Each week, we allow our people to see the realness of our walk with the Lord, to watch our spiritual growth, to have a front-row seat to our right-now struggles and victories in Him. When their leaders take this risk to be genuine before them, our people will be comforted, reassured, and inspired to know that their leaders have not yet "arrived" either. That we have not attained these things, but we press on (Phil 3:12-13).

In order to share vulnerably as a leader, we must have worked through our own freedom and received healing. We must be able to share comfortably about our own victories and struggles. It is important that we are leading from a strong place of healing and victory, and not leading from brokenness or as a means of finding healing ourselves. This is not a class for leaders to monopolize the sharing time for our own healing. We as leaders must have places for accountability, prayer, encouragement, and healing – *places other than the class that we are leading.*

Ponder, Pray, and Journal

Are you comfortable sharing vulnerably? If not, work with your *Triumph* leader to prepare for this critical assignment.

Leading With Authority

I have led in classrooms where chaos reigned. Where no one obeyed me as leader or listened respectfully to others, and where gossip and criticism ran rampant. One of the reasons this occurred was because of my sins of people pleasing, idolatry, and fear of rejection. As Patrick Lencioni explains in *The Five Temptations of a CEO*, my problem was "the need to be liked and popular with my [people], at the expense of holding them accountable."[2]

But an even deeper reason was because I did not understand the authority that God had delegated to me. It took me many years to learn how to lead with authority. Stand on my shoulders and learn right from the start what the Holy Spirit has taught me.

God has called you to lead this class. You have been prayerfully chosen by your leaders. Just as, when the church was praying, the Holy Spirit set aside Saul and Barnabas for missionary work (Acts 13:2), the Holy Spirit has set aside you for *Triumph Ministry*. Just as the Holy Spirit selects overseers (Acts 20:28), He has selected you. The Lord has set your feet on high places (Ps 18:33). He has appointed and anointed *you* (2Cor 1:21-22, 1Jn 2:27).

It is *His* class. He chose you as leader, and *He* brought the participants (Acts 17:26-27). *He* is in charge. And you are His *delegated authority* in this class (2Cor 5:20). He did not assign someone else. *He assigned you.* This means you do not lead with your own authority, *but with the authority God has assigned to you* (Mt 28:18-20, Eph 2:6).

God has given you the gift of leadership; He has assigned you here and requires you to lead with diligence (Rom 12:8). He commands you to serve with the strength that He supplies (1Pt 4:11). You are in charge of the class as *His representative* (2Cor 5:20). He holds you responsible for each individual participant, *and for the class as a whole*.

"... but whoever causes one of these little ones who believe in Me to stumble, it would be better for him to have a heavy millstone hung around his neck, and to be drowned in the depth of the sea."

Matthew 18:6

You have the anointing. You are in charge. It is a heavy responsibility.

When you step up and lead with authority, you will create a safe environment and establish trust. You will create an environment where participants will have courage to share, and will be open to hear from the Holy Spirit. Here are some specifics:

- Crush gossiping and criticizing. Remind participants to keep the focus on their own heart and their encounters with the Lord.
- Require respectful behavior and words. Do not allow participants to interrupt each other, and require that they treat each other with compassion.
- Do not allow graphic descriptions, offensive language, or use of the Lord's name in vain.
- Do not allow fixing, counseling, coaching, preaching, advising, or cross-talk. (We will define each of these in the next chapter, and learn how to handle them.)

The *Triumph* Class Guidelines are located in Appendix II. Turn to it and read through it now. Requiring each participant to sign these guidelines prior to the first class will send a strong message that these behaviors will not be tolerated.

To follow are some additional components that also promote a sense of safety in the classroom and create an encouraging place to grow. As leaders, we will also be responsible to ...

- Create a place where the Holy Spirit is invited and welcomed.
- Affirm each one who shares. (More on this in the next section below.)
- Separate classes by gender to create a safe place to share & grow (exception married couples *Triumph*.)
- Primarily, leaders should pray. Even strong Christians may not be able to pray aloud when they are hurting .

- Be sensitive to your participants' time constraints and other commitments, and, without quenching the Holy Spirit, make every effort to start on time and end on time.

A regular format for class time also gives a sense of predictability and safety. This leads us right into our next section, *The Structure of the Class*.

The Structure of the Class

I have provided a suggested layout for a two hour class time. Please don't adhere to this structure in a legalistic way! The Holy Spirit will tailor your classroom time for you as a leader, and will also individually adjust His plan for each group you lead, and then fine tune it even more for each individual chapter. Abide in Him, ask Him, listen to Him, be led by Him.

Suggested Structure for Class Time

- Announcements
- Worship and Soaking
- Prayer
- Leader's vulnerable sharing
- *Each person* shares
- Leader responds *after each person* shares
- Set up excitement for next week
- Close in prayer

Announcements

Not weekly! Keep these occasional and brief, limiting them to important information.

I recommend doing announcements *before* worship, soaking, and prayer, because we don't want to interrupt the flow of the Holy Spirit. After worship and prayer we will want to go directly into discussion time.

If someone is late, don't hold up the start of class, and don't repeat the announcements when the person arrives. Remember, we are responsible for our participants individually, but we are also responsible for the class *as a whole*. Instruct the latecomer to check with a classmate to find out what they missed.

Worship, Soaking, and Prayer

This is critical to help quiet minds and hearts, to draw everyone's focus on the Lord, and to invite the Holy Spirit into class to take His rightful place as Teacher and Leader. I generally will bring two songs. (I use my cell phone and Bluetooth speaker.) The first song is usually upbeat; I bring lyrics and invite them to sing. The second one is for soaking; I play a quiet contemplative song and have them sit in stillness to allow the message to penetrate their souls. I teach them about soaking by providing time to do it right there in the classroom. For some, this will be the first time they have ever rested in His Presence in this way.

After the music, one of the leaders will open in prayer.

You may arrange for participants to open or close in prayer, but wait a few weeks into the course. Often, I find that those coming into *Triumph Over Suffering* for the first time, even strong prayer warriors, have a need to be prayed over before they can step up and pray for the group. Often people come in very hurting, and prayer for them by the leaders can be very healing.

If you will be asking a participant to open or close in prayer, be sure to ask ahead of time. Some participants may be uncomfortable praying out loud, and we don't want to put them on the spot or embarrass them.

Leader's Vulnerable Sharing

We discussed our transparent sharing at length above. Be creative and highlight something from the chapter as you share each week.

Our goal is for our people to no longer need the leader to open the door to vulnerability by sharing first; we want *them* to have the courage to go first. It may take a number of weeks, but nudge them in that direction. If you have spoken with a participant outside of the classroom, and they have shared with you an encounter with the Lord this week, ask them if they would share that in the classroom. They may not realize this, but sharing with you on the phone can be a "practice run" for them. Also ask them if they would be courageous and share first this week.

And when the participants have taken over and don't need you to share first, don't stop sharing! We may not share weekly, but we must continue to share transparently to maintain the depth of relationship we have developed with our people.

Each Person Shares

During the first class, ask the participants to share why they are here, and what they want Jesus to do for them through the class. If we have laid the groundwork well with prayer and conversations and phone calls prior to class, we have co-labored with the Holy Spirit and will probably find them feeling more safe and willing to open up on the first day.

If they share their story but do not share what they want Jesus to do for them, I prompt them with that question. This helps to put our focus on Jesus as the only One who can heal, save, deliver, free.

Each person sharing *every week* is the goal of the class. And I don't mean superficial summaries of key points in the chapter. That is knowledge without application. I mean sharing what God has done *in their hearts* each week as they have worked through the chapter.

Remember, there are plenty of places our people will receive teaching and preaching. This is important. But *Triumph* Classes are for deep spiritual growth, *applying* the teaching of the course to their lives personally. Courageous sharing in the classroom will facilitate this. When trust is created and accepted, and our people are able to confess to one another their pain, struggles, mistakes, failures, and victories, this will be a tremendous step in their healing and freedom. Of course we know the Holy Spirit is in charge, but as far as it depends on you, don't let any participants skate through class without opening their hearts and lives to the Lord and to their classmates.

Over my years of serving, I have learned so much from my participants, and have been deeply inspired by their courage, joy, hope, and determination. Their brave walks in the midst of their trials have influenced my own walk, demolished my own doubts, and motivated me to become even more dependent upon my Savior. The ways they minister to each other have taught me much above genuine love and compassion.

As you do the math, you may wonder why, with eight or ten participants in the class, I limit sharing to only three or four minutes until everyone has had a chance to share. Good question. I'm glad you asked. Consider ....

- Although we do our best, it is not always easy to start right on time. Other times announcements infringe on the time.

- Worship, soaking, and prayer at the beginning, and time for prayer at the end, are critical parts of the class, and we don't want to shortchange them.
- Some weeks, a participant may be particularly burdened and require quite a lot longer to share their heart. We may even stop and pray for them (more on this below).
- Realistically, if we ask participants to limit to 3 or 4 minutes, some will regularly share for 5 or more.
- Finally, we will want to allow enough time for us to *respond* to each participant. We will spend considerable time on this below.

Leader Responds After Each Person Shares

Affirming and encouraging *each person after they speak* is one of our most critical jobs in the classroom. Because this is so important, I am going to wrap up the last two elements in the structure of the class time, and then return to our response.

Set Up Next Week

Generate some excitement for the next chapter. Tell them a bit what they will encounter this week. Let them know you are praying for them. If there is something you don't want them to miss, point it out.

At the end of each class, as you send them off to work on the chapter, tell them that when they return next week, you will be asking them what God has shown them through their work in the study this week.

Closing Prayer

Don't let the class degenerate into multiple side conversations without closing in prayer. Your people need that closure and wrap up. As with the opening prayer, leaders should handle all the prayer the first few weeks. Then, as the class progresses, leaders may ask a participant to close in prayer. Be sure to ask ahead of time.

Let's focus now on our response to *each participant* after they share. Get ready; this is so important that we are going to settle in and spend some time right here. We will first learn how to *listen* to a participant who is sharing, and then we will learn how to *respond* to them. Finally, we will discuss some unique issues that may come up during sharing time.

How to Listen to a Participant Who Is Sharing

I think we can easily underestimate how much courage it takes for our participants to share in class. When someone has bravely taken that step, we honor them by giving them our complete attention.

- Utterly focus on what the participant is sharing. This is not a time to flip through our book, organize our papers, or plan our next step.

- Welcoming body language is essential. Lean in gently and keep arms in a receptive position, not crossed or closed.

- We must keep our eyes on the speaker. The speaker may want to look down, or look at the leader only, or look around at the other participants also. We want to be sure that when the speaker does look at us, we are looking into the speaker's eyes. This eye contact will say, "I'm here for you," and will help to validate, encourage, and make the speaker feel heard.

- Our response will require intense listening! Therefore we must focus on what the participant is saying, *not on our response*. Remember, when it is our turn to speak, we can trust the Holy Spirit to give us the words.

"When they arrest you and hand you over, do not worry beforehand about what you are to say, but say whatever is given you in that hour; for it is not you who speak, but it is the Holy Spirit."

Mark 13:11

Critical Responses After Each Participant Speaks

We do not provide an answer; we give a *response* led by the Holy Spirit. The purpose of our response is to let them know that we have heard them, that we deeply understand their heart, that we accept them right where they are, and that we unconditionally, nonjudgmentally love them. Whether in class or on the phone with our initial connecting conversation, our response will include three things:

- Reassuring them that it was safe to share what they just said.

- Encouraging them in their walk.

- Showering them with the Lord's nonjudgmental unconditional love as it is flowing through us. For some people, this may be the first time they have experienced nonjudgmental love. An added benefit may be their eagerness to share again next class.

Give feedback after each participant contributes. Remember, these participants have put themselves in a very vulnerable place. They need to be encouraged, affirmed, and loved unconditionally and nonjudgmentally. They need to hear their leader acknowledge them in a positive way. Don't assume that a participant seems mature in the Lord and therefore does not need acknowledgment and affirmation. *Every participant* needs acknowledgment and affirmation. I am mindful of the words of Dr. John C. Maxwell: "Question: How do you know if someone needs encouragement? Answer: Are they breathing?"[3]

Work hard to find something "right" in every answer. This does not mean to compromise the truth, but to be highly encouraging. We do not want the participants to fear sharing. Instead, we want them to be *eager* to speak because of the encouragement received from the Lord through our words. The Holy Spirit will give you the words; remember, you are here on His assignment. Even if you don't know how exactly to respond, just open your mouth, rely on Holy Spirit to speak through you, and start with one of these phrases:

- Thank you for sharing: "Thank you for sharing your struggles with us. That must have taken a lot of courage to open up to us."

- That is great progress: "Last week it took a few days for you to get past the anger. But this week you surrendered the situation to the Lord in just a few hours. Your turn around time is so much quicker. That's great progress!"

- You are drawing closer to God: "You really opened yourself up to the Lord" or "You have come more in tune with the Lord" or "You are drawing so near to Him."

- I noticed: "I noticed that you have become more accepting of God's sovereign plan. You seem to be trusting Him more this week."

- It sounds like: "It sounds like you were really battling unforgiveness, and you were finally able to forgive."

- It took a lot of courage: "It took a lot of courage for you to share that. I want you to know that I've struggled a lot with pride myself. God is growing you so much, and I can see He is giving you a heart of humility."

- That must have been challenging: "That must have been a very challenging situation, and you and Jesus have won the victory" (or "Jesus isn't finished with this yet").

- "What I hear you saying is ..." Don't parrot back their words, but *reflect back their heart*. When we are able to demonstrate that we see the beauty in their heart, they will feel encouraged and affirmed. Additionally, if we haven't understood fully, reflecting back will give the participant an opportunity to correct us and express what they really wanted to convey.

- Tie it into the chapter: "Your story illustrates just what we have been reading about in Chapter 3 this week ..." Be specific here.

I am constantly astounded how, as the participants share, the Holy Spirit covers each area of the book as He intended. Be ready with what He has shown you in your preparation time that He wants to cover this week. As you reflect back to the participant, highlight the teaching in the chapter as it relates to their vulnerable sharing. At the end of sharing time, if there are areas that have not been covered and there is time, highlight those areas yourself.

Before we leave this very important topic of our response, I'd like to visit a few specific areas: ministering to holy tears, handling the gift of discernment, and calling a participant up to a new level.

Ministering to Holy Tears

When someone is crying as they share, we may be tempted to pass the tissue box. It's our natural instinct to "happy them up." But offering tissues or other actions listed below may interrupt the flow of the Holy Spirit if we extend them at the wrong time:

- Comforting or consoling.
- Hugging or otherwise physically touching them.
- Verbally reassuring them.
- Offering tissues.

When someone is tearfully sharing, if we attempt to comfort in these ways, we may stifle their emotions. Our well-intentioned gesture may cause them to feel that we cannot handle their tears.

So instead, stand back, remain silent, and pray for Light to triumph in that person's heart. Wait for *them* to reach for the tissues. This movement generally indicates that the intense work of the Holy Spirit is subsiding. (Be sure to position a box of tissues in prominent view, so they can reach for it when ready.) When the Holy Spirit is finished, *then* we can do those comforting measures.

And be sure to also teach this to all your participants on the first day!

I consider tears to be a call to drop everything and pray. When the crying has subsided, the leader may pray over the person, or ask someone in the class to pray, or even gather the class around the person and invite all to pray over them. Many participants have told me that the times they were prayed over in class were the most profoundly impacting moments of the entire course.

Handling the Gift of Discernment

Three of our paramount responsibilities as *Triumph* Servant Leaders are to expose lies, to teach participants to seek God's direction, and to guide them back on track if they have strayed from His path. If the Holy Spirit has granted you the gift of discernment, you may recognize in your participants such things as sins, strongholds, or deceptions. But the Holy Spirit has not granted you this gift to indiscriminately speak out what He has revealed to you. Because many who come into class are deeply hurting, they may not be receptive, and may perceive your words as criticism. The Holy Spirit may not necessarily have granted you this revelation for *you* to speak to the participant. He may have revealed this to you because He wants you to pray for *Him* to speak to the participant and to set them free. Discerning His plan here will require a very close walk with the Lord indeed.

There may be times when Satan's lies are spoken in the classroom by those who are blinded by the enemy. Although God holds us responsible *for the entire class,* and we are anointed as *Triumph* Servant Leaders to expose lies and teach truth, we must do so with grace and love as led by the Holy Spirit. This will be a very delicate balance indeed, requiring a solid knowledge of the Word, an ability to speak the truth with gentleness and compassion, *and a sensitivity to His timing.* Remember, the Lord has brought to us hurting hearts, and we must handle them with the utmost love and care.

Let no unwholesome word proceed from your mouth, but only such a word as is good for edification *according to the need of the moment*, so that it will give grace to those who hear.
Ephesians 4:29, emphasis added

Realize that although we don't want lies to run unchecked, not everything needs to be handled the day it arises. Sometimes, a participant may be closed in class but more receptive in a one-on-one setting outside of the classroom. Pray before you speak to the participant, and ask the Holy Spirit to go ahead of you into the conversation. I am repeatedly surprised at how often He beats me to it and exposes the lie before I even say a word – and of course the Holy Spirit always handles these issues with more grace than I ever could! If a lie is exposed and brought down, ask the participant if they would be willing to share in the next class. The Holy Spirit can use this sharing to effectively teach the entire class the truth.

When someone has shared and a course correction is needed, listen well, and give empathy first. This may facilitate receptivity. Tread carefully, and listen to the Holy Spirit. If you sense they are open, allow the Holy Spirit to use you to gently guide them into truth. If you sense that they are not open at this moment, just end on empathy, make a mental note to address this, and arrange to talk to the participant outside of class.

Let's practice. I'll set up some situations that could happen in the classroom or outside of class. I'll give you room to write an empathetic response, and then the course correction when you feel they are open. I've filled in the first one for you.

Participant: "I will never forgive them for what they've done."

Empathy: "I am so sorry for what they have done to you. I feel your pain. Forgiveness is certainly not easy in a situation like this. The world would even say you would never be expected to forgive something so horrid."

Course Correction (when they are ready): "Forgiveness is not healing or restoration; it is a choice to release into God's hands, to let it be between them and God." Pause. "God does command us to forgive, and forgiveness releases us from bondage. What is holding you back from forgiving?"

Participant: "God wants me to be happy. I just don't know why He doesn't end this trial already."

Empathy: _____

_____

Course Correction (when they are ready):

_____

_____

Participant: "How can I make my spouse return to the Lord?"

Empathy: _____

_____

Course Correction (when they are ready):

_____

_____

When the Lord takes the scales off their eyes, handle their hearts with great gentleness.

Calling a Participant Up To a New Level

One of our critical jobs as *Triumph* Servant Leaders is to bring to light when a participant is at a crossroads, and invite them to repent, surrender, and choose God's way. Sometimes, the Holy Spirit will want us to nudge a participant with a challenge. The Holy Spirit may lead us to ask:

- "Are you ready to pray to forgive right now?"
- "Are you ready to surrender (or put this all in God's hands) right now?"
- "What is God calling you to do right now?"

If a participant agrees to pray right now to forgive or to surrender or release into God's hands, be aware that the class has just stepped onto holy ground (Ex 3:5). Be in silent prayer for the participant as they pray, and ask God to give you His anointing right now too.

Sometimes it will be necessary to teach them how to pray, as Jesus taught His disciples (Lk 11:1-13, Mt 6:5-15). Before they pray, I explain that the Lord is here helping them. I instruct them to pray "I choose" instead of "help me." If I have forgotten to first instruct, or if they begin to pray, "God help me forgive" or "God help me surrender," I gently interrupt them, reminding them that God *is* here and He *is* helping them. I remind them to pray instead, "God, I *choose* to forgive" or "God, I *choose* to surrender." I don't generally recommend interrupting someone who is praying, but in this case, this is so critical that some guidance may be needed.

I find that people truly appreciate if the leader or another in the class prays over them a prayer of blessing after they have prayed to forgive or surrender.

The *Surrender* chapters and the *Forgiveness* chapters of both TOS and T2 uniquely position participants at a crossroads, and give us an opportunity to challenge them. For both TOS and T2, I set aside extra time during the weeks they will be wrestling through these chapters, because these are critical weeks to call *each person*. I tell them that the leaders will want to speak with each person this week, and will be asking them the following questions:

- What is the Lord calling you to surrender (or who is He calling you to forgive)?
- Did you surrender it (or did you forgive)?
- If not, are you willing to surrender it (or to forgive) right now on the phone?

With a little nudging and a lot of prayer, we can invite the Holy Spirit to bring tremendous breakthroughs in these chapters!

Last Class: Celebration Day

I find that most participants like to add on a final class day for closure, with each participant given five minutes to share what Jesus has done for them through the class. Tell them to pray and prepare ahead of time. Their "Admission Ticket" is their Evaluation Form (see Appendix II).

This day can be a tremendous blessing for the participants as they see how much the Lord has grown both themselves and their classmates; speaking out their victories in Jesus seems to seal it in. This day will also be a tremendous blessing for us as leaders as the Lord unveils the work He has done through our partnership with Him. And it will be a beautiful way to pause, to thank and give glory to the One who has healed and freed and transformed and delivered.

Let's wrap up this chapter discussing our participants' next steps.

Next Steps for Participants

We have a significant responsibility to direct those who have completed the course into their next steps. Some may have received some direction from the Lord, but many will be looking to us as leaders for guidance. As class nears a close, it's time to begin one-on-one conversations to see how the Lord is leading.

As I have ministered to wounded people over the years, I have come to realize that one twelve or fourteen week course is rarely enough time for discipleship and healing. It seems that much more time is necessary for deep spiritual growth, repentance, sanctification, and freedom. I am thinking how Jesus spent three years pouring into His disciples – and He surely wasn't meeting with them only once a week!

As we discussed last chapter, our intent is for these classes to be a bridge to the Lord. Our ultimate goal is to help them learn to continue their journey of spiritual growth, sanctification, and healing – *without us*. Some may learn this through one semester. But for many, this will require several semesters and even several years before they are seeking Jesus on their own and no longer relying on us.

We bring our people to the foot of the cross to meet Jesus in repentance and to receive His healing and freedom. We aim to raise up *disciples* who know how to feed themselves and are equipped to step out into their Kingdom purposes. We do not want to release them prematurely. But nor do we want to create an atmosphere that makes them dependent upon us for their spiritual growth. To accomplish this goal, my leaders and I have developed what we call the *Triumph Rhythm*. I'll lay out the suggested rhythm, and then explain the pieces of it.

Suggested Triumph Rhythm

Months	Class or Season	Number of Weeks
Jan – April	*Triumph Over Suffering*	12-13 weeks
April - May	Participants' Percolation/ Leader's Restoration	4-6 weeks
June - Aug	Bible Study	6-12 weeks
Aug - Sept	Participants' Percolation/ Leader's Restoration	4-6 weeks
Sept - Nov	*Triumph of Surrender*	9-10 weeks
Nov – Jan	Participants' Percolation/ Leader's Restoration	6-8 weeks (thru the holidays)

Participants' Percolation Time/
Leaders' Restoration Time

Many participants complete *Triumph Over Suffering* with a great hunger for more. I have found that after a season of sanctification, it can be helpful for participants to have some time for the teachings to percolate before jumping into the next class. I encourage participants to rest and process as they spend quiet time with the Lord without the intensity of a study. I caution them not to pull back from God just because they are not in the study, but to press in with soaking and Scripture and quiet time. If our participants have not yet learned to study the Word themselves, they may want to use a devotional at this time, or go back through *Triumph Over Suffering*.

During this time of percolation, as the participants apply what they have learned to their everyday lives, the Holy Spirit often seems to seal in His work. This is also a good time for participants to connect with each other in a more relaxed atmosphere. Encourage them to go for walks together, go to lunch together, or go on other outings in order to get to know each other better on a social level.

Of equal importance during percolation time is a season for *leaders* to receive the Holy Spirit's rejuvenating work. Leaders need time to take care of themselves, to rest and replenish without the responsibility of constant ministry work. To have deep times to drink of the water of the Holy Spirit without the pressures of the class.

A month or two may seem like a long time for our participants not to be in class. And indeed it is. Yet I believe it is an important time for them to test their wings, to learn how to stay connected to God on their own. Although we want all of them to succeed, realistically, some may do well, others not so well. I find that the ones who did not maintain their spiritual disciplines and keep close to the Lord may learn from their mistakes, and press in deeper the next percolation season.

Bible Study

In order to encourage spiritual growth and foster a love for the Word, I have also found that interspersing Bible study with *Triumph* Classes is a good rhythm for many. I mean *Bible* study, not book study, not devotional study. Our people need the meat of the Word, not a Bible substitute.

And I, brethren, could not speak to you as to spiritual men, but as to men of flesh, as to infants in Christ. I gave you milk to drink, not solid food; for you were not yet able to receive it. Indeed, even now you are not yet able, for you are still fleshly.
1 Corinthians 3:1-3

If our goal is to raise self-feeding disciples, this is critical time to teach them to treasure His Word, to long for it, and to hear Him speaking through it. When prayerfully selecting a book of the Bible to lead your participants through, I think the following books are a good length and depth to start for a first time Bible study: Philippians, First Thessalonians, Colossians, James, First John, or First or Second Timothy. You could also try the Sermon on the Mount (Mt Ch 5-7). In Appendix III are some instructions on *How To Study Your Bible* that you can use to teach your participants to encounter Jesus through the Word.

Repeating the Rhythm

We know from firsthand experience that the depth of the teaching in these classes cannot be grasped the first time around. Many of the participants will want to return through *Triumph Over Suffering* and *Triumph of Surrender* a second time, and I definitely encourage this. Participants going through a second time will generally process the courses on a deeper level.

I will often mix new participants and second level participants. Those coming back for second level seem to be quite an inspiration to the participants entering class for the first time. I would caution not to allow more that one fourth or one third of the participants to be repeating the class. I have found that if the preponderance of the class is second level, the new participants can feel left out of a group that has already bonded, and can sometimes feel intimidated.

I recommend participants go through this full rhythm *twice* before *Triumph in Warfare*. Teaching Volume I of *Warfare* in the spring, then a study on the Holy Spirit in the summer (e.g. John Bevere's *Holy Spirit: An Introduction),* proved to be powerful preparation for Volume II in the fall.

As each one is completing their season under our mentorship, whether it is after one course or after a series of courses, meet with each one individually in person or by phone to pray and seek God's leading for their next steps. Remember they are leaving God's spiritual hospital, and we want to be sure they have ongoing places for fellowship, accountability, encouragement, and prayer, as well as a place to serve and use the gifts God has given them.

Some goals of this discipling season under our mentorship include:

- Security in their identity in Christ.
- A deep walk into their journey of healing and freedom.
- Knowing how to walk out their freedom.
- Able to read the Word on their own and to hear from the Lord through the Word.
- Strengthened to step into their God-ordained Kingdom purposes.

We may realize that some of our participants are leaving prematurely, and would benefit from longer time in the *Triumph Rhythm*. Remind them that they can always come back for further study, sanctification, and healing as the Holy Spirit prompts them.

Other participants have received much healing and freedom and we can see they are ready to "graduate." As you meet with them to discuss their next steps, don't be surprised to see God craft their purposes using the deepest pains of their hearts and lives as He ministers His healing and brings beauty from ashes. Make yourself available and keep in touch with your "graduates" as they launch out into their callings.

Potential Triumph Servant Leaders

And of course it is very much on our hearts to raise up additional *Triumph* Servant Leaders. Keep your ears open to the Holy Spirit, and hold your heart in a position of hopeful expectation. Those who have traveled through *Triumph Rhythm* twice and especially *Warfare* are often well-positioned – and drawn to – *Triumph Leadership Training.*

> **The things which you have heard from me**
> **In the presence of many witnesses,**
> **Entrust these**
> **To faithful men**
> **Who will be able to teach others also.**
> 2 Timothy 2:2

I will extrapolate from this passage a bit.

> **The sum of these *Triumph* teachings ...**
> **Entrust as a treasure**
> **To reliable and faithful people**
> **Who are capable and qualified to teach others also.**
> Adapted from 2 Timothy 2:2 AMP

Additionally,

> **Guard, through the Holy Spirit who dwells in us, the treasure which has been entrusted to you.**
> 2 Timothy 1:14

The deep and sure understanding of the *Triumph* teachings are a treasure that God has *entrusted* to you. Guard these teachings, and entrust them to faithful, capable, and qualified teachers. Trust God to send into your class those He desires to carry on the work of *Triumph Ministry*, for we are always in prayer for the Lord to multiply our work thirty, sixty, a hundredfold (Mk 4:20).

Chapter 8
Avoiding Traps in the Classroom

*L*eading in the classroom is not easy. As you continue to seek the Lord's guidance and correction, He will develop your leadership gifting. Pray for discernment, that you may hear His voice with greater clarity. Ask Him to flow through you as you respond to each participant.

Leading the discussion in the classroom can be fraught with snares. When we fall into them, we erect barriers to the flow of the Holy Spirit. Identifying common pitfalls and becoming more aware of when we have fallen into them will help us to become stronger, more sensitive leaders – and help us to sidestep these pitfalls the next time.

In this chapter, we are going to explore some snares that I have fallen into, or allowed the class to fall into. We will then discuss ways to avoid these traps – and in the next chapter, we will learn how to get us out of traps if our participants have fallen into them. Ideally, we want to avoid these pitfalls, not only because they do not glorify God, but also because falling into them can undermine trust, shut down honest sharing, and stifle growth.

In the final part of this chapter, we will discuss how to seek unity and avoid the very dangerous trap of division between co-leaders.

Trap: Fixing

It is natural human inclination to problem solve, fix, counsel, coach, advise – especially if we have a heart for the hurting coupled with some experience ourselves in the arena in which they are struggling. Some may come into class *wanting* to be fixed, counseled, coached, or advised. But others may not be emotionally, mentally, or spiritually ready to receive any wisdom, counsel, or advice. Either way, changing people is not our job. *It is the Holy Spirit's job.*

Fixing includes dispensing advice. Providing counsel. Furnishing the answer. Offering books or other resources. Directing a participant by coaching with leading questions. All of these are fine and even good in the right setting and the proper timing. But God has not invited people into *Triumph* Classes for human problem solving, advice, counsel, or coaching. He has invited them into class to hear from His Holy Spirit. To learn to recognize His still small voice. To learn how to welcome, receive, and implement His wise counsel, direction, guidance, and strength.

Realize that we can give advice and people can receive it, carry it out, and change. But God's ultimate goal is not change. It is not behavior modification. God's intent is deep internal *heart transformation.* Caterpillar to butterfly. *Metamorphoo.*[1] And *only Jesus* can accomplish that.

Since it can be hard to discern if we are falling into any of these "fixing" traps, I've given some examples:

- Problem Solving: A participant shares about a

challenging situation with a co-worker. The leader allows the class to jump in with their recommendations on how to handle the situation.

- Counseling: A man shares about his wife's alcoholism and says he doesn't know how to handle it. The leader gives recommendations on what to do when she becomes drunk.
- Coaching: A participant shares about a demanding boss. The leader asks, "What would happen if you decided to see your boss' corrections as a desire for the entire project to succeed, instead of feeling criticized and seeing him as a perfectionist?"
- Problem Solving: A parent shares about her struggles with her teenager. The leader tells what she herself did with her teenagers, or suggests a book to address the topic.
- Leading to the answer: A participant shares about something he has stolen. The leader asks, "Did you think about returning the item?"
- Advising: A participant asks for help making a difficult decision. The leader gives his recommendations and suggestions.
- Giving advice: A participant asks how to handle her friend's betrayal. The leader begins, "When I had that issue, I ..."

While some of these suggestions in the above examples may be well-meaning and even good advice, this is not what class is for. Class is not a counseling or coaching session. Yes, at times a referral to individual counseling or to Celebrate Recovery or marital counseling, for example, may be appropriate. But for the most part, class is a time of sharing what the Lord is doing in our hearts, of learning to hear from Him, and of constantly being pointed to the Lord and His Word. The response to all of these examples that would direct the participant to the Lord for an answer would be, "What do you think God is saying to you about this?" or "How is the Lord leading you here?"

It can be a fine line between nudging someone closer to God, and *fixing*. It can be a fine line between gently speaking the truth of His Word with grace, and *dispensing advice*. To keep from crossing that line, we can evaluate with some questions. Is what we said pointing someone to God, *or dispensing our own wisdom and expertise*? Is it encouraging them to hear from the Lord, *or promoting dependence upon us to teach them or give the answers?*

We may think that because we ask a participant a question, we are not fixing. *But that is a misconception.*

Asking a question is not a protection against fixing. In asking leading questions that in essence give advice or recommendations, or provide the answer within the question, we are still trying to correct, change, or fix. This can be quite painful to a wounded soul who is not seeking to be fixed. Additionally, when we are fixing, we circumvent the work of the Holy Spirit, and interfere with opportunities for the participants to learn to hear from the Lord themselves.

Some leading questions that indicate fixing is probably happening may sound like this:

- What would happen if … ? "What would happen if you went to marriage counseling?"
- What would it look like if …? "What would it look like if you changed jobs?"
- Would you consider…? "Would you consider apologizing to him?"
- Did you ever think about doing … ? "Did you ever think about giving back the money?"

I am a physician, but I do not take care of any participants medically. That is reserved for my practice. If a participant comes to me for medical advice, I pray with the participant, asking God to reveal His will to them. I pray for His healing, and I ask Him to guide them to the right medical care.

Similarly, if you as a leader have a degree or license, perhaps as a therapist or a counselor or a coach, reserve your counseling or coaching for your practice. It is not for the classroom, or for casual use of these skills with participants outside of the classroom.

As leaders, we are not to engage in these types of fixing activities with our participants either inside or outside of class. We are leaders and facilitators, not counselors, therapists, coaches, or advisors. Remember, a key to avoiding fixing, advising, or coaching is to ask the participant, "What do you think God is saying to you about this?"

Trap: Teaching and Preaching

As *Triumph* Servant Leaders, it is not our job to teach. All the teaching is done by the Holy Spirit as our people work through the material. We trust the Word of God, **which also performs its work in you who believe** (1Thess 2:13).

As *Triumph* Servant Leaders, it is also not our job to preach or to lecture. The preaching is done by our pastors.

If the Holy Spirit has given us as leaders the gift of teaching or preaching, it may be natural human inclination to want to teach or preach in class. Yet realize that God ordains a *proper timing* when He desires to use our spiritual gifts.

Think about Jesus' life. There were times He was preaching, times He was teaching, times He was healing, times He was serving, times He was prophesying. He was completely led by the Holy Spirit, and was not preaching when the Spirit was leading Him to heal, or prophesying when the Holy Spirit was leading Him to serve. Nor was He serving when the Holy Spirit was telling Him to rest. There were also times when

He did not heal or deliver, but stood back and allowed His disciples to heal and deliver.

If, at any particular time, the Holy Spirit has not *assigned* us to use the gift He has given us, and we choose to employ that gift, we will be operating in our own strength (Jn 15:4). Imagine a pastor preaching to his wife when he took her out to dinner. He would be using his gift in the wrong place at the wrong time. If the Holy Spirit is not flowing through us, we are accomplishing ... nothing (Jn 15:5).

Since it can be hard to discern if we have fallen into teaching or preaching traps, I've given some examples:

- Teaching: Leader goes through the chapter, highlighting important points. (This can discourage participants from working through the material on their own with the Holy Spirit.)
- Teaching or Preaching: Leader is talking more than the participants. (Of course, this doesn't always indicate traps of teaching or preaching, but if you find yourself doing most of the talking, ask the Holy Spirit to reveal what is going on.)
- Teaching: Leader is summarizing the chapter because some of the participants haven't read it this week.
- Preaching: Leader or participant begins to generalize, or apply what they learned this week *to other people*.
  - "You need to ..."
  - "We all need to ..."
  - "This is for all of us ..."

Both leaders and participants can fall into teaching or preaching traps. Going over the *Triumph* Guidelines (see Appendix II) on the first day will help, but as the weeks progress it may be necessary to refer the class back to those guidelines. Take the time to teach them what fixing, teaching, and preaching is, and use concrete examples such as we have done in this chapter. If someone falls into these traps of fixing, teaching, or preaching, gently remind them to keep the focus on their own heart. We will discuss this a little further in the next chapter.

Trap: Bringing a Different Agenda Into the Class

These classes are *very full* courses. They are sacred times that God has ordained for healing, spiritual growth, surrender, and freedom. Adding additional items into the agenda may detract from the work the Lord intends through this course. There may be times when the Holy Spirit may lead in a different direction, but that is not the norm. Keep His time and His agenda sacred.

Both leaders and participants may be tempted to use the classroom as a platform to advance their own personal agenda. If the Holy Spirit has given you a teaching, a message, a book, a class – I truly encourage you to follow His leading and allow Him to develop it in you! *But it is not for this class.*

There is already so much content and Scriptures in these classes that it will become too much for participants to process if we add to it. As leaders, it is our job to ensure that the person speaking remains focused on their own heart, and that the discussion remains centered around the chapter for the week.

Trap: Cross Talk

Cross talk is a back-and-forth conversation between two or three participants that excludes others. This conversation could be two people whispering to each other in their own private side conversation. Or, it may be audible to all, going back and forth across the room, yet still shut others out. "I can relate to you because ...." could be a tip-off that cross talk is starting.

Cross talk is particularly hurtful because it is exclusive. If is also disrespectful because the ones engaging in cross talk are not listening to a participant who is sharing. Cross talk is addressed in the *Triumph* Course Guidelines, so reviewing them can help curtail this problem.

Trap: Searching for Answers

Our participants may expect us as the leaders to have all the answers. We may even expect ourselves to have all the answers. Yet although we are His appointed leaders, walking in His anointing and relying on Him to lead us and speak through us, we will certainly not have all the answers. There will be Scriptures we don't understand, problems we don't know how to solve, challenges in the classroom we don't know how to handle. Only Jesus has all the answers. He is the only Perfect One (1Jn 1:5, 3:5, Jn 14:6, 2Cor 5:21).

As someone is speaking, quietly in your heart acknowledge that you don't *know* how to respond, and ask the Holy Spirit to give you wisdom, insight, and revelation. Although the Holy Spirit will give you *His response*, He will not always give you the *answer* that you or the participants were looking for. Remember, it's not our job to fix or to provide answers. We are here to encourage and point our people to God, and help them to recognize *His* answer.

- Don't be afraid to say with humility, "I don't know the answer to that. I will do some research and get back to you."

- If you realize the answer is in dispute: "This is something the greatest theologians debate. Some believe one way; others believe the opposite."

- If one of your co-leaders can answer, move the question to them.

Be cautious about giving the class an opportunity to answer. Sometimes, particularly in those not spiritually mature, the discussion can degenerate into a free-for-all with no truth presented. Be sure you are ready to interrupt a fruitless discussion and present the truth. A good way to intervene here is to say,

"Let's pray and ask the Holy Spirit to speak to us."

I will then pray, asking Him to speak, and listen for His direction. I will bring the discussion to a conclusion as the Holy Spirit is leading me, and immediately move the discussion to the next participant to share. After praying, my answer may sound something like this:

"We may not fully understand everything right now, but we do know that God has a plan and is working for our good. Mary, you haven't had a chance to share yet. What did the Lord show you in your study of the chapter this week?"

Trap: Grumbling and Complaining

Recognize that the leaders set the tone of the class. If we are negative, complaining, or griping, our participants will behave in the same manner.

Do everything without grumbling or arguing, so that you may become blameless and pure, "children

of God without fault in a warped and crooked generation." Then you will shine among them like stars in the sky.

Philippians 2:14-15 NIV

Out of the same mouth come both blessing and cursing. These things, my brothers, should not be this way [for we have a moral obligation to speak in a manner that reflects our fear of God and profound respect for His precepts].

James 3:10 AMP

We are to do everything without complaining or arguing. We have a moral obligation to speak in a way that demonstrates our fear of the Lord and our profound respect for His Word. James also says that if we think we are devoted yet do not control our tongues, we are deluding ourselves and our devotion is worthless (Jas 1:26). God is calling us to a very high standard indeed.

Specifically,

- Keep a positive attitude.
- Be sure to have a safe place to vent so that you do not vent in class; vent in this safe place only to be accountable and to seek heart purification. In class, no complaining about anything -- not spouse, children, family, church, neighbors. (And remember, a constant venting may signal impending burnout.)
- Celebrate every breakthrough, no matter how small it may seem at the time.
- Remember, in all things, God is in control. Expect that your class will not look like you expected or planned. Be flexible and prepared for Him to change things up at any moment.

The Goal of Our Instruction is Love

We as leaders are responsible not only *for each individual participant*, but also *for the class as a whole*. We must handle these issues right away – while ensuring that all our interventions are coming out of a heart of love.

But the goal of our instruction is love from a pure heart and a good conscience and a sincere faith.
1 Timothy 1:5

Do you recall my testimony in Chapter 5 regarding my attempts to control a participant who was doing a lot of talking? I felt a strong need to be in control. I was trying to maintain control, instead of letting God be in control.

I would like to be able to share with you that this story had a good resolution, but it did not. I was so busy controlling that I did not see her wounded heart. By trying to control her, I hurt her instead of loving her. I drove her away instead of drawing her in. In the next chapter, we will discuss specifically how God would have us handle a participant who is doing a lot of talking, but for now, let's pause and do a heart check.

Ponder, Pray, and Journal

Spend some time alone with the Lord. Ask Him to show you if you are struggling with any issues of fear or control. Ponder 1 Timothy 1:5 and journal what He is showing you.

Next ask the Holy Spirit to reveal any time when you, as a leader, or a student, or even as a friend, have fallen into traps of fixing, coaching, counseling, advising, teaching, preaching, grumbling, engaging in cross talk, or bringing your own agenda to class. Let the Lord use this exercise begin to remove control and stir up compassion in your heart for participants who fall into these traps. (We will learn how to handle these participants with compassion in the next chapter.)

Guiding Participants Away from These Traps

Once our hearts are clear, we can take some specific steps to help both us as leaders and our participants to avoid these traps. Our goal in the classroom is for leaders to be listening, and participants to be talking. This class is for our participants to speak and to tell their testimonies and struggles. It is not a platform for us as leaders to tell ours.

The classroom is where accountability happens for the participants. It seems that giving voice to their pain, struggles, sins, and failures can demolish denial and promote accountability and authenticity. And as they give voice to their breakthroughs in the Lord, the Holy Spirit seems to seal those victories into their hearts. The less talking the leaders do and the more sharing the participants do, the more that honesty, accountability, and growth can happen in class.

Specifically,

- Be sure that our participants are doing the vast majority of the talking.
- After each participant shares, we as leaders limit our response to affirming them, encouraging them, loving them, and pointing them to Jesus, as we discussed at length in the previous chapter.

Realize that not only are we responsible for *our own behavior* as leaders, we are also responsible *for the class*.

Allowing these behaviors to persist unchecked in class can cause participants to fear sharing, thus destroying trust and thwarting authenticity. It is our assignment to educate our people on classroom dynamics that will create a safe environment, encourage vulnerability, and stimulate growth.

Please also understand that we are not doing participants any favors by denying the problem, ignoring it, running roughshod over it, dealing with it in a passive-aggressive manner, or not meeting it head-on. God commands us to reach down and extend a hand up to a new level of spiritual growth. We will need a deep abiding relationship with the Lord to allow the Holy Spirit to use us to speak into these people.

Realize that these behaviors that are inappropriate in class may also be behaviors that participants are engaged in outside of class. They may be pushing potential friends away by preaching and fixing. So as we guide them to more connecting ways to interact, we will not only be helping the classroom dynamic, but we may also be helping them integrate well into community.

God has entrusted us with hurting people. They have underlying brokenness that may erupt into words and actions that are not conducive to a healthy group dynamic. The leaders shutting down the unwanted behavior or attempting to control the class is not the solution. The answer is healing and transformation that only Jesus can do. Therefore we have a dual responsibility: to love this particular participant and direct them into the Lord, and to maintain a safe and healthy environment for all participants within the classroom.

With these thoughts in mind, let's talk about some specific ways to steer our participants away from these traps.

Pre-Treating

The *Triumph* Class Guidelines and Course Description (located in Appendix II) are excellent tools to lay the groundwork. Go ahead and review them again now. Distribute these to your participants prior to the first class, and have them sign in agreement to abide by them. Go over them at the beginning of the first class, and explain what it means to fix, counsel, coach, preach, teach, and bring their own agenda. My husband calls this *pre-treating*.

Redirecting

Sometimes, a participant will not be aware that they have fallen into one of these traps. The best first step is *redirection*. Gently draw their focus back to the Lord. For example, if someone starts dispensing advice or counseling, we may try something like this: "Remember to keep the focus on yourself and what the Lord has done in your heart through your study this week."

Gentle and Loving Interruption

If someone is not open to redirection, and continues to fix or preach or counsel, it may require us to *gently and lovingly interrupt*. Do this with compassion and understanding, yet with firmness. We may try something like this: "I'd like to give others a chance to share" or "I am going to bring our focus back on our study because I want everyone to have an opportunity to share."

After class, be sure to talk with them about the fact that

you interrupted them. You may want to apologize, not for what you did (remember, you were acting to take care of the entire class), but for the *abruptness* of the interruption. Take responsibility for the choice you made, and be careful not to accuse, or blame, or take false responsibility.

Avoid these phrases, because they are skirting responsibility:

- "I'm sorry I interrupted you."
- "I had no choice but to interrupt you."
- "I had to make sure everyone had a chance to share."
- "I needed to interrupt you because ..."

This is a subtle difference, but try instead, "I'm sorry my interruption was abrupt. I wanted to give everyone a chance to share today." Take responsibility. Say "I wanted to" not "I needed to" or "I had to."

One-on-One Conversations

If ...

- Redirecting was ineffective, and we were forced to resort to gentle interruption, or

- The participant was able to be redirected, but repeated the behavior and required another redirection, or

- We sense that the participant, even after redirection or interruption, still does not recognize how their behavior was not in alignment with the Guidelines ...

... then it may be necessary to meet one-on-one. It may be more loving to risk causing pain in order help that person to grow, and in order to care for the class as a whole.

Arrange for a *one-on-one conversation* outside of class, in person or on the phone. Since this meeting has potential for embarrassment, one leader is sufficient. The leader who has the greatest connection with the participant should be the one to handle this conversation. Remember, God has brought very fragile hearts into our care. Do not go into this conversation cavalierly. Be sure to pray that God will grant the participant an open teachable heart. Be sure to pray for yourself that God will grant you unconditional love, insight into the participant's heart, and the right words. Ask the Lord to reveal your own heart, to expose any judgment or control. Ask your co-leaders and your prayer team to pray over the situation also.

These conversations are best held during the days before the next class. Having this kind of conversation minutes before class starts may rattle the participant and make them feel uncomfortable or embarrassed in the classroom. They may need time to process this. Additionally, be sure the place of discussion is private, not where other participants can overhear.

We may try something like this: "When you responded to Mary in class yesterday, it seemed to me that you were giving her advice. It felt like you were trying to fix her." Give the participant time to process what you have said. Gently help her to see that what she was doing was dispensing advice and fixing. Help her to learn how to listen respectfully and to allow the Holy Spirit to provide wisdom. It may be helpful to arrange for a signal to give her if she starts advising or fixing again in class. I find that many people are receptive to this suggestion, and sincerely want to interact in class in a way that is connecting and compassionate.

As difficult as these situations are to address, if we do not, we are shirking our responsibilities as leaders and may be allowing harm to come to the class. Additionally, we may be missing an opportunity to help a participant grow up in the Lord and to learn to interact with peers in positive and loving ways. Before we move into the last chapter to study some approaches to handling these challenges, we will address one more critical classroom trap: disunity between co-leaders.

Trap: Division Between Co-Leaders

As we discussed in Chapter 5, Satan is the driving force behind division, strife, and arguments between the leaders, between the participants, between the leaders and participants. It seems Satan knows better than we do that ...

Two are better than one because they have a good return for their labor. For if either of them falls, the one will lift up his companion. But woe to the one who falls when there is not another to lift him up. Furthermore, if two lie down together they keep warm, but how can one be warm alone? And if one can overpower him who is alone, *two can resist him*. A cord of three strands is not quickly torn apart.
Ecclesiastes 4:9-12, emphasis added

Two can resist him. I am thinking of how Jesus sent out His disciples two-by-two on their missionary assignment. As the disciples worked, the enemy was overcome, and Jesus watched Satan fall from heaven like lightning (Lk 10:1-18). It seems that when it comes to spiritual battles, when we work together our power increases exponentially.

But you will chase your enemies and they will fall before you by the sword; five of you will chase a hundred, and a hundred of you will chase ten thousand, and your enemies will fall before you by the sword.
Leviticus 26:7-8

Additionally, I find that working together with a team helps to promote humility. Alone, I can be prone to start taking credit for what only the Lord has done. Working with others helps to keep my heart in check here. Pastor Henri Nouwen elaborates on this concept.

I have found over and over again how hard it is to be truly faithful to Jesus when I am alone. I need my brothers or sisters to pray with me, to speak with me about the spiritual task at hand, and to challenge me to stay pure in mind, heart, and body. But far more importantly, it is Jesus who heals, not I; Jesus who speaks words of truth, not I; Jesus who is Lord, not I. This is very clearly made visible when we proclaim the redeeming power of God together. Indeed, whenever we minister together, it is easier for people to recognize that we do not come in our own name but in the name of the Lord Jesus who sent us.[2]

I believe that Satan continually attacks relationships, so that if we are not intentionally seeking unity, it may not be long before we are offended and fall into disunity, division, and strife. So in this section we will explore some practical ways to be intentional about connecting with our co-leaders. As Pastor Tom Mullins in *The Leadership Game* explains, "Unity is not a decision; it's an action."[3]

Communication

I cannot overemphasize the need for direct and constant communication. Prayerfully discuss how often you will meet together as leaders during the length of the class. Will you come early, stay late, or both? Will you have a weekly phone call? Maybe a monthly meeting? Agree on a plan, and commit to stick with it. Remember, our connection and communication must be *intentional.*

Start meeting weekly several weeks before class for planning and prayer, and to determine shared responsibilities. Keep your time with other leaders sacred. Do not use the time for complaining, gossip, or even small talk; use it to encourage and edify and pray. Pray and seek God's guidance and wisdom to work through problems.

- Assign administrative jobs, such as creating the roster and attendance sheet.

- Pray and ask the Holy Spirit to indicate who will lead which chapter.
- Prayerfully assign each leader a list of participants to call and connect with.
- If possible, pray over the room you will be meeting in.
- Agree on what time you will arrive before class starts in order to pray over each other, over the person leading that week, and over the participants.
- You may want to select certain times or days to fast regularly together to seek spiritual strengthening and to remind yourselves of your utter reliance on the Lord.
- Handle conflict resolution according to Matthew 18:15-17.

Bonding

The stronger you are as a team, the greater protection you will have against enemy attack, and the more easily the Holy Spirit will flow through you and your class.

- Continually lift each other up in prayer.
- Watch each other's back.
- Encourage each other when down.
- Make sacrifices for each other.
- Keep each other accountable.
- Fight the enemy together in prayer.
- Celebrate victories together.

Come to Class Prepared

As we discussed in Chapter 4, serving as a *Triumph* Servant Leader is a marathon, not a sprint. It will require focus and momentum. Concentrate on one individual class at a time, without losing the overarching picture. Each class is important. Each chapter is pivotal. Every week counts. Never give up – sometimes Holy Spirit will bring everything together in a participant's understanding months after class ended.

Even if you are not the designated leader a particular week, don't come in to class without re-reading the chapter and re-familiarizing yourself with the material. This will make you a strong support for the one leading. Additionally, a leader may become sick or unavoidably detained. The enemy will be trying to wreak havoc.

Your most important preparation for each class is your deep spiritual growth, your sanctification, your continued healing, and your abiding relationship with Jesus. Spend time with Him. Read the Word. Soak. Worship. Listen. Pray for yourself, your co-leaders, and your participants. If this is all you do, you will be plenty ready. If something happens to prevent you from your usual preparation of re-familiarizing yourself with the chapter, above all else do not skimp on your time with the Lord.

A Word of Encouragement

I think every possible way I could have mishandled situations in class, I have done it. These issues are extremely challenging, and I have to admit I have not always handled them in God-honoring ways. I can't even count the number of times I went to my pastor to confess and ask for wisdom, guidance, and prayer.

Be assured that God will cover our well-intentioned mistakes. He never demands perfection, only a fully committed heart, a heart that is open to His molding and shaping. He will bring good out of our failures as we place them in His hands and ask Him, "What now?" I used to think that God's intent in these classes was only for the spiritual growth of the participants, but surprising and perhaps even more delightful is the work the Lord is doing in my own heart most of all!

Chapter 9
Handling Challenges in the Classroom

*T*he list of potential difficulties we may encounter in the classroom could be a bit daunting. From the one who dominates the discussion, to the one who doesn't say a peep, from gossiping to chronically late participants to cell phones – the list could be overwhelming. I have to admit that I don't have any quick fixes for these issues.

Although we will be tempted to do whatever we can to immediately squelch the unwanted behavior, God calls us to handle these hearts with much more love and care than that. Each topic addressed below will begin with a section entitled *What's Underlying?* As we seek the Lord on behalf of each participant, we will rely on the Holy Spirit to reveal the heart pain driving the behavior, and to show us how to minister to them in love (1Tim 1:5).

It seems that these challenges often arise because of a participant's unmet need. And our response must begin with our own heart. If there is one who is talking a lot whom we are trying to silence, we will start by asking the Holy Spirit to search our own heart. He may reveal our judgment, impatience, or need to control, requiring us to first take the log out of our own eye (Mt 7:1-5). And as we repent and He purifies our hearts, He may then reveal the participant's deep heart pain that is driving their behavior.

As we wrestle through these classroom challenges, remember the handling of each precious heart requires *our own hearts* to be clear first. If we do not start with our own hearts, the flow of the Holy Spirit through us will be blocked. We will be operating on our own strength and may even hurt people. Apart from Him we can do nothing (Jn 15:4-5).

Pay attention to your own words that will expose your heart. Out of the abundance of the heart, the mouth speaks (Mt 12:34-35). For example, I have often heard people refer to those that bring challenges as "EGR" people ("Extra Grace Required"). This is not a Christlike attitude. We *all* require extra grace (Jn 1:16). Ask the Lord to grant you a deep compassion and understanding of your people.

Additionally, because we are also responsible for the class as a whole, there will be times when God calls us to immediately put a halt to the unacceptable behavior. Therefore each topic addressed below also includes a section entitled *Tips for Handling*, which contains suggestions to use in the classroom. You will also find here recommendations for working with the participant outside of the classroom in order to help them mature in their group interactions. God does desire our participants to grow here, for these behaviors are not conducive to a healthy classroom environment, and can also thwart their connection with others outside of the classroom.

Most of these problems will not resolve spontaneously, but will require head-on addressing. Although all of these issues are best addressed as soon as possible, many times the discussions must wait until outside of class. We will want to be cautious not to shame people in front of the group. And when we are going into a one-on-one meeting to address these issues, it is paramount that we enter that meeting with lots of prayer.

Remember, the Holy Spirit is in control. You have surrendered the class to Him. It is *His* class. If there is a challenge going on in the classroom, He is most likely after something in someone's heart – and it could very well be ours. Before class, during class, after class – constantly release to His control.

One thing God has clearly shown me is that it is not about controlling and having a nice little class where everyone "behaves properly." It is about God being glorified, the Holy Spirit transforming, and Jesus touching and healing for all eternity. It's about you and I being oaks of righteousness for the display of His splendor (Isa 61:3).

As we jump into this last chapter, remember these key points:

- We are responsible for the entire group, not just one person.
- We are not helping a participant by not taking the time to gently redirect them. Educating them and guiding them in these areas is a critical part of their spiritual growth. We want them to learn to relate in community in ways that are connecting.
- As leaders, we have a God-given responsibility to help our participants to mature in Christ.

Ready? Let's go.

The One Who Shares A Lot

What's Underlying?

Although it may be easy to discern pride or even arrogance, those who dominate the discussion actually often have a deep sense of inadequacy. I know that seems counter-intuitive, because often they seem to speak with great confidence and authority and boldness, and maybe even braggadocio. But the reason they may be trying to prove themselves could be because they believe that no one will accept them unless they measure up. Or they may feel so insufficient that they feel a need to bolster their own reputation, sometimes by repeatedly sharing how God is using them for His Kingdom work.

Another factor that could contribute is a deep root of fear of rejection. They may be terrified that their classmates will not accept them because they think they are "not good enough" or "not holy enough." Additionally, they may be so starved for acceptance, love, attention, or affirmation that they may be seeking reassurance of acceptance from leaders or participants in the class. People-pleasing and idolatry of people can be intertwined here also.

I have also even had participants who were hearing impaired and were so embarrassed to ask people to repeat themselves that they compensated by excessive talking so they didn't have to do much listening.

I find most overtalkers to be operating out of deep woundedness. Until they are healed in the Lord, they will have much trouble allowing others to share.

Tips for Handling

We will face this suddenly in class without any forewarning and must be ready to handle it. Remember, *none of these tips will work if our hearts are not right*, so we must be prayed up before the semester even starts. Remain in deep abiding intimacy with Jesus. Ask the Holy Spirit to expose and cleanse you of pride, judgment, impatience, and control.

What to do during class when this happens without any warning:

- Pray in your heart while they are speaking. Ask the Holy Spirit for compassion and wisdom.

- *Listen* to what the person is saying, because they are going to need you to respond to them with very specific acknowledgment and affirmation.

- After acknowledging and affirming, maybe try, "It sounds like you have so much to *share*, and I so want to hear you. I also want to give others a chance to share in class today, so let's you and I talk after class."
  - Use *"share"* instead of "say" or "speak" or "talk."
  - Be sure to follow up on that commitment.

- If they are not verbally interruptible, and you are near them, you can put your hand gently on their arm or shoulder. Sometimes that will stop the talking long enough for you to speak and turn the conversation over to someone else.

This participant will most likely require one-on-one time outside of class – and often more than one meeting. Before that meeting, pray, and ask others to pray for you. Remember it is about *our* hearts too, not just theirs.

What to do before the next class:

It is urgent to connect with them outside of class, *before* the next class day. Give them time to tell their story. Sometimes, just having someone listen to their entire story from start to finish will be sufficient. But others may need another meeting *after the next class* in order to more directly handle the situation.

Sometimes, they are oblivious. A gentle, "Are you aware that others don't always get a chance to share in class?" or "that you share more than others?" may open their eyes.

You may also ask them, "Do you have any suggestions for how we can handle this?" Note the "we" in this sentence. Let them know that you are partnering with them here. They may come up with some good suggestions, such as a hand signal or a word that lets them know it is time to "land the plane."

Emphasize that once they've shared in class, they will want to hold back and listen to what others have to share. After everyone has shared, if there is more time, then people will be able to share again.

One last suggestion. This next tip we can use only if we can say it from the depth of our heart. If we cannot say this with all truthfulness, we shouldn't say it. They will see right through us, and we may hurt their heart: "You have so much to offer the class, and I wish that there was time for everyone to share as much as they want. But we are limited here in class."

Heart check: Be sure *you* are comfortable with silence in the classroom. If the one who shares a lot has already spoken, and you have invited the rest of the class to share what God has revealed to them this week through the chapter, give the class a good seven seconds to respond. If you are uncomfortable waiting those seven seconds of silence, you may be, with unintentional body language, inviting the overtalker to start talking again.

The One Who is Reluctant to Share

When it comes to spiritual growth, I think that there is no substitute for sharing in the classroom. Be intentional about encouraging each one to speak. When people voice what is in their hearts, with others present as witnesses, the Holy Spirit can seal in His transformation, the growth can become more real, and the roots can reach down deep because they are now in a place of accountability. Additionally, sharing makes people feel included; it makes them feel like they belong. This can inspire them to dive into the study deeper, and draw them to return next week to class.

What's Underlying?

This one is also often deeply wounded. They may have a buried root of distrust – both of people and of God. They may fear rejection, judgment, or disapproval.

These people may have been traumatized with criticism or laughter when they have opened their hearts in the past. They are treading very carefully, wondering if this class will be safe. They may have been betrayed, and are not sure that this class can be trusted.

They may be oppressed with shame. For this person, the intensity of soul pain that shame elicits may be so overwhelming that they are terrified to risk that pain.

This may not be obvious at first, but the one reluctant to share may also have a root of pride. Pride can cause intense people-pleasing and fear of what people think, leading to the reluctance to speak. Pride entwined with shame can present a difficult barrier to surmount. Much prayer may be needed to enable these participants to begin to trust.

The overtalker with obvious pride often fears rejection, and the one reluctant to share with obvious fear of rejection often wrestles with pride. Similar issues, manifested in different ways.

Tips for Handling

Make it clear from the outset that you expect everyone to share in every class. I don't mean to force them to share deep heart issues when they are not ready, but that they are expected to speak something each class. As we have discussed, sharing in class is a critical factor for spiritual breakthrough. Somehow, in a way that is hard to explain, articulating what is in one's heart promotes truthfulness, accountability, trust, and healing.

Set up expectations *before* the first class. When you are having your initial conversations, let them know that each one will be given an opportunity to share why they are here and what they want the Lord to do for them through this class.

Let the participants know what to expect in subsequent classes: "Next week when you come to class, I will ask each of you what the Lord showed you in your reading of Chapter 1 and working through the *Workbook*. We are praying for powerful encounters with the Lord. Sharing with each other invites the Lord to grow us, so I will want to hear from each one of you." And when they return to share what God has shown them from the first chapter, remind them to keep their sharing focused on their own hearts.

Earning trust will be crucial here. Meeting with them outside of class may encourage them to open up a bit to you. As you demonstrate yourself safe, that may embolden them to open up to the class also. When they have shared with you outside of class, you may say, "Your story is very impacting.

I think the whole class would benefit from hearing it. Would you pray about sharing in class?"

As we have discussed, creating a safe environment in the classroom will also help to establish trust. And when a participant who is usually reticent has opened up in one class, encourage them and allow them the time needed.

The One Who Shares – But Not Transparently

This is different than the one who is reluctant to share at all. This one may even be very wordy, without revealing their heart. They may highlight the chapter or even express how wonderful it is, but have no heart application, remaining guarded and protective of their true self. They may discuss all they have accomplished *in the past*, or what God has worked in their hearts *in the past*, or breakthroughs and healings they have had *in the past*. Acknowledge what the Lord has done in them and through them, and gently remind them that the Lord has brought them to this class to focus on something in their hearts and lives *right now*. Remind them to keep their focus on present issues, or on things of their past that are still affecting their present.

What's Underlying?

Perhaps intense fear, self-protection, or defensiveness. They may have been wounded or betrayed. Pride, fear of the people, the need to prove themselves or elevate themselves may be present also. Shame may also play a big factor here. They may not realize that a sin or failure is something they did, but not who they are. They may have failed, but they are not a failure.

I think of this as wearing a mask, or blowing smoke. They seem to throw up a smoke screen to hide their pain, their mistakes, their imperfections, their very heart. They may be seeking to control what people think of them, so they put up a façade and only allow people to see certain parts of themselves.

Tips for Handling

This participant will likely need time outside of class also. They may be dealing with a deep root of shame, so we will not want to embarrass them in class with pointed questions.

Increased vulnerable sharing on the leaders' part may help to open this one up. Or, if they have described encounters with the Lord with no real heart application, specific but gentle questions led by the Holy Spirit and directed at heart issues may help. "When you had this encounter with God, did He show you anything in your heart that you did not know?"

Sometimes, all our efforts and prayers will not bring this person to apply the teachings to their own heart during the season of the class. Although the Holy Spirit brought them here for transformation, remember, they have free will, and may choose not to partner with the Lord in His intended work.

The One Who Declines to Silence Their Phone

Triumph Guidelines require participants to silence their phone and put it out of sight during class time. Some may be shocked at this request and decline to acquiesce. I am not referring to the mom who has a sick kid at home during one particular class. I mean the one whose presence is so completely necessary in their job that they cannot silence their phone for two hours to give the Lord their undivided attention.

What's Underlying?

Possibly pride. Or the need to be indispensable. Or maybe the need to maintain control. It could be inability to delegate, fear of failure, or perfectionism.

Tips for Handling

Remember, we are responsible for the entire class. Cell phones in view will distract the entire class – and us as leaders – from the work of the Lord.

This issue is addressed in the *Triumph* Guidelines, so the Guidelines themselves may have already dealt with the problem. Be sure everyone has signed prior to the first day of class. If this issue occurs during the first class, remind them of what they have agreed to in the Guidelines, and explain the distraction cell phones are for others who are trying to focus on the Lord during this time. If they still decline to turn off their phone and put it out of view, you may be stuck that class. "I understand what you are saying; go ahead and leave it out but on silent, and please stay after class today so we can discuss it further."

After class, ask them more about why they feel they need to be completely available even during the two hours of class. After hearing their heart, and responding as the Holy Spirit leads, you may say, "As you saw today in class, this is an intense spiritual growth class. Everyone here wants to fully focus on what the Lord has for them. If you are not able to give the Lord your full attention during class time, maybe this is not the right season for you to take this class."

I recommend that you do not make an exception for this participant. Let them pray about whether this is the right season for them to participate in this class, and ask them to get back to you before the next class with their answer. Trust that if the Lord wants them in class, He will make it clear to them.

The One Who Is Chronically Late

What's Underlying?

Find out why after class. Sometimes, it is just an excuse to delay. Other times it can be simple selfishness and disrespect for the other participants. At other times, it's the best they can do. Ask with a nonjudgmental heart: "I noticed you are having trouble getting to class on time." They may have a legitimate issue, such as childcare, elderly parent care, transportation issues, or work constraints.

I have had participants chronically late because they really dreaded coming to class. They were in such a place of pain or fear that it took all they could muster just to get to class. People such as these who have been so traumatized need our support and encouragement, not our condemnation.

Tips for Handling

Don't take it personally. This issue is between them and God. Even if you feel that they are missing so much by coming in late, just let it be between them and God.

It will be disruptive enough for the participant to come in late; don't add to the distraction by calling attention to it. You can give the participant a brief head nod to acknowledge them, but do not interrupt the class or repeat anything they have missed.

The One Who Gossips or Criticizes

In general, gossip is talking about someone when they are not there. However, explaining briefly about someone may be necessary background information as our participants share. But there is a fine line between sharing the pain of a relationship as background to help the class understand their story, and *gossiping*.

Clearly gossip involves speaking about someone in a way that is disparaging, critical, or slanderous. But gossip also includes talking about the intimate, personal, private, or sensational affairs of another person.

Sometimes, it may be hard for us as leaders to discern if the line was crossed from appropriate background sharing, to gossiping. Ask for the Holy Spirit to give you that discernment. If a participant feels the need to recount details of the latest hurtful behavior in a relationship, they have probably crossed that line into gossip, slander, or criticism.

Another way to help discern gossip is to realize that gossip is a matter of the heart. If someone is sharing about another person appropriately as background information, their focus will be *on their own heart*. Details will be unnecessary. Gossip, criticism, or slander, on the other hand, gives details and puts the focus on how awful the other person's behavior was. Appropriate background sharing may sound like, "Someone said something that hurt me about the way that I parent, and I am trying to forgive and give grace. I'm also asking the Lord if there is a grain of truth in what that person said."

What's Underlying?

Often, gossip and criticism erupt out of comparisons and jealousy. Fear of not being accepted, pride, and self-idolatry feed in to this also. Low self esteem, a need to prove oneself, struggles in identity in Christ and lack of intimacy with Him can also be roots of gossip. And I have often seen that gossip, criticism and slander are signs of a wounded unforgiving heart.

Triumph Classes are not "support groups." These classes are not a place for people to whine, grumble, complain, or to air their gripes. Refer back to the *Triumph* Course Description to underscore this point.

Triumph Classes are for heart transformation, repentance, healing, and freedom. Interrupt the one gossiping or criticizing, boldly if necessary. Don't allow the discussion to deteriorate into a bashing session.

Tips for Handling

"Why do you look at the speck that is in your brother's eye, but do not notice the log that is in your own eye? Or how can you say to your brother, 'Let me take the speck out of your eye,' and behold, the log is in your own eye? You hypocrite, first take the log out of your own eye, and then you will see clearly to take the speck out of your brother's eye."
Matthew 7:3-5

It is very important to take the log out of your own eye. Are you interested in the latest gossip? That will make it hard to immediately shut it down. Have you yourself fallen into criticism, either in class or in your personal life? That will make it hard to keep someone else accountable in this issue.

When you discern that gossip or criticism has started, immediately speak out, gently the first time: "Remember to keep the focus on yourself and your heart." If the gossip continues, they really may be unaware that what they are doing constitutes gossip. Step in and educate them, speaking clearly and unequivocally:

- "Please share primarily about yourself and not about others. Talking about other people is gossip."
- "Are you part of the problem and sharing this with us for the purposes of confession, accountability, and prayer? If not, it is gossip."

If the criticism continues, they may be unaware that they are criticizing. Again, clear education is important: "You have already provided us with the background of this relationship. Giving us further details becomes criticism."

After you have told them what *not to do,* be sure to tell them what *to do.* "How about sharing with us what God is working in your own heart through this pain." If this behavior persists, it may require a discussion outside of the classroom.

If you are addressing gossip with the group, it may be a good time to remind them that we do not discuss *outside of class* what was shared in class – *even with other participants or with the leaders.* That is also gossip.

Please be aware that if someone has gossiped in the classroom, they may well be gossiping outside of the classroom as well. They could be unaware that their behavior is gossip, so clear teaching on what gossip is will be crucial. Additionally, gossip creates an unsafe atmosphere in the classroom, so it is critical that we address this issue. Participants may not be able to identify why the classroom feels unsafe, but somehow their spirit may sense that if they are vulnerable, their private issues may not remain private.

Special Notes for Triumph Leadership Meetings:

Meeting with other *Triumph* leaders for accountability, encouragement, and prayer may also be places to share your difficulties handling classroom challenges. Do not cross the line into gossip or criticism, and share only for the purposes of confession and to receive guidance and prayer.

Triumph Leadership Meetings may also be safe places for us to process the devastating stories that we have heard and the heavy encounters we have had with our participants. We will keep our hearts clear and be sure we are sharing not to gossip or criticize, but to receive encouragement and prayer as we release our participants to God.

The One Who Complains or Criticizes the Church or Church Leaders

As we discussed in Chapter 5, pastors and church leaders are anointed by God for their position, and God commands us to support them. God demands submission to our leaders and pastors and respectful speech about them. He expects us to require that our disciples have submitted hearts and respectful speech about their leaders and pastors also.

What's Underlying?

Spiritual immaturity can be a cause of criticism and complaining. Those who are young in the Lord and have not learned how to feed themselves, who expect and demand the church to feed them, may become frustrated and disappointed when their needs go unmet. If the issue is spiritual immaturity, they are in the right place, for *Triumph* Classes are discipleship classes to facilitate growing up in the Lord. Over the course of the class, take the time to educate them on grumbling and complaining vs. gratitude and contentment, on milk vs. solid food, on expecting the church to meet their needs vs. self-feeding.

Judgment, disdain, and superiority can also lead to criticism of the church and its leaders. Sometimes, those who criticize have hard hearts that are not open to the pastor's teaching of the Word. Judgment and disdain can even lead to contempt, and will require the Holy Spirit to grant humility and bring repentance for pride. Hard hearts require repentance to open them up to the Word of the Lord.

Finally, wounding by current or former church members or church leaders can result in anger and unforgiveness. Unresolved issues or unmet expectations can lead to grudges or resentment also. People can unknowingly carry over the pain from a past church to their current church. If the Lord brings someone to your class who has been wounded by someone in the Body, tread carefully here. We don't want to be dismissive of a wounding from church or church members, because these types of wounds can cut particularly deep. The wounded will truly need the Lord's healing, and coming to forgiveness will position them to receive His healing.

Tips for Handling

If you are suddenly dealing with criticism of the church or church leaders in the classroom, ask the Holy Spirit to give you quick discernment. If you sense it is due to disdain or spiritual immaturity, immediate squelching is key. But if you sense there has been some type of wounding, validate the pain they are having, and ask if you can speak with them outside of class. Out of respect for the church and church leaders, you will want to give them a safe place to share other than in the classroom.

Do not give your opinion of a preacher, church, or pastor – of your church or of another's – even when people ask. The exception to this is if your participants are listening to teachings that are not Biblically sound. You have a responsibility to teach them how to discern if what they are listening to lines up with Scripture.

If a participant's criticism is recurrent, meet with them outside of the classroom. Teach them to go to God and ask Him what is causing them to criticize.

If you have worked with a participant in this area, and they persist in criticizing, if the Holy Spirit leads, you may gently recommend that they pray and ask God if this is the right church for them. Sometimes, if they are unable to receive from the leadership in their current church, and are *really seeking* healing and growth, they may benefit from a different church. But other times, changing churches will not help, and they will simply take their critical spirit to the next church.

Similar to criticism and gossip, it is imperative that we maintain a clean heart here. Remember, we as *Triumph* Servant Leaders set the tone both in class and out. We are not to criticize any churches, pastors, preachers, or teachers.

When Another Leader Comes In as a Student

At times, God grants us the honor of ministering to someone who is a leader in a different ministry or profession, or a therapist, counselor, or coach. Sometimes, it may be challenging for these leaders to step into the role of student. Don't judge; give grace; it can be challenging when God calls us to step into student role also.

It will be wise to discuss these challenges with the participant prior to the first class as a way to pre-treat. You may say something like this:

"I admire your humility and courage to put yourself in the position of student in this season. God has brought you here for a very special reason: He wants to pour into you. You have ministered to so many for so long, and this is *your time*. A time just for you. A time when you don't need to be responsible for other people. I want you to receive all the Lord has for you in this season. It may be challenging to mindfully put yourself in the place of student in this season. Are you ready?"

If your leader-as-student is having trouble with *receiving* and continues to lead and pour into others, address this early on. As you meet with them outside the classroom, you may say something like this:

"You don't seem to be absorbing all the Lord has for you through this class. Perhaps you are feeling responsible to lead or mentor. Maybe your leadership skills are blocking you, or your strengths as a leader could be interfering with your receiving.

"God wants to work different things in your heart with you as a participant compared to the times He works in you and through you when He has positioned you as leader. Being a student takes much humility and courage! How can you transition to the position of student in this season in order to receive all God has for you?"

Dissension, Digressions, and Heated Topics

What's Underlying?

Satan may attack by causing strife and division. He may use unwitting people to criticize, step on each others' toes, and say hurtful things. He may prey on those easily offended and use others to give offense.

Satan may also be working to derail and distract and draw the focus away from the Holy Spirit's agenda. Because it is hard to confess sins and struggles, it may be easy for Satan to entice participants to talk about everything but the reason the Lord has brought them to class.

Tips for Handling

Redirect the class back to the primary focus: Jesus Christ and the teachings of the course. "Let's bring our focus back on the chapter now." Your participants are here to learn what God has to say in His Word about the topic for the week. Don't deprive them of that privilege by allowing them to talk about everything else but the lesson. I find most participants are grateful when I steer the conversation back to the lesson.

When polarizing topics come up, do not give your opinion, even when people ask. Suggest, "Let's pray for that issue, since it is so clearly on your heart." If lies or deception are being promoted, God expects us as leaders to speak and teach the truth. But if the disagreement does not involve major teachings of the faith or the Biblical teachings of the course, we do not even need to get involved in the discussion. Just bring the conversation back to Jesus and the teachings of the class.

If a participant asks a question that will require a lengthy answer, and you sense that others are not asking this same question, acknowledge that this question is important, but will require a more in-depth answer than class time allows. You can ask them to stay after class to discuss, or arrange to connect with them outside of class. If you know that this question will be addressed in the next few chapters, encourage them to stick with the course and allow the Lord to unfold the answers for them.

Don't be on a mission to discuss every single homework assignment and every single discussion question; you cannot cover it all. As each person shares, the Holy Spirit will highlight His agenda. Although the goal is to keep the class focused on God and on the lesson, there will be times when what the Holy Spirit is teaching is not exactly the lesson you planned. Be sensitive to the Holy Spirit's leading – He will direct you. There will be times that you look back and know that what was discussed is exactly the conversation God wanted; there will be other times when you will wonder; and there will be other times when you will be pretty sure the conversation went off track. Remember, it is God's class. Just be sure you are prayed up before each class; repent of pride and independence and surrender the class to Him. Trust Him to orchestrate the conversation and give you the words, and then let Him take care of the rest.

Meeting Resistance

Each person in our classroom is here by divine appointment. We have prayed for the Lord to bring only those He has ordained to be here. He has something special for each one – healing, freedom, forgiveness, revelation, understanding. Astounding breakthroughs. Profound encounters with Him. Establishment of rock solid identity in Him. Freedom from ensnaring lies. Precious truths unveiled. Ability to see Him with unclouded vision. We have seen Holy Spirit's magnificent work class after class, semester after semester.

But sometimes, a participant seems to have no breakthrough. There appears to be some type of barrier to the work of the Holy Spirit. Now what?

Ponder, Pray, and Journal

Ask the Lord why people may be resistant to change. Why they fight against His conviction, transformation, healing, or freedom. Why they sit in their prison cell when Someone has opened the door for them to walk out. Listen to the Lord and journal your thoughts – and no peeking at the next section! Meet me back here when you are finished to read some reasons my leaders and I have discovered over the years.

Pride may be at the root of much of the resistance to change. Some may not want to admit that they are wrong – and that they have been doing something wrong for a long time. Shame and guilt may also play into this.

Fear is another common barrier. They cannot imagine what life will be like on the other side of surrender; they do not know God well enough to easily trust Him; they are comfortable in their prison cell. Fear of pain or fear of the unknown can be a strong impediment.

Control can also thwart surrender. Sometimes the refusal to release control into God's hands is rebellion. Other times, a participant may be unable to surrender because they simply don't know how.

Deception may have strong impact here. Some do not see the sinfulness of their ways – or do not think their sin is all that bad. Some are in denial. The veil that lies over their mind and heart can be quite impenetrable by any human reasoning, removed only in Christ (1Jn 1:8, 2Cor 3:14-18).

Some may be ensnared in the river of culture, peer pressure, and desire to fit in.

Some may feel they have no purpose, and believe even if they change, it will not have any eternal impact.

Some may not be willing to make the sacrifices required to fully surrender. Some are trapped in grieving everything they think they will have to leave behind if they surrender.

Ponder, Pray, and Journal

Go through the list you made of why people may be unwilling to change, and for each item, write down at least one thing you can do as a leader to help break down their resistance. Don't write your list in order to create a fixed agenda for yourself. Although we will partner with the Lord as He leads, remember, only God can break through their resistance.

For those resistant to the Lord's call, having an opportunity in class to hear the testimonies of other participants' surrenders can be greatly impacting. The transparency of the leaders may also help to open the doors of their hearts. If they are afraid, teach them that the Holy Spirit does the work as they cooperate with Him.

And be patient. Encourage even small steps in the right direction. Some may simply not be ready yet. God holds the timing in His hands – and often does not reveal that timing to us. He may be laying groundwork, or orchestrating events and transformations in others' lives that will intersect with our participant's life. It's our job to simply be obedient as we present Truth through this class; it's His job to do the heart work.

If hearts are not open, if breakthroughs are not happening, receive this as His call for more prayer. Pray for the Holy Spirit to soften hearts. Pray for repentance and surrender. Pray for humility, courage, and obedience. There is a mighty battle raging in the heavenlies. Don't give up hope. Persevere to the end. Sometimes, in the very last class, you will hear, "I get it now!"

If you witness no breakthrough even to the end, do not assume that you – or God – have made a mistake inviting them into class. I have had people whose hearts seemed so hard, who didn't seem to receive any transformation or revelation the whole semester, come up to me years later and share how God just now enabled them to grasp the teachings of this class. A bountiful harvest, years after the seeds were planted.

Our Battle Is Not Against Flesh and Blood

As we are handling all these classroom challenges, it is imperative that we remember who the real enemy is.

For our struggle is not against flesh and blood, but against the rulers, against the powers, against the world forces of this darkness, against the spiritual forces of wickedness in the heavenly places.
Ephesians 6:12

In the heat of the moment, we must keep in mind that the battle is with the enemy, not with the person right in front of us. The more we try to control, the more fear may well up inside of them. We will find ourselves fighting a losing battle.

Understand that victory is not defined by getting the person to stop the unwanted behavior. Victory is defined as Jesus being glorified – and the Holy Spirit will define what that means for each situation. Victory is defined as heart transformation – theirs *and ours*.

A Final Word

Sometimes, we can be so busy serving and working that we don't take the time to pause and honor God with thanksgiving and celebration. But the Word is full of commands to stop and praise and worship with grateful hearts! Thanking and celebrating can help keep our focus on Him, remind us that He alone brings the victory, and help to keep us humble and reliant on Him. Additionally, our praise will silence the enemy attacks, which are certain to be escalating as we continue the Lord's assignment.

Remember, as we serve the Lord with all our heart, it is not our job to evaluate the results. It is our job to be obedient, to listen and love and point them to Jesus. To create a welcoming place for the Holy Spirit to rest and an atmosphere where He can work. To pray for open hearts and favor with the Lord. It's the Holy Spirit's job to transform hearts and set people free. And it's our job to celebrate His victories – both the obvious ones and the hidden ones, the ones we trust Him to reveal in His timing.

Let's end our time together with a prayer of praise and worship, from the Song of Moses, his song of praise after the Lord led Israel through the Red Sea. Stand up and read this out loud with grateful hearts and boisterous praise!

"The Lord is my strength and song,
And He has become my salvation;
This is my God, and I will praise Him;
My father's God, and I will extol Him.
The Lord is a warrior;
The Lord is His name …
Your right hand, O Lord, is majestic in power,
Your right hand, O Lord, shatters the enemy.
And in the greatness of Your excellence
You overthrow those
who rise up against You;
You send forth Your burning anger,
and it consumes them as chaff …
Who is like You among the gods, O Lord?
Who is like You, majestic in holiness,
Awesome in praises, working wonders? …
You stretched out Your right hand,
The earth swallowed them.
In Your lovingkindness You have led the people
whom You have redeemed;
In Your strength You have guided them
to Your holy habitation …
You will bring them and plant them
 in the mountain of Your inheritance,
The place, O Lord,
Which You have made for Your dwelling,
The sanctuary, O Lord,
Which Your hands have established.
The Lord shall reign forever and ever."
                    Exodus 15:2,3,6-7,11-13, 17-18

It is a great honor for God to entrust us with a hurting heart – and an equally great privilege when that heart trusts us with their pain. Pray for discernment and compassion, and hold those hearts ever so gently in your hands.

Dear Heavenly Father, I know Your sweet heart is inclined towards these men and women whom You have called into Triumph Leadership. Each of them is a letter of Christ, written not with ink but with the Spirit of the living God, not on tablets of stone but on tablets of human hearts. You have first called them to <u>be</u> Your letters, and now You have called them to <u>care for</u> Your letters.

I pray for these Triumph Servant Leaders, that You, Lord Jesus, will strengthen them with power through Your Spirit in their inner man. I pray they will decrease so You can increase. As they with all humility empty themselves of their own will and desire, please create in their hearts a great delight to carry out Your will and Your will alone. Holy Spirit, I ask You to equip them with everything necessary to carry out Your will, working in them what is pleasing in Your sight. Grant them wisdom, discernment, and revelation as they minister to the hurting hearts that You bring to them.

Lord I pray that You will fill them anew each day with an infilling of Your Holy Spirit, and they would speak the word of God with boldness. I ask that when they open their mouths, You will fill them. I pray that You will extend Your hand to heal, and through these classes that miraculous deliverances, freedoms, transformations, and healings would occur through the name of Your holy servant Jesus.

Lord God, please train their hands for war and their fingers for battle. Stretch forth Your hand from on high, flash forth Your lightning and scatter the enemy, send forth Your arrows and confuse them. I beseech You to cover these leaders with Your divine protection and shield them with Your power. Be with them like a Dread Champion, march forth on their behalf like a Mighty Man, remind them that the battle is the Lord's, and that nothing is impossible with You.

Jesus please seal them with Your Spirit, and pour onto their heads a special anointing as Your Servant Leaders. Let this anointing abide in them and teach them all things, that they will forever abide in You. I pray they will daily embrace Your will, and be led by Your Spirit.

Almighty God, keep them ever so close to You, forever dwelling in Your courts. Let those they minister to follow them as they follow Christ. I trust You to keep them from stumbling, and make them stand in the presence of Your glory blameless with great joy. May their every moment give glory, majesty, dominion, and authority to You, our Lord and Savior Jesus Christ. Amen.[1]

**I will be praying for you as you go forth,
leading others to triumph over their suffering.**

Appendix I
Investment for *Triumph Leadership*

1. *Triumph Rhythm*
2. Count the Cost
3. Qualifications To Begin *Triumph* Leadership Training

Suggested Triumph Rhythm

Months	Class or Season	Number of Weeks
Jan – April	*Triumph Over Suffering*	12-13 weeks
April - May	Participants' Percolation/ Leader's Restoration	4-6 weeks
June - Aug	Bible Study	6-12 weeks
Aug - Sept	Participants' Percolation/ Leader's Restoration	4-6 weeks
Sept - Nov	*Triumph of Surrender*	9-10 weeks
Nov – Jan	Participants' Percolation/ Leader's Restoration	6-8 weeks (thru the holidays)

Triumph classes invite in those who are hurting, meet them at their point of need, and point them to the Lord for healing, freedom, and growth in intimacy with Him. The true purpose of *Triumph Ministry* is to raise up disciples of Christ who have received His healing and equipping, and are ready to launch into their Kingdom purposes. The depth of the teaching in these classes cannot be grasped the first time around, and I encourage participants to return through TOS and T2 a second time. This will give us two years of discipleship time, and will prepare them for *Triumph in Warfare*. Of course we don't divulge all this up front! We only ask them to commit to a twelve week course – and that is a big enough initial commitment for most people. We pray the Holy Spirit will make them hungry for more.

Goals of Triumph Rhythm

- Security in their identity in Christ.
- A deep walk into their journey of healing and freedom.
- Knowing how to walk out their freedom.
- Able to read the Word on their own and to hear from the Lord through the Word.

- Strengthened and equipped to step into their God-ordained Kingdom purposes.

Additional Notes on Triumph Rhythm

- Participants' Percolation Time is an opportunity to rest and process as they spend quiet time with the Lord without the intensity of a study.

- Simultaneously, Leader's Restoration Time is a season for *leaders* to receive the Holy Spirit's rejuvenating work. Leaders need time to take care of themselves, to rest and replenish without the responsibility of constant ministry work.

- Bible Study: Since our goal is to raise self-feeding disciples, this time is for Bible study, not *book* study or *devotional* study. This is a critical time to teach participants to treasure His Word, to long for it, and to hear Him speaking through it.

I recommend participants go through this full rhythm twice before *Triumph in Warfare*. Teaching Volume I of *Warfare* in the spring, then a study on the Holy Spirit in the summer (e.g. John Bevere's *The Holy Spirit: An Introduction*), proved to be powerful preparation for Volume II in the fall.

Chapter 7, *Leading the Class*, contains more detailed information regarding the *Triumph Rhythm*.

Count the Cost

You can see from the *Triumph Rhythm* that *Triumph Leadership* involves a minimum of a one year commitment to minister to the ones the Lord brings into class. *Triump*h Leadership also involves an investment of our hearts and emotions, because we develop a level of intimacy with our participants that would make most leaders of other groups uncomfortable. This intimacy and transparency promotes trust and creates an environment conducive to vulnerable sharing in the classroom – a critical component of healing. This, of course, requires an investment of time, a Holy Spirit-created connection, and lots of prayer.

In order to evaluate the necessary time commitment, I've listed some specific elements involved in leading *Triumph* Classes. (You can find more detail in Chapters 4 and 7).

- Your own personal time alone with the Lord: I find when I am leading a class, I need more time alone with Him for spiritual strengthening.
- Inviting participants: This is a significant up-front time commitment to position yourself to meet potential participants, and to speak at length with each one to share about the material, to evaluate their readiness, and to connect deeply with them to help them to feel safe. (See Chapter 7 for more details.)
- Intercessory prayer: Before the course begins, and continually throughout the course, pray for your participants for repentance, surrender, breakthrough, revelation, freedom, deliverance, and healing.
- Seeking unity with your co-leaders:
    - Meet before a course begins for prayer and logistical preparation.
    - Pray together in the classroom before each class.
    - Discussion after each class to evaluate the class time, and pray to thank the Lord for all He has accomplished this week.

- Additional meetings with your co-leaders by phone as needed throughout the course.
- Regular meetings with *Triumph Leadership Team* for ongoing training and accountability.

- In the classroom:

  - Average length of class: 2 hours (less if the number of participants is 5 or less).
  - Available to connect with participants 15 or 20 minutes before class starts.
  - Available to connect with participants 15 or 20 minutes after class ends.

- Phone calls:

  - I encourage you to call your participants, *as the Holy Spirit leads*. That may mean some weeks you call one or two participants, and some weeks, you don't call any. Co-leaders can divide up this responsibility.
  - Since the chapters of *Surrender* in TOS and T2 are so pivotal, I recommend calling each participant those weeks. (See Chapter 7 for more details.) The *Forgiveness* chapters are also a week of additional phone calls.

- Meet with *Triumph* Leadership Team regularly for encouragement, sharing, prayer, accountability, and on-going training.

Qualifications to Begin Triumph Leadership Training
Triumph Leaders are F.A.T. = Faithful, Available, Teachable

Initial each box as it applies to you, and print and sign your name at the bottom.

Faithful: A surrendered and abiding walk with Jesus.

	Deep faith: Trusting in and relying on His goodness, power, wisdom, and grace.
	Discernment: Ability to hear from Holy Spirit and be led by Him.
	Growing in Christ: Daily time with Him - Scripture, prayer, worship, stillness, listening, journaling.
	Connection with your church family: Weekly church service, as well as regular fellowship and accountability with Christian same-gender friends.
	Strong personal support network (family, accountability partners, believing friends, pastors)
	Essentials: Believer's baptism, church membership

Available: Physically, mentally, emotionally, and spiritually available to serve those God brings into class.

	Physically available: Ready to pour into participants with prayer and time commitment starting 3 weeks before class, and throughout the course. Available to connect with other *Triumph* Leaders and with your campus pastor as needed.
	Mentally Healthy: If needed, have already sought healing for pain/ traumas. For most, taking time, perhaps a year, to process & heal from significant life events e.g. divorce, loss of loved one, addiction, family crisis, diagnosis of serious illness, major move, etc.
	Emotionally available: Stability of personal life and significant relationships. No "drama."
	Spiritually available: Have already sought healing for your own pain, and are not leading in order to fix yourself. Free from addictions, impurity, or other significant strongholds for a minimum of 6 months to a year.

Teachable: Humbly committed to on-going growth.

	TOS and T2 in the classroom, preferably taking each class at least twice. *Warfare* also in the classroom preferred. Deep processing of each course is crucial.
	Open to hear from the Lord each time you lead TOS, T2, or TIW.
	Humble and teachable heart; willing to meet with other *Triumph* leaders for training, accountability, and leadership development.
	Have read the entire Bible at least once, and continuing to immerse in Scripture study.

	If needed for deep wounds, continued pursuit of additional avenues of healing, such as seasons in counseling or in other healing classes.
	Continued meeting with *Triumph* Leadership Team for ongoing training and accountability.
	Continued leadership training in your church as available.

If you have checked most of these F.A.T. boxes, the next steps in *Triumph* Leadership Training:

-Serve Like Jesus: Triumph Leadership Training course with *Triumph* Leader or Trainer (11 weeks)

-Continue your spiritual growth to be able to check off all F.A.T boxes.

-Hands-on training in the classroom as a leader-in-training under a trained *Triumph* Leader

Sign Name: _____

Print Name: _____

Date: _____

Appendix II
Registration Paperwork

1. Registration Summary for *Triumph* Classes
2. TOS Registration Form
3. T2 Registration Form
4. TIW Registration Form
5. *Triumph* Course Description
6. *Triumph* Classroom Guidelines
7. *Triumph* Commitment and Confidentiality Agreement
8. Sample Schedule TOS
9. *Triumph* Class Evaluation Form

Email Celeste.Li.Triumph@gmail
for electronic copies of these forms.

Registration Summary for Triumph Classes

Phone Call with Interested Participant

Call each potential participant to explain about the class, the commitment, and the work and homework involved. This is also a good time to assess spiritual status. Pray together and ask the Lord if the potential participant is ready for the class, and if this is the right season to commit to immerse in the study. (See Chapter 7 for additional details.)

Forms Prior to Class

If you and the participant feel the Lord is calling them into class, ask the participant to fill out and return these forms to you prior to class. This will help you to know more about them before class starts. Additionally, participants will come to class educated about what a healthy classroom environment will look like.

- Registration Form
- *Triumph* Course Description
- *Triumph* Class Guidelines
- *Triumph* Commitment and Confidentiality Agreement

Business of the First Class

During the first class, prior to sharing time, go over these critical forms. Even though the participants have already read and signed these form prior to class, distribute another copy and go over them together. This will set the tone for an environment conducive to spiritual growth.

- *Triumph* Course Description
- *Triumph* Class Guidelines
- *Triumph* Commitment and Confidentiality Agreement

Additional Forms

- Course Schedule: Distribute on first day of class.
- Class Roster: Wait to distribute until the second class, in case there is still some fluctuation in the group.
- Maintain a record of attendance for yourself.

Triumph Over Suffering (TOS) Registration Form

Name_____ Date of Birth_____

Street Address_____

City_____ State_____ Zip _____

Home Phone_____ Cell Phone_____ Text? Yes No

Email (*please print*) _____

Emergency Contact (*name and phone #*)_____
_____

If you are a member of a church, name of church & service time:
_____

Have you been baptized as a believer? _____

Date & Age: _____

Where _____

Have you taken TOS before? If yes, please list where, when, and your leader: _____
_____

What brings you to TOS?

What would you like Jesus to do for you through this class?

Materials needed: 3rd Edition of *Triumph Over Suffering* book and *Triumph Over Suffering Workbook* (author Celeste Li), available on Amazon; contact your leader if you need scholarship money. Audiobook available.

Triumph Of Surrender, A Walk of Intimacy With Jesus (T2)
Registration Form

Name _____ Date of Birth _____

Street Address_____

City_____ State_____ Zip _____

Home Phone_____ Cell Phone_____ Text? Yes No

Email (*please print*) _____

Emergency Contact (*name and phone #*) _____

If you are a member of a church, name of church and service time:

_____

When did you complete *Triumph Over Suffering*? _____

What brings you to *Triumph of Surrender*?

What would you like Jesus to do for you during this class?

Tell me about your daily time alone with God, and your walk with Jesus right now.

Materials needed: *Triumph of Surrender, A Walk of Intimacy With Jesus*
Available on Amazon; contact your leader if you need scholarship money.
Audiobook available. You will also a notebook or journal.

Triumph In Warfare (TIW) Registration Form

Name_____ Date of Birth _____

Street Address_____

City_____ State_____ Zip _____

Home Phone_____ Cell Phone_____ Text? Yes No

Email (*please print*) _____

Emergency contact (*name and phone #*) _____
_____

If you are a member of a church, name of church and service time:
_____

When did you complete *Triumph Over Suffering*? _____

When did you complete *Triumph Of Surrender*? _____

What brings you to *Triumph in Warfare*?

What would you like Jesus to do for you during this class?

Materials needed:
Triumph in Warfare, A fight for the territory of our hearts, Vol I & II
Available on Amazon; contact your leader if you need scholarship money.
Audiobook available. You will also a notebook or journal.

Triumph Course Description

***Triumph* Classes are a time for deep spiritual growth.**

- *Triumph* courses are deep Bible studies for those who are seeking God in a profound way.

- *Triumph* courses are a season to partner with the Lord and position yourself for His transformation and healing.

- These classes will require honesty, transparency, and vulnerability – before God, and also in the safety of the classroom as the Holy Spirit leads.

- The time in the classroom is an opportunity to share the Lord's work in your heart, and to hear His work in the hearts of the other participants.

- You will probably find yourself facing crossroads during your *Triumph* journey. Growth in Christ will depend on your choice at the crossroads. Will you choose His way, or your own way? Will you forgive, or remain in unforgiveness? Will you choose surrender, or will you refuse to release it into His hands? Will you trust Him, or insist on keeping control?

***Triumph* Classes are not support groups.**

- While there will be times to share, these classes are not a time to complain about other people, to air grievances, or to grumble about your trials or circumstances.

- We will set our minds on things above, and seek God with all our hearts. To fully immerse, you may want to put aside distractions, such as social media or other activities.

- We will keep our sharing focused on the work the Lord desires to do in *our own hearts* during this season.

Triumph Class Guidelines

Each week as you study, we pray that the Holy Spirit will meet you, speak to you, heal you, and transform you. Pray for your leaders and classmates, and come to class ready to share what the Lord has done in your heart this week!

- *Triumph* leaders are not experts or professional counselors, but are here to help facilitate group discussion and to point all of us toward Jesus. The facilitators have been appointed by the Lord to lead this class. Please be respectful of the way they are guiding the class, and honor the direction they feel the Lord is leading for the group.
- Please put cell phones on silent (not just on vibrate), and put them out of sight. They are distracting to you, to your leaders, and to others in the class. Our time together is very limited, and the Lord wants your undivided attention.
- Please allow each person in the class the opportunity to share. The size of our group will determine how much time each member will have to share. Please limit your sharing to 3 minutes until everyone has an opportunity to speak.

- Treat other participants with respect and compassion. Do not interrupt them when they are sharing. Avoid graphic descriptions that could be offensive or disturbing to other participants. Avoid foul language, and do not use the Lord's name in vain.
- We are not here to teach, preach, lecture, counsel, coach, give advice or suggestions, or fix another. This is a discussion group where we share our encounters with God and how we have applied the teachings of *Triumph* to our lives right now. You may touch on past events of your life, but keep your focus on the present. Keep the focus on *your* heart and *your* experiences with the Lord.
- Please share primarily about yourself and not about others. Talking about other people is gossip. We also do not discuss with other participants outside of class what was shared in class. That is also gossip.

- If someone is crying, this is a Holy Spirit moment. Do not touch or comfort them or offer tissues. When the move of the Holy Spirit is finished, they will reach for tissues themselves, and then you can touch and comfort.

- Avoid carrying on a side conversation during class (with words, gestures, facial expressions, or eyes) – this is called cross-talk. Do not engage in a back and forth conversation with another member of the class during group time – this is also cross-talk. The leader will respond to each person after they share.

- Maintain confidentiality at all times. What is said in the group stays in the group.

I agree to abide by the *Triumph* Class Guidelines.

Name and Date: _____

Signature: _____

Triumph Commitment and Confidentiality Agreement

- *Triumph* classes are Bible studies and spiritual growth courses, and the leaders are lay ministers. *Triumph* classes are not intended to replace your physician, counselor, therapist, or other health professional.
- What you share will be held confidential by the leaders with the following exceptions:
  - The leaders may speak with their pastor and the *Triumph* Leadership Team for the purpose of guidance.
  - The leaders may ask the *Triumph* Prayer Team to pray for you by providing them your first name only.
  - The leaders are mandated by law to report to the Pastoral Staff any threats or acts of serious harm to others or to self, or if participant is suspected to be involved in physical or sexual abuse.
- God is calling you to commit to opening yourself up to the Holy Spirit's magnificent work. We understand that unexpected distractions and emergencies may occur, and it may become necessary to miss a week or two. We encourage you to complete the work even during your absence, and, if you would like, to meet with one of the leaders to discuss the missed class. Please let this commitment be between you and God.

_____ I commit to coming to all the classes.

_____ I commit to reading all the chapters of the book.

_____ I commit to completing all the homework questions.

_____ I agree to be respectful to others in my appearance, attitude, and speech. As each member comes to the class with a different perspective and background, I will be aware that my words and actions impact each group member.

_____ I agree to keep all information shared confidential. Although this cannot be guaranteed in a group, I know that trust in confidentiality is the basis for the success of this class. If I break confidentiality, I may be asked to leave the class.

_____ Initial for permission to add your name and phone to the class roster.

_____ Initial for permission to give your first name to *Triumph* Prayer Team for prayer.

Name and Date: _____

Signature: _____

Triumph Over Suffering
Sample Course Schedule
January 14 – April 7
Tuesdays, 6:30 – 8:30 PM

Please come to class ready to share what God has spoken to you through Scripture in the book or Workbook, and what He has shown you through your reading of the book and working through the Workbook.

Jan 14	Introduction	
Jan 21	Discussion of Chapter 1:	In This World You Will Have Trouble
Jan 28	Discussion of Chapter 2:	Emotions
Feb 4	Discussion of Chapter 3:	Surrender
Feb 11	Discussion of Chapter 4:	God Is Sovereign
Feb 18	Discussion of Chapter 5:	Conform Us to Christ
Feb 25	Discussion of Chapter 6:	Opening Our Eyes to Our Sin
Mar 3	Discussion of Chapter 7:	Humility, Dependence, Forgiveness
Mar 10	Discussion of Chapter 8:	Spiritual Warfare
Mar 17	Discussion of Chapter 9:	Intimacy With Christ
Mar 24	Discussion of Chapter 10:	Response to Suffering
Mar 31	Discussion of Chapters 11 & 12:	Hearing God's Voice & Seize What Jesus Seized You For
Apr 7	Celebration Day!	

Triumph Course Evaluation

Name: _____ Date _____

Leaders: _____

Dates of Class _____

Please write in number of lessons completed.
- I have attended _____ of the classes.
- I have read _____ chapters of the book.
- I have worked through and written down the answers to the questions of _____ chapters.

1) What did Jesus do for you through this class?

2) What could be done to improve the class?

Next Steps

I would like to continue to the next class: _____ Yes _____ No

If yes:
- 1) What will you do to stay deeply connected the Lord during the "Percolating Season" from now until class starts?

- 2) How will you stay connected in Christian community, with the other people from class, and/or in other places?

If no:
- 1) How will you continue to stay deeply connected to the Lord and growing in Him?

- 2) How will you stay connected in Christian community?

Whether you are coming into the next class or not, begin to seek the Lord's heart for His Kingdom plans for you now that He has brought you to new levels of healing and growth. Journal what He shows you.

Appendix III
Resources for Leaders

1. Leading Someone to Christ
2. How To Study Your Bible for Participants
3. Summary How To Study Your Bible
4. How To Study Your Bible for Leaders

Email Celeste.Li.Triumph@gmail
for electronic copies of these forms.

Leading Someone to Christ

What an incredible and holy moment, when the Holy Spirit is drawing someone to Christ! Only Jesus saves, and there is nothing we can add to His finished work on the cross. Yet God *still* invites us to partner with Him as He rescues people from the domain of Satan and transfers them to the Kingdom of Jesus Christ, granting them redemption and forgiveness of sins![1]

It is an equally incredible and holy moment when someone chooses to return to the Lord, recommit their life to Christ, or to surrender to Him in a deeper measure. *Triumph Over Suffering* is uniquely positioned to invite hurting people to come to Christ, whether as a first time commitment, a recommitment, or a deeper surrender to Him. Often, God has already used your own testimony of how He has healed and freed you to draw them to this point of desiring Christ.

What I am going to share below is directed towards people in TOS. Although the gospel remains unchanged, our presentation will be different for each person and each situation. How we share the love of Christ with someone who has little interest in the Lord will be vastly different than how we present the gospel to someone hungry for the things of God. People drawn into TOS are hurting, and the things of the world have not quieted their pain. This is a wonderful leaping off point for the gospel!

When the Lord suddenly give us the opportunity to invite someone to commit, recommit, or come to deeper surrender, it is important that we are ready and can speak with clarity.[2]

Coming to Christ

Here are the key points to cover when someone is coming to Christ. The footnotes are important Scriptures.

1. Acknowledge that we have sinned. Understand that our sin has separated us from God, we are not in relationship with God, and that we must repent of our sins.[3]

2. Recognize that we cannot make up for our sins or start a relationship with God by good deeds, prayers, or any personal effort.[4]

3. Understand that God loves us so much that He made a way for our sins to be forgiven and for us to come into relationship with Him: Jesus' death and resurrection. Jesus, fully God and fully man, perfect and sinless, died on the cross in our place to pay the penalty for our sins and make a way for us to come to be with Him in heaven.[5]

4. Jesus died for everyone, and offers His gift of salvation, forgiveness of sins, relationship with God, and eternal life to everyone. But not everyone receives His free gift.[6]

5. You *receive* His free gift by
   - Repenting of your sins.[7]
   - Trusting in Jesus' His death on the cross - not your own works - as payment for your sins.[8]
   - Asking Him to be your Savior – personally, *for you*.[9]
   - Asking Him to be Lord of your life. Giving your life to His control, putting Him in the driver's seat. Committing to follow Him and obey His will as best you can understand for the rest of your life.[10]

When someone is coming to Christ, even if I have been praying for a long time for a particular person, when the moment arrives, I pray again in my heart, asking the Lord to come to them, and to protect this time from the enemy. I then cover the first four points above. Then I ask the question,

"Would you like to receive this gift?" I find that inviting them to commit to Christ is very important. It helps them understand there is a choice to be made.

If the answer is yes, then I proceed to point number 5, and go over how to receive this free gift. I make sure they understand, and then tell them to go ahead and pray. I remind them to cover repenting, accepting His death as payment for your sins, asking Him to be your Savior, and making Him Lord of your life.

I find most people will pray from their heart in their own words. If someone needs help, you can lead them, step by step (covering repenting, accepting His death as payment for their sins, asking Him to be their Savior, and making Him Lord of their life) and have them repeat after you. If someone praying on their own misses one of those points, I prompt them and give them the words to say.

When they are finished, I pray over them a prayer of blessing and strengthening, asking the Holy Spirit to fill them, protect them, and grow them up in Him.

I have heard that the first moments after salvation are most critical, and what we say will be planted deeply by the Holy Spirit into their hearts. I take a few minutes to share some important teachings, including:

- You have now been adopted by God; you are His child.[11]
- Your sins are forgiven. When you die, you will go to heaven to be with Jesus.[12]
- You belong to God, He will never fail you or forsake you, and Satan cannot steal you away from Him.[13]
- Right at this moment, the Holy Spirit has come to live inside of your heart. He will never leave you, and He will lead you and guide you as you learn to listen to Him.[14]
- God wants you to grow up in Him – going to church, praying, and reading your Bible will help you grow in Him.[15]

Recommitting to Christ, or Deeper Surrender

As I mentioned above, TOS is uniquely positioned to draw people to the Lord, and to draw those who have fallen away back to the Lord. The Lord seems to provide two specific open doors: when we have our initial connecting conversation with them, and when we are in the surrender chapter. During these times, if we sense someone is not close to the Lord or that the Lord is calling them to a deeper surrender, it is an opportune time to *invite* them to come to the Lord. I find that often people do not realize they are at a crossroads until we *ask* them. It is our *invitation* that helps them to realize that God is calling them to a decision right now.

My discussion inviting someone to recommitment or deeper surrender is not about relationship, but about *fellowship*. I invite them to return to fellowship with God by asking a question such as one of these:

- Would you like to recommit your life to Christ right now?
- Would you like to surrender _____ to the Lord right now?
- Would you like to put _____ into His hands right now?
- Would you like to repent now and commit to live God's way?

If the answer is yes, I suggest they pray first. When they are finished, I pray over them a prayer of blessing and strengthening, asking the Holy Spirit to fill them, protect them, and grow them up in Him.

If Someone Declines the Invitation

Don't take it personally! If someone is rejecting us, they are really rejecting Jesus and His Father.[16] It is our job to be obedient in what God calls us to do; it is God's job to save.[17]

It is very important to hold a nonjudgmental heart here, and to love unconditionally. Remember how many were yelling "Crucify Him!" one day, and a few weeks later on Pentecost 3000 were saved.[18] I have heard it said that a person needs to hear the gospel message an average of 7.3 times before they are ready to receive it. I actually heard the gospel message over 150 times myself before I received Christ. Trust in God's plan and His timing.

Resources

I have found these two resources to be very helpful in learning to share the gospel:

Fay, William. *Share Jesus Without Fear*. Nashville, TN: Broadman and Holman Publishers, 1999.

Evangelism Explosion International. Their tract *Do You Know?* has been very helpful to me. EvangelismExplosion.org.

Footnotes
[1] Colossians 1:13-14.
[2] 2 Timothy 4:2, Colossians 4:2-3.
[3] Romans 3:23, Isaiah 59:2, Mark 1:14-15, 1 John 1:9, Acts 3:19, Acts 2:38.
[4] Ephesians 2:8-9, Titus 3:5-7.
[5] Isaiah 53:4, 1 Peter 2:21-24, Romans 6:23, John 14:6.
[6] John 3:16, 2 Peter 3:9.
[7] Luke 13:3.
[8] Romans 10:9-10, 13, Acts 16:31.
[9] Revelation 3:20.
[10] Matthew 7:21, John 8:31, John 14:23, 1 John 2:3.
[11] John 1:12, 1 John 3:1, Galatians 4:4-7.
[12] Ephesians 1:7, 1 John 5:11, 2 Corinthians 5:8, John 3:16.
[13] John 10:27-29, John 6:37-40, Hebrews 7:25, 1 Peter 1:3-5.
[14] Galatians 4:6, 2 Corinthians 1:21-22, Ephesians 1:13-14, John 16:13.
[15] Col 2:6-7, 1 Pet 2:2, 1 Thess 5:16-18, Eph 6:18, Jn 4:24, Heb 10:24-25.
[16] Luke 10:16.
[17] 1 Corinthians 3:6-7.
[18] Acts 2:41.

How To Study Your Bible:
Encountering God Through His Word

For the word of God is living and active and sharper than any two-edged sword, and piercing as far as the division of soul and spirit, of both joints and marrow, and able to judge the thoughts and intentions of the heart.

Hebrews 4:12

The goal of reading your Bible is to encounter Jesus. To experience the Word as alive. To hear the Holy Spirit speak, to understand our Creator and Redeemer in greater depth, to watch Him unfold mysteries before our eyes. To comprehend how He thinks and acts and moves and loves. To learn how He responds when we cry out to Him. To receive His conviction and sanctification as He purifies our hearts so we can see Him more clearly. To be blessed with His unshakable peace, His tender comfort, His wise counsel and perfect guidance. And most importantly, to see His *heart*.[1]

As Rick Warren in *Bible Study Methods* explains, our souls need the Word in various different ways.[2] Following his pattern, the first moments of my day are a sweet time of worship, reading the Word, stillness, and prayer. And I set aside other times for Bible *study*, times to research, meditate, interpret, and draw conclusions. The method of Bible *study* that I share in this Appendix is a melding of many Bible study teachers and authors who have taught me how to study my Bible over the years; some of them are listed in the Resources.

Although background information about the culture, geography, and times relating to the book is important, I like to put aside all commentaries when I'm in this type of Bible study, because I am seeking the *Holy Spirit's* revelation and interpretation.

But the Advocate, the Holy Spirit, whom the Father will send in my name, will teach you all things and will remind you of everything I have said to you.

John 14:26 NIV

Commentaries provide more than merely background information; they are *interpretations* of the Word, formatted as books, teachings, lectures, online videos, etc. Although commentaries are valuable ways to learn and grow when used at the right time, if we rely on them when we are diving into a Bible study, we can circumvent the voice of the Holy Spirit.

Bible study is hard work! Kay Arthur, in *How To Study Your Bible*, emphasizes:

If you long to know God, if you yearn for a deep and abiding relationship with Jesus Christ, if you want to live the Christian life faithfully and know what God requires of you, you must do more than merely read the Bible and study what someone else has said about it. You must interact with God's word personally, absorbing its message and letting God engrave His truth on your heart and mind and life. That is the very heart of inductive study: seeing truth for yourself, discerning what it means, and applying that truth to your life.[3]

How To Study Your Bible

The intent of studying Scripture is growing in our *relationship* with the Lord. Each time you go to your Bible, pause and ask the Holy Spirit what He desires to speak to you today. Avoid studying Scripture simply as an intellectual exercise. If we read and study without contemplation, listening, and serious application, we may open the door to spiritual dangers, such as becoming legalistic or puffed up with pride – much like the Pharisees of Jesus' day.[4]

The method that I will share with you involves six steps:

1. Overview
2. Observation
3. Interpretation

4. Meditation
5. Application
6. Repeat Overview

Step One: Overview

An overview gives a bird's eye view of the book in order to understand the scope and purpose of the book. Try to read through the entire book in one sitting, without stopping to ponder any one passage. It's helpful to read through it several times over a few days.

Step Two: Observation

Work on one small section at a time, learning as much as you can from the passage. These are the kinds of things to journal in observation time:

- "The 5 W's and an H": Who, What, When, Where, Why, and How. This works well for narratives such as Acts or Exodus.
- Commands.
- Key words that seem to be repeated throughout the book. You may also research Greek and Hebrew words, or look up unfamiliar words in the dictionary.
- *Connective words* (therefore, if/then, because, but, when, since, as, for, so that, however) and determine what those words connect.
- Questions about the passage.
- Parallels and contrasts within this book, or in other books of the Bible. If this is your first Bible study, you may not know any other Scriptures to relate to the book you are studying. That's okay! As you begin to study the Word more, and implant it in your heart, the Holy Spirit will bring to your remembrance additional passages that relate.[5]

In order to observe the Word in this way, you will be reading the passage again and again. That is exactly the plan! As the Holy Spirit reveals, you may notice something new *each time you read through the section*.

Keep in mind that although each passage will have important principles and timeless truths, it was initially written to address the unique issues of those times. Many passages relate directly to us. Other passages are unique to the people and culture addressed; they may not *relate directly* to us, but they may *relate in principle*.[6] How we determine if a passage relates directly or in principle is not always easy and will require prayerful wisdom and discernment.

Step Three: Interpretation

Paraphrase the section using your own words.[7] Then journal the meaning of the passage, any new understandings, your interpretations and conclusions. Finally, write a concise one sentence summary. Generally, the more time we have spent observing, the easier it will be to write a concise summary.

Step Four: Meditation

The purpose of meditation is to open your heart to receive revelation. Biblical meditation is a *conscious* process that involves *actively focusing* on who God is, and what He has done.[8]

**On the glorious splendor of Your majesty
And on Your wonderful works, I will meditate.**
Psalm 145:5

Some religions suggest that meditation requires emptying your mind – but that is not Biblical meditation. Biblical meditation is prayerfully reflecting on God's person and His work, specifically through the Scripture passage you have just studied.

In stillness, open your heart to hear what He wants to reveal to you through this passage. Who is God? What does this passage say about His heart, or how He works? What new understanding has the Holy Spirit given you regarding *your relationship* with Him? What is He revealing to you *personally* right now?

The Holy Spirit will be giving different revelations to different people, and will speak different things to you about this passage in different seasons of your life, also.

Step Five: Application

This is the *action plan*. Ask the Lord what *His will* is for you right now. He may want to expose a sin or a lie, to bring you to repentance and to purify your heart. He may want to give you an assignment, or guide you down His path. He may want to encourage or strengthen you, or call you to specific prayer.

"One of the biggest enemies to applying Scripture is vagueness."[9] Applications such as "I need to be more kind" will probably not lead to any concrete actions. So if you feel the Holy Spirit is focusing on kindness, don't leave His Presence too quickly and miss the specifics. Ask Him how, when, and with whom He wants you to show kindness to today.

Step Six: Repeat Overview

Finally, pull back and read the chapter as a whole, summarizing it and selecting key verses. Do the same for the book as a whole, reading it in its entirety again, marveling at how the Holy Spirit has opened your understanding to passages that you did not know the meaning of a few weeks ago. Take some time to write a brief synopsis of the book and choose one or two verses that seem to represent the theme of the book.

I am praying for you, that immersing in His Word will bring you to know the heart and nature of God in more profound ways. That the Word will become a precious door to entering into more delightful relationship with Him, and enable you to understand His will for your life with greater clarity. And I am praying for you, that as you learn to study His Word, you will find it sweeter than honey to your lips.

> **O how I love Your law!**
> **It is my meditation all the day.**
> **Your commandments make me**
>   **wiser than my enemies,**
> **For they are ever mine.**
> **I have more insight than all my teachers,**
> **For Your testimonies are my meditation ...**
> **How sweet are Your words to my taste!**
> **Yes, sweeter than honey to my mouth!**
>   Psalm 119:97-99, 103

Resources

Arthur, Kay, *How To Study Your Bible: Discover the Life-Changing Approach to God's Word*, Eugene, OR: Harvest House Publishers, 1994, 2010.

Warren, Rick, *Rick Warren's Bible Study Methods: Twelve Ways You Can Unlock God's Word*, Grand Rapids, Michigan: Zondervan, 1981, 2006.

Helpful websites:

manuscriptbiblestudy.com/wp-content/uploads/ 2012/08/Inductive-Bible-Study-Guide.pdf, accessed 4/6/2020. Additional resources can be found at manuscriptbiblestudy.com

navigators.org/resource/inductive-bible-study

Footnotes

[1] Psalm 25:14, Hebrews 12:14, Matthew 5:8, John 14:27, 2 Corinthians 1:3-4, Isaiah 9:6, Psalm 143:8,10.

[2] Rick Warren, Rick Warren's Bible Study Methods: Twelve Ways You Can Unlock God's Word, Grand Rapids, Michigan, Zondervan, 1981, 2006, p 19.

[3] Kay Arthur, How To Study Your Bible: Discover the Life-Changing Approach to God's Word, Eugene, OR, Harvest House Publishers, 1994, 2010, p 8.

[4] manuscriptbiblestudy.com/wp-content/uploads/ 2012/08/Inductive-Bible-Study-Guide.pdf, p 16, on 4/6/20.

[5] James 1:21, John 14:26.

[6] manuscriptbiblestudy.com/wp-content/uploads/ 2012/08/Inductive-Bible-Study-Guide.pdf, p 14, on 4/6/20.

[7] navigators.org/resource/inductive-bible-study, on 8/27/20.

[8] 1 Peter 5:8, 2 Corinthians 10:5, Romans 8:6.

[9] manuscriptbiblestudy.com/wp-content/uploads/ 2012/08/Inductive-Bible-Study-Guide.pdf, p 16, on 4/6/20.

Summary How To Study Your Bible: Encountering God Through His Word

Step One: Overview: First, ask the Holy Spirit what He desires to speak to you. Read through the entire book in one sitting to understand the scope and purpose of the book.

Step Two: Observation: Work on one small section at a time.
- "The 5 W's and an H": Who, What, When, Where, Why, and How.
- Commands.
- Key words.
- *Connective words* (therefore, if/then, because, but, when, since, as, for, so that, however) and determine *what* those words connect.
- Questions about the passage.
- Parallels and contrasts within this book, or in other books of the Bible.

Step Three: Interpretation: Paraphrase the section using your own words. Then journal the meaning of the passage, any new understandings, your interpretations and conclusions. Finally, write a concise one sentence summary.

Step Four: Meditation: Consciously focus on who God is and what He has done, opening your heart to hear what He wants to reveal to you through this passage. Who is God? What does this passage say about His heart, or how He works? What new understanding has the Holy Spirit given you regarding *your relationship* with Him? What is He revealing to you *personally* right now?

Step Five: Application: This is the action plan. Ask the Lord what *His will* is for you right now. He may want to expose a sin or a lie, to bring you to repentance and to purify your heart. He may want to give you an assignment, or guide you down His path. He may want to encourage or strengthen you, or call you to specific prayer.

Step Six: Repeat Overview: Pull back and read the chapter as a whole, and then the book as a whole, summarizing and selecting key verses. Write a brief synopsis of the book and choose one or two verses that represent the theme of the book.

Resources

Arthur, Kay, How To Study Your Bible: Discover the Life-Changing Approach to God's Word, Eugene, OR: Harvest House Publishers, 1994, 2010.

Warren, Rick, Rick Warren's Bible Study Methods: Twelve Ways You Can Unlock God's Word, Grand Rapids, Michigan: Zondervan, 1981, 2006.

Websites: manuscriptbiblestudy.com and navigators.org/resource/inductive-bible-study

How To Study Your Bible: Instructions for Leaders

If our goal is to raise self-feeding disciples, the time our people spend under our discipleship is a critical time to teach them to treasure His Word, to long for it, and to hear Him speaking through it. The *Triumph Series* is packed with Scriptures, but the Bible study seasons established in the *Triumph Rhythm* are uniquely designed to teach our people how to study their Bible in order to receive Truth themselves.

Commentaries, devotionals, books, and videos can be stepping stones into reading the Word, but if we never step off those stepping stones, we will be missing the opportunity to be taught by God Himself! We can become stuck looking to others to feed us, never learning to feed ourselves.[1]

I strongly believe we need the Word at a minimum *daily*, and realistically *multiple times a day*. If the Word called Himself the true bread out of heaven that gives life to the world,[2] I think our spirits must need to eat this bread as regularly as our bodies need to eat food.

Choosing a Book of the Bible

When choosing a book of the Bible to lead your participants in study, it is important to consider what books of the Bible would be a good length and depth for people who are new at this. I would recommend perhaps Philippians, First Thessalonians, Colossians, First or Second Timothy, First John, or the Sermon on the Mount (Matthew Chapters 5-7).

Preparation Work

Before the first day of class, read through the book in its entirely several times, and begin to section off the divisions for your participants. Generally, a half a chapter or even less is sufficient material for one week. Divide the week's assignment into three or four small sections.

Copy the participants' *How To Study Our Bibles* Appendix and instruct them to read through it before your first day of class.

I have found it helpful to have all participants reading from the same translation. I recommend a more literal translation when doing this kind of deep Bible study. NIV can be a good choice for those who are new at this, because it is a thought translation (easier to understand) yet is fairly close to literal translation. Select a translation and print it out for each participant. (I use YouVersion.) This will ensure you are all reading the same translation, and will allow participants to take notes or highlight with ease.

I would recommend that you as leader look up background information and provide it to your participants. You can use a *Bible Dictionary* to learn about the culture, geography, and times of this particular book of the Bible. The participants may not have the resources for this, or may become overwhelmed with the research. Additionally, they may end up reading commentary instead of just background information.

On some weeks, you may want to provide some additional resources that will be helpful in their study of the passage for the upcoming week, such as

- Additional background information
- Greek word study
- Scripture references that complement the upcoming passage. If you don't know any references yourself, you can find some references in Bibles that have parallel references included.

Class Time

On the first day of class, distribute the book of the Bible and provide them with an outline of how you will be sectioning off this chapter of the Bible. Also provide the background information. Go over *How To Study Your Bible* to be sure they understand it.

Plan to meet weekly and ask, as you do with *Triumph* Classes, "What did the Lord show you this week in your Bible study?" Application is very important, so be sure you ask each week how they are *applying* what they are learning to their lives right now. If we read and reflect without applying what we have just learned to our own hearts and lives, we will have walked away from an opportunity for transformation and direction.

For if anyone is a hearer of the word and not a doer, he is like a man who looks at his natural face in a mirror; for once he has looked at himself and gone away, he has immediately forgotten what kind of person he was.

James 1:23-24

Celebration Day

As we do with *Triumph* Classes, it is very valuable to have a Celebration Day when you have completed studying a book of the Bible. This can be a sweet time for your participants to share how this study has brought transformation to their hearts and lives.

Footnotes
[1] 1 Corinthians 3:1-2.
[2] John 6:32-33.

Appendix IV
Triumph Prayer Guide

1. Your *Triumph* Prayer Team
2. Prayer Guide: TOS
3. Prayer Guide: Percolation Time/Leader's Restoration
4. Prayer Guide: Bible Study
5. Prayer Guide: T2

Email Celeste.Li.Triumph@gmail
for electronic copies of these forms.

Your Triumph Prayer Team

Your *Triumph* Prayer Team is a critical component for your class. Ask some of your prayer partners to commit to praying for you and for your class for the length of the course, and establish your own *Triumph* Prayer Team. Request that they pray daily at home, and meet regularly (once a week, or once or twice a month) to pray together. Ideally, the leaders take part in the prayer gatherings also. Your Prayer Team need not be large, only devoted to prayer. Even two or three gathered together in Jesus' name is a prayer team.

Although my current *Triumph* Prayer Team is composed of graduates of my *Triumph* classes, it wasn't always this way. My children, still in grade school at the time, were my very first Prayer Team. They took their responsibility very seriously, held confidential each prayer request, and brought the participants before the throne of God day after day. God worked deep miracles through their sweet prayers.

My current Prayer Team consists of women who know how to hold the deepest of confidences. They pray for the participants, but they also pray for me personally. I treasure their prayerful labor, and I do not ever take them for granted.

Here are some requests you may want to give to your Prayer Team.

1. Ask your Prayer Team to commit to praying sacrificially. This means praying daily for you and your class, and when they meet for prayer, to use that time not for talk, but to pray. This also means keeping prayer requests strictly confidential. Prayer requests are not an invitation to gossip or judge.

2. Ask them to commit to pray for the length of the course – starting at least a week before the course begins, and continuing until the last class.

3. If your Prayer Team is not familiar with the material, give them a summary of each chapter to help direct their

prayers. You may even want to give them the *Triumph* books. I have included a Prayer Guide for TOS and T2 in this Appendix.

4. Provide them with a list of participants, and ask them to pray for each one by name. Ask them to pray for specific prayer requests from participants.

5. Request prayer for yourself. This is something we may be reluctant to do, perhaps because we are too proud and don't want to admit our weaknesses, or perhaps we feel selfish for asking. Asking for prayer is stepping forth in humility. Recall how often Paul asked for prayer for himself. Humbly ask for their prayers, admitting your weakness, declaring you cannot do His Kingdom work without the power of the Holy Spirit. Asking for prayer for yourself is acknowledging that we are members of the body of Christ and need the uplifting prayers of our brothers and sisters in Christ.

6. Expect warfare. Pray for, and ask for prayer, for protection from Satan. *Triumph* Classes have been taught since 2005, and God has used these books to change lives in magnificent and miraculous ways. These books are brimming with Scripture, and Satan knows that God's Word convicts, heals, transforms, and turns hearts to Him. Anticipate a battle and prepare for it.

Triumph Over Suffering Prayer Guide

Dear Prayer Team,

You cannot imagine our gratitude that you have come forth to pray for these participants and us as leaders. Thank you for your hearts so willing to draw near to God and to intercede on our behalf.

Please pray by name each day for these participants and leaders. If you are able, pray during the actual classes. We will pray for you as you pray for us.

This weekly Prayer Guide includes the title of the chapter they will be studying, a Scripture from that chapter, and some specific prayer points for the week. We are sure the Holy Spirit will lead your prayers.

In Him,
Triumph Leadership Team

In the same way the Spirit also helps our weakness; for we do not know how to pray as we should, but the Spirit Himself intercedes for us with groanings too deep for words; and He who searches the hearts knows what the mind of the Spirit is, because He intercedes for the saints according to the will of God.
Romans 8:26-27

Leaders: _____

Dates and Time of Classes: _____

Names of Participants:

Before Class Starts

... having determined their appointed times and the boundaries of their habitation, that they would seek God, if perhaps they might grope for Him and find Him, though He is not far from each one of us.

Acts 17:26-27

- Pray that God would bring to these classes exactly whom He desires, and that He would soften their hearts to hear His message.
- Pray for the leaders of the class, that God will equip them with everything necessary to do His will, by working in them what is pleasing in His sight.[1]

Introductory Class

"In this world you will have trouble. But take heart! I have overcome the world."

John 16:33 NIV

- Pray that the Holy Spirit will bring the participants open and ready to share from the first day. Pray for Holy Spirit-led connections between the participants.
- Pray that the Holy Spirit would be with the mouths of the leaders and give them the His response to each participant as they share their stories.[2]

Chapter 1: "In This World You Will Have Trouble"

"When he lies, he speaks his native language, for he is a liar and the father of lies."

John 8:44 NIV

- Pray that the participants will uproot Satan's lies and replace them with God's truths that they will hear in His Word throughout this course. Pray that God will strengthen them to implement the physical, mental, and spiritual disciplines taught this week, and give them a great hunger to read His Word, to pray, and to worship in church.

- Pray that the Holy Spirit will give the leaders discernment to see when participants are entrapped in lies, and the gentleness to expose those lies.[3] Pray the Lord will give them wisdom to handle problems and challenges in the classroom with love and grace.

Chapter 2: Experiencing and Expressing Emotions

"In your anger do not sin": Do not let the sun go down while you are still angry, and do not give the devil a foothold.
Ephesians 4:26-27 NIV

- Pray that God will unmask their hidden emotions and gently guide them through the pain of experiencing these emotions. Pray God will connect them with people to support them in this difficult time of processing painful emotions. Pray God will teach them how to express their emotions righteously and without sin.

- Pray that God will give the leaders hearts that are full of compassion for these participants and able to love and accept them no matter where they are spiritually.[4]

Chapter 3: Surrender

And he died for all, that those who live should no longer live for themselves but for him who died for them and was raised again.
2 Corinthians 5:15 NIV

- Pray that God will reach down from heaven and draw each of these participants into a deep surrender to Him. Pray that those who have not yet come to Christ will give their lives and hearts to Him, and that their commitment will not be superficial but such a piercing and passionate commitment that they will never stray to the right or to the left. Pray that those who do already know the Lord will come into a deeper surrender to Him, and the rewards of that complete surrender would be such a sweet intimacy with Jesus that they will wonder why they had been holding back.

- Pray that the leaders will reach a new level of surrender to Him also, and that the love of Christ would control them.[5]

Chapter 4: God Is Sovereign

**The LORD Almighty has sworn,
"Surely, as I have planned, so it will be,
and as I have purposed, so it will happen ..."
For the LORD Almighty has purposed,
and who can thwart him?
His hand is stretched out,
and who can turn it back?**

Isaiah 14:24,27 NIV

- Pray that the Holy Spirit will bring them to truly grasp these two defining characteristics of God: His infinite love and His absolute sovereignty. Pray that they would come to always see both of those characteristics simultaneously, and will be accepting of His sovereignty because they can trust His infinite love.

- Pray that the leaders will come to a new level of embracing God's sovereignty, trusting that it is the purposes *of His heart* that will stand.[6]

Chapter 5: Suffering Works to Conform Us To the Image of Christ

And we know that God causes all things to work together for good to those who love God, to those who are called according to His purpose. For those whom He foreknew, He also predestined to become conformed to the image of His Son.

Romans 8:28-29

- Pray that these participants would realize that God is always working for their good, and that His definition of "good" is that they are conformed to the image of Christ. Pray that they will be accepting of the work the Potter is doing as He conforms them. Pray they will consider their suffering to be joy because God is using it to grow their faith in order to prepare them for Kingdom work on earth and for their rewards and responsibilities in heaven.[7]

- Pray that the leaders will continue to invite God to work in their hearts until Christ is formed in them.[8]

Chapter 6: *Suffering Opens Our Eyes to Our Sin*

Before I was afflicted I went astray,
but now I obey your word ...
It was good for me to be afflicted
so that I might learn your decrees.

Psalm 119:67, 71 NIV

- Pray that their pain will slow them down enough to listen, and that they will be open to conviction of the Holy Spirit. Pray that they understand that their adversity is not a punishment for their sins, that hardships are not matched up with their sins, but that God will be using their trials to get their attention. Pray that they understand they were created to glorify God, and that they would desire God will reveal to them any aspect of their lives that is not bringing Him glory.[9]

- Pray that the leaders will allow the Holy Spirit to work in their own heart so they may share His holiness and humbly serve Him.[10]

Chapter 7: *Suffering Teaches Us Humility, Dependence, and Forgiveness*

... bearing with one another, and forgiving each other, whoever has a complaint against anyone; just as the Lord forgave you, so also should you.

Colossians 3:13

- Pray that God will use their times of trial and physical dependence to teach them humility and spiritual dependence. Pray also that the Holy Spirit would reveal to them anyone they are not forgiving, and will teach them what it means to forgive as Jesus forgives.

- Pray that the leaders will be open to the Holy Spirit's conviction, and if they remember that anyone has something against them, they will go and be reconciled.[11]

Chapter 8: Spiritual Warfare: Suffering To Advance the Kingdom

... and we sent Timothy, our brother and God's fellow worker in the gospel of Christ, to strengthen and encourage you as to your faith, so that no one would be disturbed by these afflictions; for you yourselves know that we have been destined for this.
1 Thessalonians 3:2-3

- Pray that they will recognize that suffering is inevitable for Christians because they have stepped into the heat of the spiritual warfare. Pray that God will give them spiritual eyes to discern the spiritual warfare they are enmeshed in, and that He would teach them to fight with spiritual weapons and not weapons of the flesh. Pray that they will realize that suffering is God counting them worthy of the Kingdom of Heaven.[12]

- Pray that the leaders will learn how to demolish strongholds, and will comprehend in greater measure that He who is in them is greater than he who is in the world.[13]

Chapter 9: Suffering To Know Jesus Intimately

I count all things to be loss in view of the surpassing value of knowing Christ Jesus my Lord, for whom I have suffered the loss of all things, and count them but rubbish so that I may gain Christ, and may be found in Him ... that I may know Him and the power of

His resurrection and the fellowship of His sufferings, being conformed to His death.

Philippians 3:8-10

- Pray that God will use their hardships to bring them into penetrating fellowship with Jesus because they have shared in His suffering and they can relate to this Man of Sorrows who is familiar with grief.[14]

- Pray that the leaders will truly consider all their earthly treasures rubbish compared to their relationship with Jesus, and that the Holy Spirit will enable them to live this so completely that they are a powerful witness to any who are still gripping earthly things.[15]

Chapter 10: How Will You Respond To Your Suffering?

So we fix our eyes not on what is seen, but on what is unseen, since what is seen is temporary, but what is unseen is eternal.

2 Corinthians 4:18

- Pray that these participants would grasp the threefold response to trials that pleases God: face forward, learn contentment, and rejoice, and that they would have a burning desire to glorify God with their response.[16]

- Pray that the Holy Spirit will enable the leaders to still rejoice even if the *only* reason for their suffering is to glorify God.[17]

Chapter 11 and 12: Hearing the Voice of God and Seize What Jesus Seized You For

"He who has My commandments and keeps them is the one who loves Me; and he who loves Me will be loved by My Father, and I will love him and will disclose Myself to him."

John 14:21

- We cover two chapters in this last class. Pray that these participants will hear God's voice and seize what Jesus seized them for. Pray that the Holy Spirit will teach them to hear His voice, that they will develop a spirit sensitive to His Spirit and will obey His call immediately. Pray that God will give each one a calling *through* their suffering, and that He would begin to reveal this calling even now. Pray they will not be afraid of the enormity of their calling, but will immediately step out in obedience to the call.[18]

- Pray that the leaders would realize afresh that each participant is a letter of Christ, written on their hearts and cared for by them, written not with ink on tablets of stone, but with the Spirit of the living God on tablets of human hearts.[19]

Celebration Day

I press on to take hold of that for which Christ Jesus took hold of me.
Philippians 3:12 NIV

- This is the wrap up class where they will share how the Lord has worked in their hearts *through* this course, and the purpose through their suffering that God has revealed to them. Pray they will have courage to share, and that God will pour His Spirit into them to enable them to fulfill their calling. Pray God will draw them all into the next Bible study to continue their spiritual growth.[20]

- Thank God for these leaders that have poured themselves out like a drink offering upon the participants of this class. Pray they will encourage the participants in the calling God has laid on their hearts.[21]

Footnotes
[1] Hebrews 13:20-21.
[2] Exodus 4:12.
[3] 2 Timothy 2:24-26.
[4] Colossians 3:12-13.
[5] 2 Corinthians 5:14.
[6] Psalm 33:10-11.
[7] Isaiah 64:8, James 1:2-4.
[8] Galatians 4:19.
[9] Revelation 4:11, Romans 8:7-8.
[10] Hebrews 12:10.
[11] Matthew 5:23-24.
[12] Ephesians 6:12-13, 2 Thessalonians 1:5.
[13] 2 Corinthians 10:3-6, 1 John 4:4.
[14] Isaiah 53:3.
[15] Matthew 5:16.
[16] Philippians 3:13-14, 2 Corinthians 12:10, 1 Peter 1:6.
[17] John 9:1-3.
[18] Philippians 3:12, John 10:27, Ephesians 2:10.
[19] 2 Corinthians 3:2-3.
[20] Acts 4:29-31.
[21] 2 Timothy 4:6, 1 Thessalonians 5:11.

Prayer Guide For
Percolation Time/Restoration Time (4-6 wks)

Dear Prayer Team,

Over these next few weeks, the participants will be processing, and the leaders resting, and we ask you to please continue to pray! Thank you for living out what the Lord commands, **Pray without ceasing** (1Thess 5:17). We are humbly grateful, and want you to know that your prayers make all the difference.

Please pray by name each day for these participants and leaders. We will continue to pray for you as you pray for us.

In Him,
Triumph Leadership Team

With all prayer and petition pray at all times in the Spirit, and with this in view, be on the alert with all perseverance and petition for all the saints.
Ephesians 6:18

Leaders: _____

Names of Participants:

> "**Come to Me, all who are weary and heavy-laden, and I will give you rest. Take My yoke upon you and learn from Me, for I am gentle and humble in heart, and you will find rest for your souls. For My yoke is easy and My burden is light.**"
>
> Matthew 11:28-30

Participants have a time to rest and process all they have learned as they spend quiet time with the Lord without the intensity of a study. Pray they will not pull back from God, but will press into Him with soaking, Scripture, and quiet time. Pray the Holy Spirit will seal in what they have learned as they apply it to their lives. Pray the participants will continue to connect with each other in a more relaxed atmosphere.[1]

Pray for the leaders, for rest, that they would have time to care for themselves, to rest and replenish without the responsibility of constant ministry work. Pray that the Holy Spirit would restore and heal them, and prepare them for the next class.[2] Pray that the Holy Spirit will show the leaders which book of the Bible He desires for Bible study season.

Footnotes
[1] John 15:4-5, Hebrews 10:24-25.
[2] Psalm 85:6-7.

Prayer Guide For Bible Study (6-12 wks)

Leaders: _____

Book of the Bible to Study: _____

Dates and Time of Classes: _____

Names of Participants:

One of the goal of the *Triumph* Series is to raise up self-feeding disciples. The *Triumph Series* is packed with Scriptures, but Bible study seasons interspersed between *Triumph* Classes are uniquely designed to teach the participants how to study their Bible in order to receive Truth themselves.

For the word of God is living and active and sharper than any two-edged sword, and piercing as far as the division of soul and spirit, of both joints and marrow, and able to judge the thoughts and intentions of the heart.

Hebrews 4:12

Pray for the participants, that they would experience the Word as *alive*. That they would hear the Holy Spirit speak, and would come to understand our Creator and Redeemer in greater depth. Pray they will learn how He responds when they cry out to Him. Pray they will receive His conviction and sanctification as He purifies their hearts so they can see Him more clearly. Pray He will bless them with His unshakeable peace, His tender comfort, His wise counsel and perfect guidance. And most importantly, pray they will see His *heart*.[1]

As for you, the anointing which you received from Him abides in you, and you have no need for anyone to teach you; but as His anointing teaches you about all things, and is true and is not a lie, and just as it has taught you, you abide in Him.

1 John 2:27

Pray for the leaders, that the anointing of the Holy Spirit will abide in them and teach them all they need to know to lead this study. Pray that they too will *encounter* Jesus as never before. Pray their hearts will be continually open to the Lord, and that they will come out of this study with a new depth of understanding of passages they could not previously grasp.

After Bible Study, the participants and leaders go back into Percolation and Restoration Time for 6-8 weeks. I know you know how to pray! Please also pray that the Lord will bring into *Triumph of Surrender* exactly whom He has ordained, and that the enemy will not be able to steal any away from this deep course.

Footnotes
[1] Psalm 25:14, Hebrews 12:14, Matthew 5:8, John 14:27, 2 Corinthians 1:3-4, Isaiah 9:6, Psalm 143:8,10.

Triumph of Surrender Prayer Guide

Dear Prayer Team,

We are eternally grateful that you labor in prayer for us, and for our participants. We actually feel your prayers. We see the Lord move mountains, break chains, and do the impossible right before our eyes in response to your humble Spirit-led prayers. We see His hand of protection upon us as we race to the battlefront.

Please pray by name each day for these participants and leaders. If you are able, pray during the actual classes. We will pray for you as you pray for us.

This weekly Prayer Guide includes the title of the chapter they will be studying, a Scripture from that chapter, and some specific prayer points for the week. We are trusting the Holy Spirit to lead your prayers in accordance with His will.

In Him,
Triumph Leadership Team

This is the confidence which we have before Him, that, if we ask anything according to His will, He hears us. And if we know that He hears us in whatever we ask, we know that we have the requests which we have asked from Him.
1 John 5:14-15

Leaders: _____

Dates and Time of Classes: _____

Names of Participants:

Before Class Starts

> "I, the LORD, search the heart,
> I test the mind,
> Even to give to each man according to his ways,
> According to the results of his deeds."
>
> Jeremiah 17:10

- Pray that God will begin to stir in the hearts of both the participants and leaders, preparing them for the deep sanctification work He will be doing in this class. Pray the Lord will protect them and nothing will thwart them from coming in to class.

- Pray for the leaders, that they will open their hearts to Him and be just as much a student as a leader through this season.

Introductory Class

> Deep calls to deep
> in the roar of your waterfalls;
> all your waves and breakers
> have swept over me.
> By day the LORD directs his love,
> at night his song is with me—
> a prayer to the God of my life.
>
> Psalm 42:7-8 NIV

- Pray that the participants will return rested and eager for a deep level of sanctification. That they will have a tremendous hunger to know You more and hear Your voice. Pray they will reconnect easily and love each other with gentleness. Please pray they will give each other grace.[1]

- Please pray the leaders will run with endurance this race marked out for them. That they will learn how to throw off anything that is hindering them from the work of the Lord, and that they would learn to pace themselves.[2]

Chapter 1: "My Sheep Hear My Voice"

"Be still and know that I am God."
Psalm 46:10 NIV

- Pray that the participants would evaluate if they are feeding their flesh or feeding their spirit, and will prioritize their lives according to God's priorities. Pray they would begin to recognize Your voice as they quiet themselves to hear You.[3]

- Pray that the leaders will recognize if they are approaching burn out, and they would seek the Lord for His pruning. Pray for increased sensitivity to Your still small voice.[4]

Chapter 2: Heaven Touches Earth

Planted in the house of the LORD,
They will flourish in the courts of our God.
Psalm 92:13

- Pray that the participants would learn what is means to be *planted* in their church, and that they would take the necessary steps to plant themselves. Pray that they would establish a secret place of His Presence, a sacred place to meet with Him daily.[5] Pray they would make stillness, listening, and soaking a regular part of their time with the Lord. Pray that they would begin to experience sweet intimacy with Him.

- Pray that the leaders would seek the Lord for balance in their lives, and would spend quality time in great quantity with Him. Pray that they would spend deep contemplative times with the Lord, and would soak in Him, humbly receiving His love without giving anything back. Pray that if they have fallen away from that deep intimate place with you because of work or busyness or distractions, they would return to abiding in you.

Chapter 3: Toppling Barriers to Intimacy

What, then, shall we say in response to these things? If God is for us, who can be against us? He who did not spare his own Son, but gave him up for us all—how will he not also, along with him, graciously give us all things?

Romans 8:31-32 NIV

- Pray that God will use this chapter to firmly establish their identity in Christ. That they would demolish all lies about their identity and *choose* to believe the truth of who God says they are, even the lies of their circumstances, their past, their own mind, and the enemy's voice seem louder than the voice of God.

- Pray for the leaders, that the Holy Spirit would enable them to recognize when their participants are ensnared in Satan's lies, and would with gentleness point them to the truth and pray for God to set them free.[6]

Chapter 4: Surrendering To His Sovereignty

He does as He pleases with the powers of heaven and the peoples of the earth ... He humbled Himself by becoming obedient to the point of death, even death on a cross ... As many as received Him, to them He gave the right to become children of God.

Daniel 4:35 NIV, Philippians 2:8, John 1:12

- Pray the Holy Spirit will miraculously enable the participants to grasp God's sovereignty as an interplay between His purposes and our free will that is infused with His irrevocable love. Pray they come to a new surrender, a surrender of their entire lives to Him.

- Pray that any areas in their lives where the leaders are under attack, they will bow their hearts in surrender to the sovereignty of God, trusting that what Satan means for evil, God intends for good.[7]

Chapter 5: Demolishing Idols That Thwart Our Fellowship

You adulteresses, do you not know that friendship with the world is hostility toward God? Therefore whoever wishes to be a friend of the world makes himself an enemy of God.

James 4:4

- Pray that the participants would be open to exposure of any idols, would not fall into denial, and would recognize how their idolatry grieves God's heart. Pray they will cast down these idols and that Jesus would fully consume them.[8]

- Pray for the leaders, that if they think they are standing firm, they would be careful not to fall. That they would realize that people-pleasing is idolatry. That they would choose to decrease so He can increase.[9]

Chapter 6: To Forgive as Jesus Forgives

"Father, forgive them; for they do not know what they are doing.

Luke 23:34

- Pray that the participants would recognize what forgiveness is, and what it is not. That anything that is blocking the forgiveness process (such as pride, control, fear, shame, anger, judgment, confusion) would be exposed as Satan's traps and lies and renounced. That they would deeply in their hearts choose to release the wrongdoer. Pray that they will also fully forgive themselves.

- Pray that the leaders will not skate through this chapter, but will open their hearts to the Lord's conviction and wrestle through yet another layer of forgiveness.

Chapter 7: The Life of the Heart

Above all else, guard your heart, for it is the wellspring of life.

Proverbs 4:23 NIV

- Pray that the participants will admit and recognize their emotions, and use their difficult emotions to drive them to God. Pray they will trust God with the wounds they experienced, trust Him to hold their hearts and heal them.

- Pray for the leaders, that the burdens of the participants' stories would not cause them to harden their hearts. That they would have safe places to process and heal, to pray and release their participants to God.

Chapter 8: A Walk of Repentance

"Blessed are the pure in heart, for they shall see God."

Matthew 5:8

- Pray for the participants, that they would see God's call to repentance as His gift. That as they seek His sanctification above all else, and that they will be able to comprehend the depth of His love as never before.[10] Pray that they would understand that abiding equals obedience, and they would choose obedience at every crossroads.

- Pray for the leaders, that they would daily walk in the Light as He is in the Light, that they would lead the way in breaking down strongholds, and as they are sanctified, out of their hearts will gush rivers of living water.[11]

Chapter 9: From Roots to Fruit

"Abide in Me, and I in you. As the branch cannot bear fruit of itself unless it abides in the vine, so

neither can you unless you abide in Me. I am the vine, you are the branches; he who abides in Me and I in him, he bears much fruit, for apart from Me you can do nothing."

John 15:4-5

- Pray that the good work the Lord started in the participants He will carry through to completion.[12] Pray they would be eager to continue this journey of sanctification and abiding, and that the fire of the Holy Spirit within them would burn brightly and drive them to live for Jesus and Him alone.

- Pray that the leaders will continue to pursue a walk of sanctification, knowing that is the only way to know Him more. Pray they will recognize the bushels of fruit the Lord has brought forth as they have co-labored with Him through this course.[13]

Celebration Day

Faithful is He Who is calling you [to Himself] and utterly trustworthy, and He will also do it [fulfill His call by hallowing and keeping you].

1 Thessalonians 5:24 AMPC

- Pray that the Holy Spirit will enable the participants to see how far they have come! That He will bring to remembrance the state of their heart at the beginning of this class, and at the end of this class. That He will show them how they are hearing from Him with greater clarity and abiding in deeper ways. That He will encourage them and strengthen them and draw them to return to TOS and T2 on a second level.

- Pray the leaders will be so blessed as the participants share their testimonies. Pray that these testimonies would be all the reward and encouragement they need to persevere in this calling as *Triumph* Servant Leaders. Pray the Holy Spirit will highlight those from this class that He is calling into *Triumph Leadership*.

The class will go into Percolation Time/Restoration Time again, and we treasure your continued prayers. I pray the Lord will shower you with blessings and will shield you from enemy attack. I am eager to see the day in heaven when the Lord unveils to you all the work He has performed, you partnering with Him by your prayers. I'd like to pray a blessing over you, from Psalm 121:

Lord God, I lift these precious prayer warriors up to You, and ask that You will forever be their Help and their Shield, and the Sustainer of their Souls. You who made the heavens and the earth, and who hold our times in Your hands, You see all things and establish Your will by Your mighty right arm. Please do not allow their feet to slip; hold their hands tightly in Yours and keep them steadily on Your path. Guard them with Your strength, shield them with Your power, protect them day and night, for You never slumber and You never sleep.

Lord You are their Keeper, and their shade at their right hand. When the intensity of the sun is too great, do not let it burn them. When the terrors of the night arise, do not let any evil touch them. Surround them with favor as with a shield, protecting them from enemy attack. Blind the enemy to their whereabouts, and let the enemy's arrows be as headless shafts. Keep their souls, don't allow the pain and destruction of this world penetrate their hearts or souls; fill them with Your peace and love and joy that nothing on this earth could possibly steal away. Guard their every movement, their going out and their coming in, from this time forth and forever. Amen.

Footnotes

[1] Ephesians 4:2-3.
[2] Hebrews 12:1-3.
[3] Romans 8:1-14.
[4] John 15:1-5.
[5] Psalm 31:20.
[6] 2 Timothy 2:24-26.
[7] Genesis 50:20.
[8] Hebrews 12:29, Exodus 34:14.
[9] 1 Corinthians 10:12, Galatians 1:10, John 3:30.
[10] Romans 2:4, Ephesians 3:16-21.
[11] 1 John 1:6-7, 2 Corinthians 10:4-6, John 7:38-39.
[12] Philippians 1:6.
[13] Hebrews 12:14, John 15:2.

Resources

Arthur, Kay, Arthur, David, De Lacy, Pete, *How To Study Your Bible: Discover the Life-Changing Approach to God's Word*, Eugene, OR: Harvest House Publishers, 1994, 2010.

Blanchard, Ken and Hodges, Phil. *The Servant Leader: Transforming Your Heart, Head, Hands, and Habits*. Nashville, TN: Thomas Nelson, Inc. 2003.

Lencoini, Patrick. *The Five Temptation of a CEO: A Leadership Fable*. San Francisco, CA: Jossey-Bass, 1998.

Maxwell, John C. *Developing the Leader within You 2.0:* New York, New York: HarperCollins Leadership, 2018.

Maxwell, John C. *Failing Forward: Turning Mistakes into Stepping Stones for Success*. Nashville, TN: Thomas Nelson, Inc., 2000.

Maxwell, John C. *The Maxwell Leadership Bible: Lessons in Leadership from the Word of God, New International Version*. Nashville, TN: Thomas Nelson, Inc., 2007.

Mullins, Tom. *The Leadership Game*. Nashville, Tennessee: Thomas Nelson, Inc., 2005.

Nouwen, Henri J.M. *In the Name of Jesus: Reflections on Christian Leadership*. New York, New York: The Crossroads Publishing Company, 1989.

Warren, Rick, *Rick Warren's Bible Study Methods: Twelve Ways You Can Unlock God's Word*, Grand Rapids, Michigan: Zondervan, 1981, 2006.

Endnotes

Foreword
[1] Eugene H. Peterson, *A Long Obedience in the Same Direction: Discipleship in an Instant Society*, Downers Grove, IL, InterVarsity Press, 2000, p 202.

Introduction
[1] Romans 12:1-2. Celeste Li, M.D., *Triumph Over Suffering, A Spiritual Guide to Conquering Adversity, Third Edition*, Jupiter, FL, Plum Tree Ministries, 2009, 2010, 2013, p 289.

[2] These Scriptures came to my heart as I was praying for you: Isaiah 12:2-3, 55:12; Psalm 103:17.

Chapter 1: You Are Called and Anointed

[1] James Strong, *The New Strong's Exhaustive Concordance of the Bible, Concise Dictionary of the Words in the Greek Testament*, Nashville, TN, Thomas Nelson Publishers, 1995, p 64 (no. 3718 to cut or divide).

[2] John C. Maxwell, *Developing the Leader Within You 2.0*, Nashville, TN, Harper Collins Leadership, 2018, p 156-157.

[3] Spiros Zodhiates, *The Complete Word Study Dictionary, New Testament*, Chattanooga, TN, AMG Publishers, 1992, p 483 (no. 1401 *doulos*).

[4] Maxwell, p 151. The entire chapter entitled "The Heart of Leadership: Serving People" was very impacting to me.

[5] Maxwell, p 161.

Chapter 2: To Set the Captives Free

[1] Zodhiates, p 155 (no. 366 come to their senses).

[2] Li, M.D., *Triumph Over Suffering*, p 289.

[3] Zodhiates, p 232 (no. 629 redemption).

[4] Zodhiates, p 842 (no. 2675 restoration).

[5] www.dictionary.com/browse/restoration?s=t on 8/21/20

⁶www.history.com/news/6-things-you-may-not-know-about-the-dead-sea-scrolls on 4/29/20.

⁷Celeste Li, M.D., *Triumph of Surrender, A Walk of Intimacy with Jesus*, Jupiter, FL, Plum Tree Ministries, 2016, p 318.

⁸ John Bevere, *The Holy Spirit: An Introduction*, Palmer Lake, CO, Messenger International, 2013, p 5.

Chapter 3: Establishing Our Identity in Christ

¹These Scriptures came to my heart as I was praying for you: 2 Corinthians 4:6, Psalm 139:23-24, 1 John 2:21, Ephesians 5:14, 1 John 1:7, 1Thessalonians 4:3.

²Bevere, p 8.

³Li, M.D., *Triumph Over Suffering*, p 8.

⁴Li, M.D., *Triumph Over Suffering*, p 186-187 and *Triumph of Surrender*, p 203.

⁵ Li, M.D., *Triumph Over Suffering*, p 44. Zodhiates p 969 (no. 3340 repent).

⁶Christ Fellowship's *Freedom Study* (p 91 and 92) and their accompanying *Freedom Encounter* teaches about renouncing lies and declaring truth.

⁷Zodhiates, p 968 (no. 3339 *metamorphoo*).

⁸Li, M.D., *Triumph of Surrender*, p 292.

Chapter 4: Running With Endurance

¹Zodhiates p 960 (no. 3306 meno); Li, M.D., *Triumph Over Suffering*, p 255.

²Li, M.D., *Triumph of Surrender*, p 16-17.

³Strong, p 78 (no. 4434 poor).

⁴medium.com/@BaysideChurch/the-cost-of-a-margin-less-life-38c4b070f483 on 8/12/20.

⁵From John C. Maxwell's message to Kingdom Builders at Chris^t Fellowship Church on 7/18/20.

⁶Some of the thoughts and ideas in this section come from Wohlever, MD Amaryllis Sanchez, "Burnout in the Workplace: Strategies, Omissions, and Lessons From Wounded Hearts", *American Journal of Health Promotion*, published May 12, 2020, and also from www.aafp.org/fpm/2015/0900/p42.html, on 5/16/20.

⁷www.aafp.org/fpm/2015/0900/p42.html, on 5/16/20.

Chapter 5: Temptations Leaders Face

¹https://www.merriam-webster.com/dictionary/hypocrisy, on 5/20/20.

²Zodhiates p 129 (no. 264 sin).

³Ken Blanchard, *The Servant Leader: Transforming Your Heart, Head, Hands, & Habits*, Nashville, TN, Thomas Nelson, Inc., 2003, p 17.

⁴Zodhiates, p 323 (no. 922, burden).

⁵Zodhiates, p 1452 (no. 5413, load).

⁶Stormie Omartian, *The Power of Praying for Your Adult Children*, Eugene, OR, Harvest House Publishers, 2009, 2014, p 35.

⁷I read this somewhere, in a book on prayer, but I cannot find the reference at this time.

⁸Watchman Nee, *Spiritual Authority*, Richmond, Virginia, Christian Fellowship Publishers, Inc., 1972, p 69.

⁹Nee, p 15.

Chapter 6: In Step With the Spirit

[1] Li, M.D., *Triumph of Surrender*, p 31.

Chapter 7: Leading the Class

[1] Henri J.M. Nouwen, *In the Name of Jesus: Reflections on Christian Leadership*, New York, New York, the Crossroads Publishing Company, 1989, p 30.

[2] Patrick Lencoini, *The Five Temptations of a CEO: A Leadership Fable*, San Francisco, CA, Jossey-Bass, 1998, p 71.

[3] John C. Maxwell taught this in one of his messages to Christ Fellowship Church a number of years ago.

Chapter 8: Avoiding Traps in the Classroom

[1] Romans 12:1-2. Li, M.D., *Triumph Over Suffering*, p 289. Zodhiates p 968 (no. 3339 *metamorphoo*).

[2] Nouwen, p 58-59.

[3] Tom Mullins, *The Leadership Game,* Nashville, Tennessee, Thomas Nelson, Inc., 2005, 76.

A Final Word

[1] These Scriptures came to my heart as I was praying for you: Psalm 17:6, 2Corinthians 3:2-3, Ephesians 3:16m John 3:30, Philippians 2:5-7, Psalm 51:10, Psalm 40:8, Hebrews 13:20-21, 2 Chronicles 1:10, Acts 4:31, Psalm 81:10, Acts 4:30, Psalm 144:1, 6-7, Psalm 3:3, Psalm 28:7, Jeremiah 20:11, Isaiah 42:13, 2 Chronicles 20:15, Luke 1:37, Ephesians 1:13, 1 John 2:27, Romans 12:1-2, 8:14, Psalm 73:28, Psalm 84:1-2, Corinthians 11:1, Jude 1:24-25.

With Heartfelt Appreciation

I first thank my Lord and my God, who rescued me from the domain of Satan and transferred me to the Kingdom of my Savior Jesus Christ, who died in my place to grant me redemption and forgiveness of my sins (Col 1:13-14).

Then, as I stand back and see the army He has raised up to complete this book, it is with grateful tears that I thank my God in all my remembrance of you. I am always offering prayer with joy in my every prayer for you all, in view of your participation in this mighty Kingdom work (Phil 1:3-4).

- To my husband John, beloved and ever so trustworthy, who loves me in a First Corinthians 13 way: Your steady and sure walk with the Lord continues to inspire me.

- To my son Alec, whose intense relationship with the Lord is like the quiet depths of a deep pool: God has put skill in your heart and blessed the work of your hands as He birthed the cover through you.

- To my daughter Jenna, whose expansive heart is unfailing in its capacity to love: You were undeniably the Holy Spirit's vessel as He edited through your gifted mind and willing heart, giving you penetrating insight right from the Lord.

- To my incredible *Triumph* Prayer Team, faithful to pray for me and for the *Triumph Ministry* day after day, year after year: Through your prayers the Lord held back the Red Sea and enabled me to hear His still small voice as I wrote.

- To Anna, who has received a double helping of the Holy Spirit's fruit of patience: You have run with endurance, working tirelessly on the layout and keeping in step with the Holy Spirit the whole way.

- To God's *Triumph* Servant Leaders, past, present, and future, who *are* a letter of Christ, and who are *caring for* His letters: You have answered God's call, and I trust He will fully equip you, shield you, and lead you on His perfect path.

- To all who have had a hand in editing, advising, input, and prayer: You have been uniquely positioned for these moments. Thank you for being His available and willing servants.

---

www.ingramcontent.com/pod-product-compliance
Lightning Source LLC
LaVergne TN
LVHW041606070426
835507LV00008B/158